Powers
and Prospects

Powers and Prospects

Reflections on Human Nature and the Social Order

Noam Chomsky

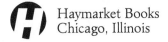
Haymarket Books
Chicago, Illinois

Copyright 1996 © Diane Chomsky Irrevocable Trust
Original edition published by South End Press in Boston, Massachusetts.

This edition published in 2015 by
Haymarket Books
P.O. Box 180165
Chicago, IL 60618
773-583-7884
www.haymarketbooks.org
info@haymarketbooks.org

ISBN: 978-1-60846-424-1

Distributed to the trade in the US through Consortium Book Sales and
Distribution (www.cbsd.com) and internationally through Ingram
Publisher Services International (www.ingramcontent.com).

This book was published with the generous support of Lannan Foundation
and Wallace Action Fund.

Special discounts are available for bulk purchases by organizations and
institutions. Please call 773-583-7884 or email info@haymarketbooks.org for
more information.

Cover design by Josh On. Cover photo of the aircraft of the U.S. President,
Airforce One, shows the executive configuration in the annex, which can be
converted to an emergency medical facility. (AP Photo)

Printed in the United States.

Entered into digital printing July 2020.

Library of Congress Cataloging-in-Publication data is available.

10 9 8 7 6 5 4 3 2

Contents

Foreword

by Agio Pereira

Professor Noam Chomsky is not a single issue activist. His range of influence transcends the boundaries of campaigns for social justice and self-determination, the field in which the East Timorese have been forced by war to learn and to become specialists.

It was with great honour that a small team embraced the gigantic role of coordinating the visit of Professor Chomsky to Australia in January 1995. Gigantic, not only because it was the first visit to Australia from a man with the stature of Professor Chomsky, but also because of the timing of the visit itself—it took place in the usual period of 'summer holidays' of the mainstream Australian media. It also coincided with the visits of Pope John Paul II and the visit of the Microsoft tycoon, Bill Gates—you could say Chomsky completed the trinity.

The consolation for us was that, at an early stage, it was clear that the focus of Professor Chomsky's visit to Australia was to be the issue of East Timor. It was therefore a litmus test for the support the Australian people have been lending to the

20-year-old struggle of the Timorese people to conquer their piece of freedom.

Having a controversial person like Noam Chomsky in Australia associated with yet another controversial issue such as East Timor, no one could foresee exactly how everything was going to play out. There were many people speculating about possible outcomes, but a clear picture was far off from even the most experienced organisers of public events. However, no one could have predicted the enormous response to his visit.

Being Timorese, as a matter of tradition, we pay tribute to those who support and respect us, by making sure that our role as hosts becomes as effective as possible to the point where when a guest departs, the feeling of returning is stronger than that carried in their arrival.

The first I heard of Professor Chomsky was in the late 1970s when I'd heard he paid from his own pocket for some Timorese refugees to fly to the USA to speak out about the tragedy of the people of East Timor.

I was later very delighted when I learnt that he presented a paper in the first session of the 'People's Tribunal' for East Timor, held in Lisbon in 1981. That was the time when the Resistance of East Timor was going through extremely difficult times. The deaths of charismatic leaders such as President Nicolau Lobato, Vicente Sahe and many others, brought the morale of the Maubere Resistance to a very low point. This was at the time when Kay Rala Xanana Gusmao was reorganising the struggle. At that time of 'soul searching' Professor Chomsky lent his undeniable support for the people of East Timor.

On meeting Professor Chomsky for the first time at the Sydney International Airport, his humbleness was so familiar to me that I felt we had known each other for many years. His approach to human interaction was as Maubere as one can reach, and this made our task much easier.

As the program of public addresses and media work was implemented, we learnt that the Chomsky factor and East Timor were a deadly combination. The Chomsky factor was critical in the sixties and still is critical today for those who search for basic explanations of the increasingly sophisticated machine of manipulation of public opinion. East Timor after 20 years has become a thorn in the conscience of those in the world who struggle for fundamental justice and values of human beings.

In this struggle, both Professor Chomsky and East Timor are Davids against Goliath. The combination of the conscience of the people of East Timor and Professor Chomsky has proved to be too powerful for those who tried to defeat us.

Perhaps it was this sense of being in the same trench and defending fundamental justice that made us feel that Professor Chomsky is part of us; and that was a turning point in the way we perceive Chomsky. Because, in the end, our sense of being hosts of a special guest was replaced with a much bigger one: that our home was richer with the sense of freedom Chomsky's visit helped us reach.

Even though Noam Chomsky is no longer in Australia fighting for the people of East Timor, we do rely on his support. We know that wherever he is, he will fight for the freedom for our people. That was the impression he left not only with the 16 000 or more people he spoke directly to during his visit, but also with those he reached through the media, and I hope now through this book.

This book testifies to how dedicated Professor Chomsky is to the issues he embraces in his active pursuit of freedom and fundamental justice.

From linguistics to the Middle East, from foreign affairs to the role of the media, from intellectual responsibility to East Timor, Noam—as he asked us to call him—refuses to accept complexity and imperfection as an excuse to violate fundamental principles of human beings.

Agio Pereira is the executive director of the East Timor Relief Association, and an adviser to the National Council for Maubere Resistance (CNRM).

Preface

In January 1995, after efforts that go back almost 20 years, I was finally able to arrange a week's visit to Australia, something I have long wanted to do but had not been able to work into a very demanding schedule. The immediate impetus was a suggestion by an old friend, José Ramos-Horta, that I visit under the auspices of the East Timor Relief Association (ETRA) to speak about the issue of East Timor—always urgent, but at that moment of special significance because of the impending World Court case on the Australia–Indonesia Timor Gap treaty and the 20th anniversary of the Western-backed Indonesian invasion a few months later, in December. ETRA had planned a six-month initiative to bring all of these matters to public attention, and I was more than pleased—more accurately, delighted and honoured—to be able to take part in the opening days of this project. Other events happened to converge on the same moment of time, among them, the publication of some of the fine essays of another old friend, Alex Carey, who pioneered the inquiry into one of the most significant and least-studied phenomena of the modern era: corporate propaganda. Again, I was more than pleased to be able to be present when the University of New South Wales Press launched the long-awaited publication of these essays, the first of many such volumes, I hope.

During far too few days in Australia, I had the opportunity to give talks in Sydney, Melbourne and Canberra on a variety of topics. These serve as the basis for the essays presented here, which are reconstructed from informal notes and transcripts, and updated in some cases to include material from following months. Chapters 1 and 2 form more or less an integrated unit, concerned with problems of language and mind, based on lectures at the University of New South Wales and the Science Museum in Sydney, respectively. Chapter 3 is based on notes for a talk at the Writers' Centre in Sydney; chapter 4, on notes and transcript of a talk at the Visions of Freedom conference of Australian anarchists, also in Sydney. Chapter 5 is reconstructed from notes for the Wallace Wurth Memorial Lecture at the University of New South Wales and a lecture sponsored by Deakin University, updated with some material from following months. Chapter 6 is based on a talk at the Middle East Centre of Macquarie University, also updated. Chapters 7 and 8 again form a natural unit. The former is based on talks at the town halls in Sydney and Melbourne organised by ETRA as part of the launching of their campaign; chapter 8 on a talk at the National Press Club in Canberra.

It was a great pleasure to meet old friends, some of whom I knew mainly or sometimes only from extensive correspondence; and many new ones, too numerous to mention, as are those whom I should thank for organising a most exhilarating and rewarding visit. I am particularly grateful to the many wonderful people I met from the Timorese community, several of whom I can hardly thank enough for ensuring that an intense and complex schedule proceeded with remarkable facility (for me, if not for them): Ines Almeida, Agio Pereira, and many others. I am no less indebted to other friends, old and new, among them Peter Slezak, Peter Cronau, Scott Burchill, Peter McGregor, and Wilson da Silva. To Peter Cronau I owe an additional debt of gratitude for the efforts he has undertaken to arrange and implement publication of these essays. For their help in organising the visit, I would also like to thank Ceu Brites, Benilde Brites and Arianne Rummery. It was also a great pleasure to be able to meet again—or in some cases, at last—people whose work and activities had long been a source of inspiration and understanding: José Ramos-Horta, Shirley Shackleton, Jim Dunn, Stephen Langford, Ken Fry, Brian Toohey, Michele Turner, Pat Walsh, Tom Uren, and many others.

These are hardly happy times for most of the world, apart from a privileged few in narrowing sectors. But it should also be a time of hope and even optimism. That extends from the topics of the opening essays, which discuss some prospects, which I think are real, for considerably deeper understanding about at least certain aspects of essential human nature and powers, to those of the final chapters. Quite apart from the critical importance of their own struggle, the remarkable courage of the Timorese people, and the growing numbers of Indonesians who are supporting them and demanding justice and freedom in their own country, should be an inspiration to all of those who recognise the urgent need to reverse the efforts to undermine fundamental human rights and functioning democracy that have taken such an ugly and ominous form in the past few years, and to move on to construct a social order in which a decent human being would want to live.

Noam Chomsky
Cambridge, Massachusetts

1

Language and Thought: Some Reflections on Venerable Themes

The study of language and mind goes back to classical antiquity—
to Classical Greece and India in the pre-Christian era. It has
often been assumed over these millennia that the two inquiries
have some intimate relation. Language has sometimes been described as a 'mirror of mind', so that the study of language should
then give unique insight into human thought. That convergence,
which has been repeated over the centuries, took place again
about 40 years ago, at the origins of what is sometimes called the
'Cognitive Revolution'. I will use the term intending you to hear
quotes around the phrase 'cognitive revolution', expressing some
scepticism; it wasn't all that much of a revolution in my opinion.

In any event, however one assesses it, an important change
of perspective took place: from the study of behaviour and its
products (texts, and so on) to the internal processes that underlie
what people are doing, and their origin in the human biological
endowment. The approach to the study of language that I want
to consider here has developed in that context, and was a significant factor in its emergence and subsequent progress.

The First Cognitive Revolution

Much the same convergence had taken place in the seventeenth century, in what we might call 'the first cognitive revolution', perhaps the only real one. This was part of the general scientific revolution of the period—the 'Galilean revolution', as it is sometimes called. There are interesting features in common between the contemporary cognitive revolution and its predecessor. The resemblance was not appreciated at the outset (and still is hardly well known) because the history had been largely forgotten. Such scholarly work as existed was misleading or worse, and even basic texts were not available, or considered of any interest. The topic merits attention, in my opinion, not just for antiquarian reasons. My own view is that we have much to learn from the earlier history, and that there has even been some regression in the modern period. I will come back to that.

One element of similarity is the stimulus to the scientific imagination provided by complex machines. Today that means computers. In the seventeenth and eighteenth centuries it meant the automata that were being constructed by skilled artisans, a marvel to everyone. Both then and now the apparent achievements of these artefacts raises a rather obvious question: Are humans simply more complex machines? That is a topic of lively debate today, and the same was true in the earlier period. It was at the core of Cartesian philosophy—but it is worth remembering that the distinction between science and philosophy did not exist at the time: a large part of philosophy was what we call 'science'. Cartesian science arose in part from puzzlement over the difference—if any— between humans and machines. The questions went well beyond curiosity about human nature and the physical world, reaching to the immortality of the soul, the unchallengeable truths of established religion, and so on—not trivial matters.

In the background was 'the mechanical philosophy', the idea that the world is a complex machine, which could in principle be constructed by a master craftsman. The basic principle was drawn from simple common sense: to interact, two objects must be in direct contact. To carry through the program of 'mechanisation of the world view', it was necessary to rid science of neoscholastic sympathies and antipathies and substantial forms, and other mystical baggage, and to show that contact mechanics suffices. This endeavour was considerably advanced by Descartes' physics and physiology, which he regarded as the heart of his achievement. In a letter to Mersenne, his confidant and most influential supporter in the respectable intellectual world of the day, Descartes wrote that his *Meditations*, today commonly considered his fundamental contribution, was a work of propaganda, designed to lead readers step-by-step to accept his physics without realising it, so that by the end, being entirely convinced, they would renounce the dominant Aristotelian picture of the world and accept the mechanical world view. Within this context, the question of limits of automata could not fail to be a prominent one.

The Cartesians argued that the mechanical world view extended to all of the inorganic and organic world apart from humans, even to a substantial part of human physiology and psychology. But humans nevertheless transcend the boundaries of any possible machine, hence are fundamentally different from animals, who are indeed mere automata, differing from clocks only in complexity. But however intricate a mechanical device might be, the Cartesians argued, crucial aspects of what humans think and do would lie beyond its scope, in particular, voluntary action. Set the machine in a certain state in a particular external situation, and it will be 'compelled' to act in a certain way (random elements aside). But under comparable circumstances, a human is only 'incited and inclined' to do so. People may tend to do what they are incited and inclined to do; their behaviour may be predictable, and a practical account of motivation may be possible. But theories of behaviour will always miss the crucial point: the person could have chosen to act otherwise. In this analysis, the properties of language played a central role. For Descartes and his followers, notably Géraud de Cordemoy, the ability to use language in the normal way is a criterion for possession of mind—for being beyond the limits of any possible mechanism. Experimental procedures were devised that could be used to determine whether some object that looks like us is actually a complicated machine, or really has a mind like ours. The tests typically had to do with what I have called elsewhere the 'creative aspect of language use', a normal feature of everyday usage: the fact that it is typically innovative, guided but not determined by internal state and external conditions, appropriate to circumstances but uncaused, eliciting thoughts that the hearer might have expressed the same way. If an object passes all the tests we can devise to determine whether it manifests these properties, it would only be reasonable to attribute to it a mind like ours, the Cartesians argued.

Notice that this is normal science. The available evidence suggests that some aspects of the world, notably the normal use of language, do not fall within the mechanical philosophy—hence cannot be duplicated by a machine. We therefore postulate some further principle, a kind of 'creative principle', that lies beyond mechanism. The logic was not unlike Newton's, to which I'll return. In the framework of the substance metaphysics of the day, the natural move was to postulate a second substance, mind, a 'thinking substance' alongside of body. Next comes the problem of unification: how do we relate these two components of the world? This was a major problem of the period.

These intellectual moves were not only normal science, but also pretty reasonable. The arguments that were given are not without force. We would frame the issues and possible answers differently today, but the fundamental questions remain unanswered, and puzzling.

Fascination with the (possible) limits of automata is one respect in which the first cognitive revolution has been in part relived in recent years, though the usual preoccupation today is the nature of consciousness, not the properties of normal human action that concerned the Cartesians; crucially, the apparent fact that it is coherent and appropriate, but uncaused. Another similarity has to do with what are nowadays called 'computational theories of mind'. In a different form, these were also a salient feature of the first cognitive revolution. Perhaps Descartes' most lasting scientific contribution lies right here: his outline of a theory of perception with a computational flair (though our notions of computation were unavailable), along with proposals about its realisation in bodily mechanisms.

To establish the mechanical philosophy, Descartes sought to eliminate the 'occult properties' invoked by the science of the day to account for what happens in the world. The study of perception was an important case. How, for example, can we see a cube rotating in space when the surface of the body—the retina, in this case—records only a sequence of two-dimensional displays? What is happening in the outside world and in the brain to bring about this result?

Prevailing orthodoxy held that, somehow, the form of the cube rotating in space passes into your brain. So there is a cube in your brain, rotating presumably, when you see a cube rotating. Descartes ridiculed these fanciful and mysterious notions, suggesting a mechanical alternative. He asked us to consider the analogy of a blind man with a stick. Suppose there is an object before him, say a chair, and he taps on it with the end of his stick, receiving a sequence of tactile sensations in his hand. This sequence engages the internal resources of his mind, which compute in some manner, producing the image of a chair by means of their inner resources. In this way, the blind man perceives a chair, Descartes reasoned. He proposed that vision is much the same. According to the mechanical world view, there can be no empty space: motion is caused by direct contact. When Jones sees a chair, a physical rod extends from his retina to the chair. If Jones's eye is scanning the surface of the chair, his retina is receiving a series of sensations from the rod that extends to it, just as the fingers of the blind man are stimulated when he taps on the chair with a stick. And the mind, using its intrinsic computational resources, constructs the image of a chair—or a cube rotating in space, or whatever it may be. In this way, the problem of perception might be solved without mysterious forms flitting through space in some immaterial mode and mystical fashion.

That was an important step towards eliminating occult ideas and establishing the mechanical world view. It also opened the way to modern neurophysiology and theory of perception. Of course, Descartes' efforts to work all of this out have a quaint tone: tubes with animal spirits flowing through them and so on. But it's not very hard to translate them into contemporary accounts in terms of neural systems transmitting signals which somehow do the same thing—still just stories in a certain measure, in that not a great deal is understood. The logic is rather similar whether it is instantiated by tubes with animal spirits or neural nets with chemical transmitters. A good deal of the modern theory of vision and other sensorimotor activities can be seen as a development of these ideas, obviously a huge improvement, but based on similar thinking. The mechanisms are no longer mechanical; rather, electrical and chemical. But the pictures are similar. And at a more abstract level, explicit computational theories of the operations of the internal mechanisms have now been devised, providing much insight into these matters: for example, Shimon Ullman's demonstration that remarkably sparse stimulation can lead to rich perception when intrinsic design interprets it in terms of rigid objects in motion—his 'rigidity principle'.

These two achievements—the establishment of the mechanical world view and of the basis for modern neurophysiology and theory of perception—fared very differently. The latter was developed in the medical sciences and physiology of the years that followed, and has in a certain sense been revived today. But the mechanical philosophy collapsed within a generation. Newton demonstrated that the world is not a machine. Rather, it has occult forces after all. Contact mechanics simply does not work for terrestrial and planetary motion. Some mystical concept of 'action at a distance' is required. That was the great scandal of Newtonian physics. Newton was harshly criticised by leading scientists of the day for retreating to mysticism and undermining the achievements of the mechanical philosophy. He seems to have agreed, regarding the idea of action at a distance as an 'absurdity', though one must come to terms somehow with the refutation of the mechanical philosophy.

Notice that Newton's invocation of immaterial forces to account for ordinary events is similar in its basic logic to the invocation of a second substance by the Cartesians to overcome the limits of mechanism. There were, of course, fundamental differences. Newton *demonstrated* that the mechanical philosophy could not account for the phenomena of nature; the Cartesians only argued—not implausibly, but not conclusively—that aspects of the world fell beyond these limits. Most importantly, Newton provided a powerful theoretical account of the operation of his occult force and its effects, whereas the Cartesians had little to say about the nature of mind—at least, in what records we have (some were destroyed).

The problems that Newton sought to overcome remained very troubling for centuries, and many physicists feel that they still are. But it was soon understood that the world is not a machine that could in principle be constructed by a skilled craftsman: the mechanical philosophy is untenable. Later discoveries demolished the picture even more fully as science moved on.

We are left with no concept of body, or physical, or material, and no coherent mind-body problem. The world is what it is, with its various aspects: mechanical, chemical, electrical, optical, mental, and so on. We may study them and seek to relate them, but there is no more a mind-body problem than an electricity-body problem or a valence-body problem. One can doubtless devise artificial distinctions that allow such problems to be formulated, but the exercise seems to make little sense, and indeed is never undertaken apart from the mental aspects of the world. Why it has been commonly felt that these must somehow be treated differently from others is an interesting question, but I am aware of no justification for the belief, nor even much recognition that it is problematic.

So the most important thesis—the mechanical philosophy—did not last; it was gone in a generation, much to the consternation of leading scientists. On the other hand, Cartesian physiology had a lasting impact, and ideas of a somewhat similar cast about neurophysiology and perception have re-emerged in modern theories in the cognitive and brain sciences.

An interest in language provides a third point of contact between the first and second cognitive revolutions. The study of language was greatly stimulated by Cartesian thought, leading to a good deal of productive work which, in a rational world, would have provided much of the foundations of modern linguistics, had it not been forgotten. This work had two components: particular grammar and rational grammar, also called 'universal grammar' or sometimes 'philosophical grammar', a phrase that translates as 'scientific grammar' in modern terminology (these notions did not mean quite the same thing, but we can abstract from the differences). Rational grammar was the study of the basic principles of human language, to which each particular language must conform. Particular grammar was the study of individual cases: French, German, etc. By the mid-seventeenth century, studies of the vernacular were being undertaken, and interesting discoveries were made about French, notably 'the rule of Vaugelas', which was the focus of inquiry for many years. The first explanation for it was given by the linguists and logicians of Port Royal in the 1660s, in terms of concepts of meaning, reference, and indexicals in pretty much their contemporary sense. Much influenced by Cartesian thought along with earlier traditions that remained alive, these same investigators also formulated the first clear notions of phrase structure, along with something similar to grammatical transformations in the modern sense. They also developed a partial theory of relations and inference involving relations, among other achievements. In the case of language, these early modern contributions were scarcely known, even to scholarship, until they were rediscovered during the second cognitive revolution, after somewhat similar ideas had been independently developed.

The last prominent inheritor of this tradition before it was swept aside by behaviourist and structuralist currents was the Danish linguist Otto Jespersen, who argued 75 years ago that the fundamental goal of linguistics is to discover the 'notion of structure' of sentences that every speaker has internalised, enabling the speaker to produce and understand 'free expressions' that are typically new to speaker and hearer or even the history of the language, a regular occurrence of everyday life. A specific 'notion of structure' is the topic of particular grammar, in the sense of the tradition.

This 'notion of structure' in the mind of the speaker finds its way there without instruction. There would be no way to teach it to anyone, even if we knew what it is; parents certainly don't, and linguists have only limited understanding of what is a very hard problem, only recently studied beyond the surface of phenomena. The 'notion of structure' somehow grows in the mind, providing the means for infinite use, for the ability to form and comprehend free expressions.

This observation brings us to a much deeper problem of the
study of language: to discover the basis in the human mind for
this remarkable achievement. Interest in this problem leads to
the study of universal grammar. A theory of universal grammar
can be envisaged for syntax, Jespersen believed, but not for morphology, which varies among languages in accidental ways.

These ideas seem basically correct, but they made little sense
within the prevailing behaviourist or structuralist assumptions of
Jespersen's day. They were forgotten—or worse, rejected with
much scorn and little comprehension—until new understanding
made it possible to rediscover something similar, and still later,
to discover that they entered into a rich tradition.

It makes sense, I think, to view what happened in the 1950s
as a confluence between ideas that have a traditional flavour but
that had been long forgotten, and new understanding that made it
possible to approach at least some of the traditional questions in a
more serious way than heretofore. Previously, fundamental problems could be posed, though obscurely, but it was impossible to
do very much with them. The core idea about language, to borrow Wilhelm von Humboldt's formulation in the early eighteenth
century, is that language involves 'the infinite use of finite means',
something that seemed paradoxical. The means must be finite, because the brain is finite. But the use of these means is infinite,
without bounds; one can always say something new, and the array
of expressions from which normal usage is drawn is astronomical
in scale—far beyond any possibility of storage, and unbounded in
principle, so that storage is impossible. These are trivially obvious
aspects of ordinary language and its use, though it was not clear
how to come to grips with them.

The new understanding had to do with computational
processes, sometimes called 'generative' processes. These ideas
had been clarified enormously in the formal sciences. By the mid-
twentieth century, the concept of 'infinite use of finite means'

was very well understood, at least in one of its aspects. It is a core part of the foundations of mathematics and led to startling discoveries about decidability, completeness, and mathematical truth; and it underlies the theory of computers. The ideas were implicit as far back as Euclidean geometry and classical logic, but it wasn't until the late nineteenth and early twentieth century that they became really clarified and enriched. By the 1950s, certainly, they could readily be applied to traditional problems of language that had seemed paradoxical before, and that could only be vaguely formulated, not really addressed. That made it possible to return to some of the traditional insights—or more accurately, to reinvent them, since everything had unfortunately been forgotten; and to take up the work that constitutes much of the contemporary study of language.

In these terms, the 'notion of structure' in the mind is a generative procedure, a finite object that characterises an infinite array of 'free expressions', each a mental structure with a certain form and meaning. In this sense, the generative procedure provides for 'infinite use of finite means'. Particular grammar becomes the study of these generative procedures for English, Hungarian, Warlpiri, Swahili, or whatever. Rational or universal grammar is the study of the innate basis for the growth of these systems in the mind when presented with the scattered, limited, and ambiguous data of experience. Such data fall far short of determining one or another language without rigid and narrow initial restrictions.

While the newly available ideas opened the way to very productive study of traditional problems, it is important to recognise that they only partially capture traditional concerns. Take the concepts 'infinite use of finite means' and production of 'free expressions'. A generative procedure incorporated in the mind/brain may provide the *means* for such 'infinite use', but that still leaves us far from what traditional investigators sought to understand: ultimately, the creative aspect of language use in something like the Cartesian sense. To put it differently, the insights of the formal sciences allow us to identify and to investigate only one of two very different ideas that are conflated in traditional formulations: the infinite scope of finite means (now a topic of inquiry), and whatever enters into the normal use of the objects that fall within this infinite scope (still a mystery). The distinction is crucial. It is basically the difference between a cognitive system that stores an infinite array of information in a finite mind/brain, and systems that access that information to carry out the various actions of our lives. It is the distinction between knowledge and action—between competence and performance, in standard technical usage.

The problem is general, not restricted to the study of language. The cognitive and biological sciences have discovered a lot about vision and motor control, but these discoveries are limited to mechanisms. No one even thinks of asking why a person looks at a sunset or reaches for a banana, and how such decisions are made. The same is true of language. A modern generative grammar seeks to determine the mechanisms that underlie the fact that the sentence I am now producing has the form and meaning it does, but has nothing to say about how I chose to form it, or why.

Yet another respect in which the contemporary cognitive revolution is similar to its predecessor is in the importance assigned to innate structure. Here the ideas are of much more ancient vintage, traceable back to Plato, who famously argued that what people know cannot possibly be the result of experience. They must have far-reaching prior knowledge.

Terminology aside, the point is hardly controversial, and has only been considered so in recent years—one of those examples of regression that I mentioned earlier (I put aside here the traditional doctrine that 'nothing is in the mind that is not first in the senses', to be understood, I think, in terms of rich metaphysical assumptions that are properly to be reframed in epistemological terms). Hume is considered the arch- empiricist, but his inquiry into 'the science of human nature' recognised that we must discover those 'parts of [our] knowledge' that are derived 'by the original hand of nature'—innate knowledge, in other terms. To question this is about as sensible as to suppose that the growth of an embryo to a chicken rather than a giraffe is determined by nutritional inputs.

Plato went on to offer an explanation of the fact that experience scarcely accounts for the fringes of knowledge attained: the reminiscence theory, which holds that knowledge is remembered from an earlier existence. Today many are inclined to ridicule that proposal, but mistakenly. It is correct, in essence, though we would put it differently. Through the centuries, it has been understood that there must be something right about the idea. Leibniz, for example, argued that Plato's conception of innate knowledge is basically correct, though it must be 'purged of the error of reminiscence'—how, he could not really say. Modern biology offers a way to do so: the genetic endowment constitutes what we 'remember from an earlier existence'. Like the neurophysiological rephrasing of Cartesian tubes with animal spirits, this too is a kind of a story, because so little is known about the matter, even in far simpler domains than language. Nevertheless, the story does provide a plausible indication of where to look for an answer to the question of how we remember things from an earlier existence, bringing it from the domain of mysteries to that of possible scientific inquiry.

As in the theory of vision, and the cognitive sciences generally (in fact, much of science), we can study these questions at various levels. At one level, we can seek to identify the cellular structures involved in these operations. Or we can study the properties of these objects more abstractly—in this case, in terms of computational theories of mind and the symbolic representations they make available. Such investigations have something of the character of the study of structural formulas of chemistry or the Periodic table. In the case of language, we can be reasonably confident that the computational structure is largely innate; otherwise, no language could be acquired. A reasonable conjecture is that at root, there is only one fixed computational procedure that underlies all languages, and enough is understood for us to be able to spell out some of its likely properties. These have been major topics of inquiry during the past 40 years. From the 1950s, and particularly in the past fifteen years as new theoretical ideas became available, languages of a very broad typological range have come under intensive scrutiny, and surprising properties have been discovered, sometimes fairly plausible explanations for them. Vastly more is known about languages as a result of this work, and some of the leading questions on the research agenda today could not have been formulated or even imagined not many years ago.

The Second Cognitive Revolution

In such ways as these, the second cognitive revolution has rediscovered, reformulated, and to some extent addressed some of the most venerable themes of our cultural tradition, back to its early origins.

As I mentioned, the second cognitive revolution involved a shift of perspective from the behaviourist, structuralist approaches that constituted the orthodoxy of the day: a shift from the study of behaviour and its products to the study of states and properties of the mind that enter into thought and action. Reconsidered in these terms, the study of language is not the study of texts or their elements, or of procedures for identifying such elements and their arrangement, the primary concerns of European and American structuralism. Still less so is it the study of 'dispositions to respond' or other constructs of behaviourist doctrine that cannot even be coherently formulated, in my opinion, though they have been taken seriously in philosophy of mind—to its detriment, I believe. What had been the topic of inquiry—behaviour, texts, etc.— is now just data, with no privileged status, standing alongside any other data that might prove relevant for the investigation of the mind. Behaviour and texts are of no more intrinsic interest than, say, observations of electrical activity of the brain, which has become quite suggestive in recent years. We cannot know in advance what data will advance the study of the 'notion of structure' that enters into the normal use of language, and its origins in initial endowment.

The perceptual judgments called 'linguistic intuitions' are also just data, to be evaluated alongside other kinds: they do not constitute *the* data base for the study of language, any more than observed behaviour and its products do. The contrary is widely argued, but mistakenly, I think. These data may have a special status, however, in a different sense. A theory that departs too radically from linguistic intuitions will not be an account of language, but of something else. Furthermore, we cannot exclude the possibility that a future science of mind may simply dispense with the concept of language in our sense, or those of other cultures that relate to the same obscure and complex domain. That has already happened in contemporary linguistics. It is also the norm, as understanding progresses.

The shift of perspective was, in essence, a shift from something like natural history to at least potential natural science. It should also not be controversial, in my opinion. Contrary to what is often maintained, sometimes with great passion, it in no way conflicts with pursuit of other interests. If anything, it may facilitate them, insofar as it progresses.

Also pointless, in my opinion, is the controversy that has arisen over the abstract (in this case, computational) approach to the study of mind. Efforts to allay uneasiness about the approach commonly introduce computer metaphors: the hardware–software distinction, for example. A computer has hardware and we write software for it; the brain is the hardware and the mind the software. The metaphors are harmless if not taken too seriously but it should be borne in mind that the proposed analogues are much more obscure than the original they are supposed to clarify. The hardware–software distinction raises all sorts of problems that do not arise in the study of an organic object. What is hardware and what is software is largely a matter of decision and convenience. But the brain is a real natural object, just as a molecule is, whether we study its abstract properties (say, structural formulas) or its postulated components. The problems that plague the hardware–software distinction, which are probably unanswerable, do not arise in the study of the mind/brain. So the metaphor should not be pressed beyond the point where it may be helpful.

The second cognitive revolution has led to real advances in certain areas, among them, language and vision, which also figured prominently in the first cognitive revolution. It is less clear that there have been advances in second-order reflection about these matters. I'll come back to that, but first a few comments about the study of language.

The Language Faculty

It seems now reasonably well established that there is a special component of the human brain (call it 'the language faculty') that is specifically dedicated to language. That subsystem of the brain (or the mind, from the abstract perspective) has an initial state which is genetically determined, like all other components of the body: the kidney, the circulatory system, and so on. The study of that initial state is a contemporary version of traditional universal (rational, philosophical) grammar. This aspect of biological endowment appears to be close to uniform across the species, apart from pathology. It also seems to be unique in essentials. That is, its essential properties do not seem to be found in other organisms, perhaps even elsewhere in the organic world.

The language faculty changes from its initial state during early life, as do other biological systems. It 'grows' from the initial state through childhood, reaching a relatively steady state at some stage of maturation. This is the process of language acquisition, sometimes misleadingly called 'language learning'; the process seems to bear little resemblance to what is called 'learning'. It seems that growth levels off before puberty, perhaps as early as six to eight, some investigators believe. After the system stabilises, changes still take place, but they seem to be at the margins: acquisition of new words, social conventions of usage, and so on. Other organs develop in rather similar ways.

The steady state incorporates a computational (generative) procedure that characterises an infinity of possible expressions, each of which has properties that determine its sound, its meaning, its structural organisation, and so on. We could reasonably call the computational procedure itself the 'language', thinking of a language more or less as 'a way of speaking', one traditional notion.

Adopting this terminology, we take a language to be—to first approximation—a particular state of the language faculty. For Jones to have (know) a language is simply for the language faculty of Jones's mind to be in a particular state. If the state of your language faculty is similar enough to the state of mine, you may understand what I say. Spelling it out a bit further, when my mind produces something that induces my articulatory apparatus to produce noises, and those signals hit your ear, they stimulate your mind to construct some sort of an 'image' (a symbolic structure of some sort), your counterpart to what I was trying to express. If our systems are similar enough you may understand me, more or less, comprehension being a 'more or less' affair.

How does perception of language work? A common assumption is that one component of the mind is a 'parser', which takes a signal and turns it into a symbolic representation. Clearly the parser accesses the language. When you interpret what I say you are using your knowledge of English, not Japanese (if you happen to know Japanese). What the parser yields is of course enhanced and enriched by other systems; you interpret what I say on the basis of beliefs, expectations, and so on, which reach far beyond language.

This approach embodies a number of assumptions that are less than obvious. One is that a parser exists at all—that there is a faculty of the mind that interprets signals independently of other features of the environment. That may well be true, but it need not be. It is commonly assumed that we can be fairly confident of the existence of the parser, while the status of the generative procedure is more problematic. But that is incorrect; the opposite is true. The existence of the generative procedure is far better established from a scientific point of view, and embedded in a much richer theoretical matrix.

A second assumption is that parsers do not grow. Unlike languages and organs of the body generally, they are fixed. The parser for Japanese is the same as for English. The reason for this rather implausible assumption is that we do not know that it is wrong. In a situation of ignorance, one begins with the simplest assumption, expecting it to be disproven as more is learned.

On these assumptions, the changes that take place during language acquisition are in the cognitive state alone; in the 'storage of information', the language, the generative procedure that distinguishes English from Japanese.

A third assumption is that the parser works very efficiently: parsing is 'easy and quick', according to a slogan that has motivated a good deal of research seeking to show that language design yields this result. But the belief is incorrect. Parsing is often

difficult, and often fails, in the sense that the symbolic representation produced by the perceptual mechanism is not the one determined by the language, and may well be incoherent even for
expressions with a determinate and sensible meaning. Many
cases are known, including quite simple ones. Thus all sorts of
problems arise in interpretation of expressions involving some
kind of negative meaning, with such words as 'unless', or 'doubt',
or 'miss'. If I had hoped to see you last summer, but did not, do
I say 'I missed seeing you'? 'I missed not seeing you'? Neither?
Confusion is so compelling that it has even been established in
idiomatic usage. If two aeroplanes pass too close for comfort,
they nearly hit; they don't nearly miss. But the event is called a
'near miss', not a 'near hit'.

For many categories of expressions, parsing fails completely
or is extremely difficult. Such 'parsing failures' have been a major
topic of inquiry in recent years, because they provide a good deal
of evidence into the nature of language processing.

Why then does parsing seem so easy and quick, giving rise
to the conventional false belief? The reason is that when I say
something, you ordinarily understand it instantaneously, without
effort. That much is generally true. In practice, the perceptual
process is close to instantaneous and effortless. But from that
fact we cannot conclude that language is designed for quick and
easy parsing. It shows only that there is a part of language that
we parse easily, and that is the part we tend to use. As a speaker,
I draw from the same scattered part that you are able to deal
with as a hearer, giving rise to the illusion that the system is
somehow 'designed for efficient use'. In fact, the system is 'inef-
ficient', in the sense that large parts of the language—even short
and simple expressions—are unusable, though they have quite
definite sound and meaning, determined by the generative procedure of the language faculty. The language is simply not well
adapted to parsing.

In the background there is a familiar fairy tale sometimes called 'Darwinism' that probably would have shocked Darwin: that the systems of the body are well adapted to their functions, perhaps superbly so. What that is supposed to mean is unclear. It is no principle of biology. On some interpretations, the statement just seems false. Nothing follows about the theory of evolution, which in no way suggests that the systems that have developed should be well adapted to conditions of life. They may be the best that nature could do under the constraints within which organisms evolve, but the outcome may be far from ideal. For all sorts of reasons, specific organs might turn out to be more poorly designed than is possible even within these constraints; perhaps because such design failures contribute to modifications elsewhere in the highly integrated system that improve reproductive capacity. Organs do not evolve independently, of course, and a viable organism has to hang together in complicated ways; breeders know how to breed bigger horses, but it won't help if size increases without highly intricate corresponding changes in the brain, the circulatory system, and much more. In general, little can be said without an understanding of the physical and chemical properties of complex organisms, and if we had that understanding, it would hardly be a surprise to discover significant 'design errors' in organisms that are a 'biological success' (meaning, plenty of them are around).

A familiar example is the human skeleton. Few people escape back problems, because the system is poorly designed from an engineering standpoint. That may be true for large vertebrates generally (though cows don't know how to complain about back pains). The system works well enough for reproductive success, and perhaps it is the 'best solution' under the conditions of vertebrate evolution. But that's as far as the theory of evolution reaches. In the case of language, there would be no reason to expect the system to be 'well adapted to its functions', and it seems not to be (at least, if we try to give some natural meaning to these obscure notions). The fact that large parts of language are unusable doesn't bother us; we use the parts that are usable, hardly an interesting fact.

There are similar assumptions in the theory of learnability. It's often assumed that languages must be learnable. Natural languages are sometimes defined as those learnable under normal conditions. But that need not be true. We could have all sorts of possible languages in our heads, which we cannot access. There would be no way to acquire them, though they are possible states of our language faculty. There is recent work suggesting that languages may indeed be learnable, but if so, that's an empirical discovery. It is not a conceptual necessity.

I've said nothing so far about the production of language. The reason is that there is little to say of any interest. Apart from peripheral aspects, it remains largely a mystery. As I've already discussed, that is no small gap in our understanding: it has to do with the very criterion of mind, from the Cartesian perspective— not an unreasonable one, though unformulable today in anything like their terms.

Unification Problems

A last issue that was of great importance during the first cognitive revolution and that arises again today, though in a very different form, is the unification problem. This has two aspects. One has to do with the hardware–software relation (to adopt the metaphor): How do the computational procedures of the mind relate to cells and their organisation, or whatever is the proper way to understand the functioning of the brain at this level? A second kind of unification problem is internal to the cognitive sciences. Is there a 'problem-solving' system, or a 'science-forming' system, as a component of the mind, and, if so, are they distinct? Is there some kind of overarching unity?

For the first unification problem, a general faith in unity of science leads to the expectation that an answer exists, whether humans can find it or not. But the second need not have a solution. It could turn out there is no theory of 'mental organs' any more than there is an 'organ theory' for other components of the body: the kidney, the circulatory system, etc. Their fundamental building blocks are the same, but they may not fall together above the cellular level. If that is the case for cognitive systems, then there will be no 'cognitive science' in any very useful sense of the phrase.

Let's turn to the first unification problem: finding the 'physical basis' for computational systems of the mind, to borrow the conventional (but, as noted, highly misleading) terminology. There are several ways to approach the problem. The standard method of the sciences is to study each of these levels, try to discover their properties, and seek some kind of convergence. The problem arises constantly and might be solved (if at all) in quite different ways. Reduction of one system to another is a possible outcome, but it may not be possible: the theory of electricity and magnetism is not reducible to mechanics, and the elementary properties of motion are not reducible to 'the mechanical world view'. Consider chemistry and physics, long separated by what seemed to be an unbridgeable divide. Unification finally took place, though rather recently; in my lifetime, in fact. But it was not reduction of chemistry to physics. Rather, chemistry was unified with a radically altered physics, a step made possible by the quantum-theoretic revolution. What had seemed to be a gap was a real one. A few years later, parts of biology were unified with biochemistry, this time by genuine reduction. In the case of the mental aspects of the world, we have no idea how unification might proceed. Some believe it will be by means of the intermediate level of neurophysiology, perhaps neural nets. Perhaps so, perhaps not. Perhaps the contemporary brain sciences do not yet have the right way of looking at the brain and its function, so that unification in terms of contemporary understanding is impossible. If so, that should not come as a great surprise. The history of science provides many such examples.

This seems a perfectly reasonable way to address the first unification problem, though whether it can succeed, and if so how, we cannot know in advance, any more than in any other case.

There is also a different approach to the problem, which is highly influential though it seems to me not only foreign to the sciences but also close to senseless. This approach divorces the cognitive sciences from a biological setting, and seeks tests to determine whether some object 'manifests intelligence' ('plays chess', 'understands Chinese', or whatever). The approach relies on the 'Turing Test', devised by mathematician Alan Turing, who did much of the fundamental work on the modern theory of computation. In a famous paper of 1950, he proposed a way of evaluating the performance of a computer—basically, by determining whether observers will be able to distinguish it from the performance of people. If they cannot, the device passes the test. There is no fixed Turing Test; rather, a battery of devices constructed on this model. The details need not concern us.

Adopting this approach, suppose we are interested in deciding whether a programmed computer can play chess or understand Chinese. We construct a variant of the Turing Test, and see whether a jury can be fooled into thinking that a human is carrying out the observed performance. If so, we will have 'empirically established' that the computer can play chess, understand Chinese, think, etc., according to proponents of this version of artificial intelligence, while their critics deny that this result would establish the conclusion.

There is a great deal of often heated debate about these matters in the literature of the cognitive sciences, artificial intelligence, and philosophy of mind, but it is hard to see that any serious question has been posed. The question of whether a computer is playing chess, or doing long division, or translating Chinese, is like the question of whether robots can murder or aeroplanes can fly—or people; after all, the 'flight' of the Olympic long jump champion is only an order of magnitude short of that of the chicken champion (so I'm told). These are questions of decision, not fact; decision as to whether to adopt a certain metaphoric extension of common usage.

There is no answer to the question whether aeroplanes *really* fly (though perhaps not space shuttles). Fooling people into mistaking a submarine for a whale doesn't show that submarines really swim; nor does it fail to establish the fact. There is no fact, no meaningful question to be answered, as all agree, in this case. The same is true of computer programs, as Turing took pains to make clear in the 1950 paper that is regularly invoked in these discussions. Here he pointed out that the question whether machines think 'may be too meaningless to deserve discussion', being a question of decision, not fact, though he speculated that in 50 years, usage may have 'altered so much that one will be able to speak of machines thinking without expecting to be contradicted'—as in the case of aeroplanes flying (in English, at least), but not submarines swimming. Such alteration of usage amounts to the replacement of one lexical item by another one with somewhat different properties. There is no empirical question as to whether this is the right or wrong decision.

In this regard, there has been serious regression since the first cognitive revolution, in my opinion. Superficially, reliance on the Turing Test is reminiscent of the Cartesian approach to the existence of other minds. But the comparison is misleading. The Cartesian experiments were something like a litmus test for acidity: they sought to determine whether an object has a certain property, in this case, possession of mind, one aspect of the world. But that is not true of the artificial intelligence debate.

Another superficial similarity is the interest in simulation of behaviour, again only apparent, I think. As I mentioned earlier, the first cognitive revolution was stimulated by the achievements of automata, much as today, and complex devices were constructed to simulate real objects and their functioning: the digestion of a duck, a flying bird, and so on. But the purpose was not to determine whether machines can digest or fly. Jacques de Vaucanson, the great artificer of the period, was concerned to understand the animate systems he was modelling; he constructed mechanical devices in order to formulate and validate theories of his animate models, not to satisfy some performance criterion. His clockwork duck, for example, was intended to be a model of the actual digestion of a duck, not a facsimile that might fool his audience. In short, this was simulation in the manner of normal science: construction of models (in this case, mechanical models) to enhance understanding, not a confused attempt to answer a question that has no meaning.

Computer simulation of course proceeds in a similar way today: the approach to the theory of vision by David Marr and his colleagues, Robert Berwick's investigation of universal parsers, the study of robotics to determine how a person reaches for a cup, and so on. That is all perfectly sensible, and has often been very revealing as well. Also perfectly sensible is the development of robots for factories, or expert systems. That is as legitimate as making bulldozers. But it would be of no interest to show that the performance of a bulldozer could be mistaken for that of a person, and a computer program that could 'beat' a grandmaster in chess is about as interesting as a bulldozer that can 'win' the Olympic weight-lifting competition.

Returning to the second unification problem, there is, as I mentioned, no particular reason to expect a solution. It has been assumed over a fairly broad range—from Skinner to Piaget in psychology, and very commonly in the philosophy of mind—that

people (or perhaps organisms generally) have a uniform array of
learning and problem- solving procedures that apply indifferently
in all domains; general mechanisms of intelligence, or whatever
(perhaps changing through childhood, as Piaget thought, but at
each stage, uniformly applicable to any task or problem). The
more we learn about human or animal intelligence, the less that
seems likely. There are no serious proposals as to what such 'general mechanisms' might be. It seems that the brain is like other
known biological systems: modular, constituted of highly specialised subsystems that have their particular character and domains of operation, interacting in all sorts of ways. There is a
good deal to say about the topic, but I will have to leave the matter here.

Knowledge of Language

Let me end with a few words about the kinds of questions that
arise today in the study of language specifically, and the kinds
of answers that can now be offered. Here things become interesting and intricate, and I will only be able to illustrate with a
few examples.

Take some simple phrase, say, 'brown house'. What do we
know about it? We know that it consists of two words; children
have such understanding well before they can articulate it directly. In my speech, probably yours, the two words have the
same vowel; they are in the formal relation of assonance. Similarly, 'house' and 'mouse' are in the fuller formal relation of
rhyme. We know further that if I tell you about a brown house,
I want you to understand that its exterior is brown, not necessarily its interior. So a brown house is something with a brown
exterior. Similarly, if you see a house, you see its exterior. We cannot now see the building in which we are meeting, unless perhaps
there were a window and a mirror outside reflecting its outer surface. Then we could see the building much in the way we can see

the aeroplane in which we are flying if we can look out the window and see the surface of the wing.

The same is true of a very wide range of objects: boxes, igloos, mountains, etc. Suppose there is a lighted cave inside a mountain with a straight tunnel leading to it, so we can see into the cave when standing in the entrance to the tunnel. But we do not see the mountain in that case. If we are inside the cave, we cannot see the mountain, though we could if a mirror outside the entrance reflected its surface. Over a large range of cases, we think of an object somehow as its exterior surface, almost like a geometrical surface. This is even true of invented objects, even impossible ones. If I tell you that I painted my spherical cube brown, I intend you to understand that I painted its exterior surface brown.

But we do not think of a brown house just as a surface. If it were a surface, you could be near the house even if you were inside it. If a box were really a surface, then a marble in the box and another marble outside it at the same distance from the surface would be equidistant from the box. But they are not. So an object of this kind is at least an exterior surface with a distinguished interior.

A further look shows that the meanings of such terms are still more complex. If I say I painted my house brown, you understand me to mean that I painted the exterior surface brown; but I can say, perfectly intelligibly, that I painted my house brown *on the inside*. So we can think of the house as an interior surface, with the background circumstances complicated slightly. In technical jargon, this is called *marked* and *unmarked* usage; in the unmarked case, with a null context, we take the house to be the exterior surface, but a marked usage is allowed when the context provides the proper conditions. This is a pervasive feature of the semantics of natural language. If I say 'I climbed the mountain', you know that I went up—generally; I may at the moment be going down even if I am climbing the mountain, yet another fact about meaning that we know. But I can say 'I climbed *down* the mountain', adding extra information that permits the marked usage. The same holds quite generally.

Notice that my house is perfectly concrete. When I return to my house at night, I am returning to a concrete physical thing. On the other hand, it is also abstract: an exterior surface with a designated interior and a marked property that allows it to be an interior surface. We can refer to the house as simultaneously abstract and concrete, as when I say I painted my wooden house brown just before it was blown down by a tornado. And I can say that after my house blew down, leaving just rubble, I rebuilt *it* (my house) somewhere else, although it is no longer the same house; such terms of dependent reference as 'same', 'it', and 're-' function rather differently in this case, and differently still when we consider other objects. Take London, also both concrete and abstract; it can be destroyed by a fire or an administrative decision. If London is reduced to dust, *it*—that is, London—can be *re*-built elsewhere and still be the *same* city, London, unlike my house, which won't be the same house if it is reduced to dust and *it* is *re*-built somewhere else. The motor of my car is still different. If it is reduced to dust, it cannot be rebuilt, though if only partially damaged, it can be. If a physically indistinguishable motor is built from the same dust, it is not the same motor, but a different one. Judgments can be rather delicate, involving factors that have barely been explored.

These remarks only scratch the surface, but they perhaps suffice to indicate that there need be no objects in the world that correspond to what we talk about, even in the simplest cases, nor does anyone believe that there are. About all we can say at a general level is that the words of our language provide complex perspectives that offer us highly special ways to think about things—to ask for them, tell people about them, etc. Real natural language semantics will seek to discover these perspectives and the principles that underlie them. *People* use words to refer to things in complex ways, reflecting interests and circumstances, but the *words* do not refer; there is no word–thing relation of the Fregean variety, nor a more complex word–thing–person relation of the kind proposed by Charles Sanders Peirce in equally classic work in the foundations of semantics. These approaches may be quite appropriate for the study of invented symbolic systems (for which they were initially designed, at least in the case of Frege). But they do not seem to provide appropriate concepts for the study of natural language. A word–thing(–person) relation seems as much of an illusion as a word–molecular motion(– person) relation, though it is true that each use of a word by a person is associated with a specific motion of molecules, and sometimes with a specific thing, viewed in a particular way. The study of speech production and analysis postulates no such mythical relations, but rather asks how the person's mental representations enter into articulation and perception. The study of the meaning of expressions should proceed along similar lines, I believe. This does not mean that the study of meaning is the study of use, any more than the study of motor control is the study of particular actions. Usage and other actions provide evidence about the systems we hope to understand, as may information from other domains, but nothing more than that.

What we know about such simple words as 'brown', 'house', 'climb', 'London', 'it', 'same', etc., must be almost entirely unlearned. We are unaware of what we know without inquiry, and it could well turn out to be inaccessible to consciousness, so that we can learn about it only as we learn about circulation of the blood and visual perception. Even if experience were rich and extensive, it could not possibly provide information of the kind just barely sampled, or account for its uniformity among people with differing experience. But the question is academic, since experience is very limited. At the peak period of language acquisition, from ages two to six, a child is picking up words at an average of about one an hour, hence on a single exposure under highly ambiguous circumstances. Miracles aside, it must be that the child is relying on those 'parts of [its] knowledge' that are derived 'by the original hand of nature', in Hume's terms—on 'memory from an earlier existence', as reformulated within the framework of genetic endowment (in some as yet unknown manner).

It is sometimes argued that genes do not carry enough information to yield such highly intricate results, but that argument is without force. One could say the same, with equal merit, about any other component of the body. Knowing nothing about the relevant physical–chemical constraints, one might be led to conclude (absurdly) that it takes infinite information to determine that an embryo will have two arms (rather than 11 or 93), so that it must be 'learned' or determined by the nutritional environment of the embryo. Just how the genes determine the specific number of arms, or the delicate structure of the visual system, or the properties of human language, is a matter for discovery, not idle speculation. What seems evident from the most elementary observations is that interaction with the environment can have at most a marginally shaping and triggering effect. The assumption is taken for granted (virtually without direct evidence) in the case of development 'below the neck', metaphorically speaking. The conclusions should be no different in the case of mental aspects of the world, unless we adopt illegitimate forms of methodological dualism, which are all too prevalent.

Notice further that we learn little about these matters from dictionaries, even the most elaborate. The entry for the word 'house' will say nothing about what I just reviewed, a bare beginning. Until very recently, there was little recognition of the rich complexity of the semantics of words, though, for accuracy, we should recall that there had been some penetrating discussion of the matter in the past, mostly forgotten. Even very elementary features of the meaning and sound of words are not presented in the most extensive dictionaries, which are useful only for people who already know the answers, apart from the further details that the dictionary provides.

That is not a defect of dictionaries; rather, their merit. It would be pointless—in fact, highly confusing—for a dictionary of English, Spanish, Japanese, or whatever, to present the actual meanings of words, even if they had been discovered. Similarly, someone studying English as a second language would only be confused by instruction about the real principles of grammar; these they already know, being human. Though not by conscious design, dictionaries rightly focus on what a person could not know, namely superficial details of the kind provided by experience; not on what comes to us 'by the original hand of nature'. The latter is the topic of a different inquiry, the study of human nature, which is part of the sciences. Its aims are virtually complementary to those of the practical lexicographer. Dictionaries intended for use should—and in practice do—fill in gaps in the innate knowledge that dictionary users bring with them.

We expect that the basic semantic properties of words, being unlearned and unlearnable, will be shared with little variation across languages. These are aspects of human nature, which provides us with specific ways to think about the world, highly intricate and curious ones. That is clear even from the simplest cases, such as those just briefly reviewed.

When we turn to more complex expressions, the gap between what the speaker/hearer knows and the evidence available becomes a chasm, and the richness of innate endowment is still more evident. Take simple sentences, say, the following:

1 John is eating an apple.
2 John is eating.

In 2, the grammatical object of 'eat' is missing, and we understand the sentence on the analogy of 1, to mean (more or less) that John is eating something-or-other. The mind fills the gap, postulating an unspecified object of the verb.

Actually, that is not quite true. Consider the following brief discourse:

3 John is eating his shoe. He must have lost his mind.

But the sentence 2 does not include the case of eating one's shoe. If I say that John is eating, I mean that he is eating in a normal way; having dinner, perhaps, but not eating his shoe. What the mind fills in is not an unspecified grammatical object, but something normal; that's part of the meaning of the constructions (though what counts as normal is not).

Let's suppose that this is roughly correct, and turn to a slightly more complex case. Consider the sentence 4:

4 John is too stubborn to talk to Bill.

What it means is that John is too stubborn for him (John) to talk to Bill—he is so stubborn he refuses to talk to Bill. Suppose we drop 'Bill' from 4, yielding 5:

5 John is too stubborn to talk to.

Following the principle illustrated by 1 and 2, we expect 5 to be understood on the analogy of 4, with the mind filling the gap with some (normal) object of 'talk to'. The sentence 5, then, should mean that John is too stubborn for him (John) to talk to someone-or-other. But it doesn't mean that at all. Rather, it means that John is too stubborn for anyone (maybe us) to talk to him, John.

For some reason, the semantic relations invert when the object of 'talk to' in 4 is deleted, unlike 1, where they remain unchanged. The same holds for more complex cases, as in 6:

6 John is too stubborn to expect the teacher to talk to.

The meaning is that John is too stubborn for anyone (maybe us) to expect the teacher to talk to him (John). In this case, parsing difficulties may make the facts harder to detect, though the sentence is still a very simple one, well below average sentence length in normal discourse.

We know all of these things, though without awareness. The reasons lie beyond even possible consciousness. None of this could have been learned. The facts are known to people who have had no relevant experience with such constructions. Parents and peers who impart knowledge of language (to the limited extent that they do), have no awareness of such facts. If a child made errors using such expressions, it would be virtually impossible to correct them, even if the errors were noticed (which is most unlikely, and surely rare to the point of nonexistence). We expect that interpretations will be similar in every language, and, so far as is known, that is indeed true.

Just as dictionaries do not even begin to provide the meanings of words, so the most elaborate multi-volume traditional grammars do not recognise, let alone try to explain, even elementary phenomena of the kind just illustrated. It is only in very recent years, in the course of attempts to construct explicit generative procedures, that such properties have come to light. Correspondingly, it has become clear how little is known of the elementary phenomena of language. That's not a surprising discovery. As long as people were satisfied that an apple falls to the ground because that is its natural place, even the basic properties of motion remained hidden. A willingness to be puzzled by the simplest phenomena is the very beginning of science. The attempt to formulate questions about simple phenomena has led to remarkable discoveries about elementary aspects of nature, previously unsuspected.

In the course of the second cognitive revolution, myriad facts of the kind just illustrated have been discovered in well-studied languages, and increasingly a fair sample of others; and, more importantly, some understanding has been gained of the innate principles of the language faculty that account for what people know in such cases. The examples just given are simple ones, but it has been no trivial matter to discover the principles of universal grammar that interact to account for their properties. When we move on, complexities mount very quickly. As tentative answers have been developed, they have sometimes opened the way to the discovery of hitherto unknown phenomena, often very puzzling ones; and, in not a few cases, new understanding as well. Nothing similar has happened in the rich tradition of 2500 years of research into language. It is an exciting development, with few parallels in the study of the mind, I think it is fair to say.

As I mentioned earlier, the conditions of language acquisition lead us to expect that, in some fundamental sense, there must be only one language. There are two basic reasons. First, most of what we know must be 'pre-existent', in a modern version of Plato's insights; people lack evidence for even simple aspects of what they know. Furthermore, there is strong reason to suppose that no one is designed to speak one or another language. If my children were to have grown up in Japan, they would have spoken Japanese, indistinguishably from natives. The ability to acquire language is basically a fixed, uniform species property.

For such reasons, we expect all languages to be fundamentally alike, cast to the same mold, differing only in marginal ways that limited and ambiguous experience suffices to determine. We are now able to see how this might be so. It is now possible to formulate at least the outlines of a uniform, invariant computational procedure that assigns the meanings of arbitrary expressions for any language, and provides them with sensorimotor properties within a restricted range. At last, we may be approaching a period when the expectations of rational grammarians from Port Royal to Jespersen may be given a clear formulation and empirical support.

While this uniform procedure—in essence, *the* human language—is common to all the specific manifestations of the human language faculty, it is not completely fixed. Variations at the periphery distinguish English from the Australian language Warlpiri, to take two cases that have been studied in considerable depth because they look so different on the surface. There are now some plausible hypotheses about where in the nature of language such differences reside. It seems (as we would anticipate) that they lie in restricted areas of language. One range of differences is in inflectional systems, as Jespersen suggested when he questioned the possibility of a universal morphology alongside a universal syntax. That is why so much of second-language learning is devoted to such morphological properties (in contrast, no Japanese- speaking student of English wastes time studying the properties of the words we looked at earlier, or the sentences 1–6). An English speaker studying German has to learn about the case system, mostly lacking in English. Sanskrit and Finnish have a richer array, while Chinese has even more meagre resources than English.

Or so it appears, on the surface. Work of the past few years suggests that these appearances may be illusions. The languages may have similar case systems, perhaps the same one. There may be a universal morphology after all. It is just that in Chinese (and, mostly, in English) the cases are present only in the mental computations, not reaching the sensorimotor organs, while in German they partially reach these performance systems (and in Sanskrit and Finnish, still more so). The effects of case are seen in English and Chinese, even if nothing 'comes out of the mouth'. The languages do not differ much in inflection (if at all), but the sensorimotor systems access the mental computation at different points, so that there are differences in what is articulated. It may be that much of the typological variation of language reduces to factors of this kind.

Suppose we succeed in identifying the points of potential variation among languages—call them *parameters*, their values to be set by experience. Then it should be possible literally to deduce Hungarian or Swahili or any other possible human language by setting the values of the parameters one way or another. And the process of language acquisition would be just the process of fixing those parameters—finding out the answers to a specific 'list of questions', in effect. It must be that these questions are readily answered, given the empirical conditions on language acquisition. A large part of the empirical study of language acquisition in varied languages has been framed in these terms in recent years, with encouraging progress, and plenty of new dilemmas.

If all of this turns out to be on the right track, it will follow that languages are learnable—a non-obvious conclusion, as noted. To discover the language of a community, the child has to determine how the values of the parameters are set. With the answers given, the full language is determined, lexicon aside. The properties of such sentences as 'John is too stubborn to talk to' need not be learned—fortunately, or no one would know them; they are determined in advance, as part of the biological endowment. As for the lexicon, it is unnecessary to learn properties of the kind discussed earlier—again, fortunately—because these too are determined in advance. Languages will be learnable, because there is little to learn.

What about the matter of usability? We know that parts of language are unusable, posing no problem for daily life because we keep to what is usable, naturally. But some recent work suggests that the unusability property may be more deeply rooted in the nature of language than previously suspected. It appears that the computations of language have to be optimal, in a certain well-defined sense. Suppose we think of the process of constructing an expression as selection of words from the mental lexicon, combining them, and performing certain operations on the structures so formed, continuing until an expression is constructed with a sound and meaning. It seems that some such processes are blocked, even if legitimate at each step, because others are more optimal. If so, a linguistic expression is not just a symbolic object constructed by the computational system, but rather an object constructed in an optimal fashion.

Those familiar with problems of computational complexity will recognise that there are dangers lurking here. Optimality considerations of the kind just sketched require comparison of computations to determine whether some object is a valid linguistic expression. Unless sharp constraints are introduced, the complexity of such computations will explode, and it will be virtually impossible to know what is an expression of the language. The search for such constraints, and for empirical evidence from varied languages that bears on them, raises difficult and intriguing problems, now just being considered seriously.

If such optimality properties exist, and it seems they do, then still further questions arise: Can we show that the usable expressions do not raise problems of unfeasible computation, while unusable ones may do so—perhaps the source of their unusability? These are hard and interesting questions. We understand enough to formulate them intelligibly today, but not much more.

If language design has something like this character, then the unusability property may be rather deep.

Recent work also suggests that languages may be optimal in a different sense. The language faculty is part of the overall architecture of the mind/brain, interacting with other components: the sensorimotor apparatus and the systems that enter into thought, imagination, and other mental processes, and their expression and interpretation. The language faculty *interfaces* with other components of the mind/brain. The interface properties, imposed by the systems among which language is embedded, set constraints on what this faculty must be if it is to function within the mind/brain. The articulatory and perceptual systems, for example, require that expressions of the language have a linear (temporal, 'left-to-right') order at the interface; sensorimotor systems that operated in parallel would allow richer modes of expression of higher dimensionality.

Suppose we have some account of general properties P of the systems with which language interacts at the interface. We can now ask a question that is not precise, but is not vacuous either: How good a solution is language to the conditions P? How perfectly does language satisfy the general conditions imposed at the interface? If a divine architect were faced with the problem of designing something to satisfy these conditions, would actual human language be one of the candidates, or close to it?

Recent work suggests that language is surprisingly 'perfect' in this sense, satisfying in a near-optimal way some rather general conditions imposed at the interface. Insofar as that is true, language seems unlike other objects of the biological world, which are typically a rather messy solution to some class of problems, given the physical constraints and the materials that history and accident have made available. Evolution is a 'tinkerer', in the phrase of evolutionary biologist François Jacob, and the results of its tinkering may not be what a skilled engineer would construct from scratch to satisfy existing conditions. In the study of the inorganic world, for mysterious reasons, it has been a valuable heuristic to assume that things are very elegant and beautiful. If physicists run across a number like 7, they may assume that they have missed something, because 7 is too ridiculous a number: it must really be 2^3, or something like that. A standard quip is that the only actual numbers are 1, 2, infinity, and maybe 3—but not 79. And asymmetries, independent principles with much the same explanatory force, and other oddities that deface the picture of nature are viewed with a degree of scepticism. Similar intuitions have been reasonably successful in the study of language. If they are on target, it may mean that language is rather special and unique, or that we do not understand enough about other organic systems to see that they are much the same, in their basic structure and organisation.

Possibly all of this is mere artefact; we are just not looking at things correctly. That would hardly be surprising. But the conclusions look reasonable, and if they are correct, they pose new mysteries to add to the ancient ones.

2

Language and Nature

I would like to discuss two aspects of an ancient and perplexing topic. The first has to do with the mind generally: What is its place in nature (if any)? The second has to do with language specifically: How do its elements (words, sentences, etc.) relate to the world? The first topic leads to questions of materialism, dualism, and the mind-body problem. The second to questions of reference, meaning, intentionality, and the like.

Let me begin with simple proposals concerning each of these topics. Both theses should, I think, be uncontroversial, though they are often vigorously denied, sometimes implicitly. I'd like to proceed to contrast them with other theses that are much more far-reaching and significant, and are widely held, though I think untenable.

Naturalism and Language–World Relations: Weak and Strong Theses

The first of the uncontroversial theses has to do with the first and more general aspect of the topic. It is a methodological proposal about the study of mind and nature. The world has many aspects: mechanical, chemical, optical, electrical, and so on. Among these are its mental aspects. The thesis is that all should be studied in the same way, whether we are considering the motion of the planets, fields of force, structural formulas for complex mole-

41

cules, or computational properties of the language faculty. Let's call this a 'naturalistic approach to mind', meaning that we seek to investigate the mental aspects of the world by the methods of rational inquiry characteristic of the natural sciences. Whether the results of a naturalistic approach merit the honorific term 'science' depends on the results it achieves. One can sensibly ask how far a naturalistic approach might carry us towards topics of human concern and intellectual significance, but there is no question about its legitimacy, I will assume.

We expect to find quite different sorts of things as we study the various aspects of the world, but the burden of proof is surely on any demand for different modes of inquiry or standards of evaluation. The methodological proposal is that this burden has not been met, nor is there any reason to attempt to do so.

Such categories as chemical, optical, etc., are neither clear nor deep, a matter of no concern. We begin any inquiry with puzzles about unexplained phenomena, which we try to sort out into categories that seem to fall together, caring little about boundaries, and not expecting the categories to survive inquiry. They are not intended to cut nature at its joints; rather, to serve as a convenience. Conventional categories may be useful for administrative purposes in universities or government funding agencies. But in serious work, they are not intended to delimit the scope of inquiry. Consider, say, chemistry and biology. The distinguished biologist François Jacob observes that 'for the biologist, the living begins only with what was able to constitute a genetic program', while 'for the chemist, in contrast, it is somewhat arbitrary to make a demarcation where there can only be continuity'. Others might want to add crystals to the mix, or self-replicating automata of the kind pioneered by John von Neumann. There is no 'right answer', no reason to seek sharper boundaries to distinguish among physical, biological, chemical, and other aspects of the world. No discipline has any prior claim to particular objects in the world, whether they are complex molecules, stars, or human language.

I should make it clear that these remarks are not uncontentious. There is much vigorous debate about the matter in the case of language, though rarely about other objects of the world. It is also commonly argued that language must be construed in some fundamentally different way from other objects, perhaps as a 'Platonic entity' or in accord with 'Grandma's view' (understood to be a kind of 'folk psychology'), keeping to certain kinds of evidence but not others. A standard argument is that 'linguistics' must keep to the perceptual judgments called 'linguistic intuitions' but not discoveries about the electrical activity of the brain or language processing; only 'psychology' can introduce this further evidence. I won't pursue the matter here (I have elsewhere, to some extent), but will only state (unfairly) that the arguments presented seem to me fallacious, sometimes quite irrational, and commonly based on serious misinterpretation.

Given preliminary guesses about kinds of phenomena, we pose questions about them and try to answer them, if possible by constructing explanatory theories that postulate often-hidden entities and principles that they obey. We also seek unification: that is, we try to discover how these theories are related, perhaps in terms of more fundamental entities or overarching principles from which the results of particular theoretical inquiries are derived. One kind of unification is literal reduction; the demonstration that one theory can literally be incorporated within a more fundamental one. That is a possibility, though one that is rare in the history of science on any large scale (in narrower spheres it happens all the time). In general, unification proceeds along various paths, a fact worth bearing in mind when we consider the 'mind-body problem'.

Consider two classical examples: (1) Newton's account of the principles of mechanics, and (2) the unification of chemistry and physics.

Newton's achievement took place in the context of the effort to establish 'the mechanical philosophy', the idea that animated the seventeenth century scientific revolution. The guiding thesis was that the world is a complicated machine that could in principle be built by a skilled artisan—and indeed had been, in some manner that had to be resolved. The goal was to eliminate the mystical baggage of the prevailing neoscholastic physics: mysterious 'sympathies and antipathies' that drew objects together or kept them apart, and so on. One basic task was to show that interaction of objects could be explained in terms of direct contact, as in the workings of a clock: success in that endeavour would solve the unification problem by reduction to the mechanical world view.

In this case, there was no unification. Newton demonstrated that the mechanical world view is false. Terrestrial and planetary motion escape the bounds of contact mechanics. There are occult forces after all. The discovery was a major turning point in the history of Western thought. Newton's conclusion, which he himself considered 'absurd', ultimately became scientific 'common sense', though not without turmoil, anguish, and intellectual struggle.

The unification of chemistry and physics followed a somewhat similar course. It is rather recent, dating to Linus Pauling's discovery of the physical nature of the chemical bond just 60 years ago, in terms of radically changed notions of 'physical'. Before Max Planck, there seemed to be an unbridgeable divide; a standard history of chemistry observes: 'The chemist's matter was discrete and discontinuous, the physicist's energy continuous', a 'nebulous mathematical world of energy and electromagnetic waves . . .' (William Brock). Well into this century, the chemist's atoms were considered 'theoretical, metaphysical entities'; interpreted operationally, they provided a 'conceptual basis for assigning relative elementary weights and for assigning molecular formulae', and these instrumental devices were distinguished from 'a highly controversial physical atomism, which made claims concerning the ultimate mechanical nature of all substances'. Unification was achieved only after revolutionary changes in the concepts of physics, including Bohr's model of the atom and quantum theory. As recently as the 1920s, the very idea of explaining the instrumental notions of chemical atomism in physical terms—in terms of the Bohr model, for example— was ridiculed by distinguished scientists. Earlier, eminent scientists had made fun of attempts to find physical accounts of fields and molecules, regarding them as basically calculating devices, to be given only an instrumental interpretation.

Such attitudes, and their fate, are worth keeping in mind when we turn to assessments of the status of the cognitive sciences and the 'mind-body problem' today. Thus Nobel Prize-winning biologist Gerald Edelman points out that 'The variance of neural maps is not discrete or two-valued but rather continuous, fine-grained, and extensive', concluding that computational or connectionist theories of the mind, with their discrete models, face a 'crisis', and must be wrong. History, however, suggests caution. There may be a 'crisis', but the chips will fall where they may.

Nineteenth century physics was far better established than the brain sciences of today. One reason is that physics keeps to very simple structures; other scientists do not have that luxury, but must deal with the complexity of the objects of their 'special sciences' so that understanding drops off very quickly—one of several reasons why physics is not a good model for other sciences, perhaps even for the general philosophy of science. In the case of the brain, despite impressive progress, one still scarcely knows where to look, and it would hardly be surprising if today's guesses turned out to be far from the mark. But physics had to undergo radical revisions before physical and chemical atoms could be related, and the 'discrete and discontinuous' matter of the chemist integrated with the apparent continuity of the physicist's universe. Even today, with fundamental unification achieved, advanced texts describe chemistry as a 'quirky science', based on unsolvable quantum-theoretic equations, using different models for different purposes for no very satisfying reason. The history of the hard sciences should not be forgotten when we turn to discussions of 'materialism' and 'the mind-body problem'. The debates over the mechanical philosophy, the nature of fields and molecules, the relation of physical and chemical atoms and principles, and much else in the history of science, have interesting resemblances to those underway today at the current frontiers of understanding. I think there is much to be learned from a careful look at how classic problems were eventually resolved. History suggests only that one should pursue inquiry where it leads, develop explanatory theory as one can with an eye towards eventual unification but without much concern about gaps that may appear unbridgeable at a particular moment, and recognising that the path towards eventual unification is unpredictable.

It might also be worth attending to the fact that at the outer limits of physical inquiry, there is even controversy as to whether unification is generally possible at all. Silvan Schweber alleges that work in condensed matter physics, which has created phenomena such as superconductivity that are 'genuine novelties in the universe', has raised earlier scepticism about the possibility of reduction to 'an almost rigorously proved assertion', so that there might be 'emergent laws' in some more fundamental sense than had been supposed. Whatever the validity of the conclusion, intuitions about unity of science, or philosophical doctrines about the matter, have nothing to say about it, still less so when we turn to the domain of mind and brain, where understanding is far more meagre.

To repeat, the first thesis is a form of methodological monism: mental phenomena (events, entities, etc.) can be studied naturalistically, like chemical, optical, or other phenomena. We construct explanatory theories as best we can, taking as *real* whatever is postulated in the best theories we can devise (because there is no other relevant notion of 'real'), seeking unification with studies of other aspects of the world—the one and only world—while recognising that it might take many paths. And that it might even be unattainable, either because there is no unified account, or there is one but it lies beyond our cognitive reach. We are biological organisms, with scope and limits, not angels, and these epistemic limits may leave questions we pose (perhaps inaccurately) as permanent mysteries to us, just as some problems are beyond the cognitive scope of a rat. It is hardly reasonable to adopt the traditional idea that God was kind enough to design the universe so that humans can understand it, or an absurd modern variant which holds that natural selection achieved this miraculous result—a proposal that is clearer, therefore more readily refuted (there is also a quantum-theoretic variant, which I'll ignore).

To avoid misunderstanding, I am keeping clear of the concepts of 'foundationalism' and 'objectivity' that are the target of much vigorous rhetoric in postmodernist literature, whatever they are supposed to be (I confess failure to understand, for the most part). To my knowledge, there has been little departure from the seventeenth century reaction to the contemporary sceptical crisis, described by the outstanding historian of philosophy Richard Popkin: 'the recognition that absolutely certain grounds could not be given for our knowledge, and yet that we possess standards for evaluating the reliability and applicability of what we have found out about the world', thus 'accepting and increasing the knowledge itself' while recognising that 'the secrets of nature, of things-in-themselves, are forever hidden from us'.

These attitudes towards 'foundationalism', 'objectivity', and 'certainty' are part of the standard outlook of modern science, and other rational inquiry, as far as I am aware. It is sometimes held that Rudolf Carnap and the Vienna Circle had on occasion taken foundationalist positions in some sense relevant here, but that is dubious, a fact clarified particularly in recent scholarly work by Thomas Uebel, Christopher Hookway, and others. In any event, I am assuming that what Popkin describes is accurate, and not seriously questioned.

The thesis of methodological naturalism must be distinguished from a different one that seems much more far-reaching and profound: 'metaphysical naturalism'. Or in other usages, 'materialism', 'physicalism', or 'the naturalisation of philosophy', a position formulated by W.V. Quine that has become 'one of the few orthodoxies in American philosophy' (and beyond) since the 1960s, Tyler Burge comments in a recent review of a century of American philosophy of mind: the view that there are no mental entities (states, events, properties, etc.) 'over and above ordinary physical entities, entities identifiable in the physical sciences or entities that common sense would regard as physical'. This is the idea that 'philosophical accounts of our minds, our knowledge, and our language must in the end be continuous with, or harmonious with, the natural sciences', Daniel Dennett adds, 'one of the happiest trends in philosophy since the 1960s'. With regard to these related theses, we find advocates, sceptics, critics, and conciliators who seek a more sophisticated resolution (Donald Davidson, for one). I'll suggest in a moment that the entire discussion may be misconceived: that no sensible question has been formulated, or can be, at least if the science of the past few centuries is anywhere near accurate.

Let's turn to the second and narrower of the two topics with which I began: the question of how elements of language relate to other things in the world. Perhaps the simplest, least controversial, and weakest thesis is this: the semantic properties of linguistic expressions focus attention on selected aspects of the world as it is taken to be by various cognitive systems, and provide perspectives from which to view them, as we use language for expressing or clarifying our thoughts, inducing others whose language resembles ours to do likewise, making requests, and in other ordinary ways. I think this is also probably the *strongest* general statement that can be made about the language–world relation. Beyond that, we inquire into these semantic properties and perspectives. We discover that they are complex and intricate, involving human interests and concerns in fundamental ways even at the most elementary level, and fixed in substantial measure as part of our nature, independently of the experience that leads a child to acquire one or another of the possible human languages—a highly restricted category of mental objects, it appears.

Again, we should distinguish this weak thesis from far stronger ones, in particular, the following:

1. The *representational* thesis that the central fact about language is that it represents the world, and the central question of semantics is how it does so.

2. The *externalist* thesis that 'meaning isn't in the head', as Hilary Putnam put it; rather meaning, reference, and the content of expressions (and of thought) are fixed by properties of the world and of society.

These are true orthodoxies; the representational thesis quite generally, the externalist thesis in the past 20 years. One finds few critics or sceptics, unlike the case of the varieties of 'physicalism'.

These orthodoxies also seem to me highly dubious, for reasons elaborated in the seventeenth and eighteenth centuries. There seems to be no general relation of the postulated kind that holds between expressions of language and parts of the world, so the nature of that relation cannot be the central question of semantics. And the externalist orthodoxy seems false insofar as it is coherent.

In contrast, internalist semantics is a rich and intriguing subject, though it should really be considered part of syntax in the technical sense: the study of mental events and entities, including those called 'symbolic representations', which provide 'instructions' for systems of language use much as 'phonetic representations' do. Note that in neither case is there any suggestion that these mental objects 'represent' anything, in the sense of traditional philosophical usage, beyond their contribution to thought and action. The task of discovering how such instructions work at the semantic level is not likely to be easier than comparable ones about the sensorimotor aspects of language and the phonetic representations that relate to them, a problem that has been studied intensively for half a century, with advanced technology, and that turns out to be difficult and complex. There is little reason to believe that representational theories of semantics have any validity, and much to suggest that they do not.

Note that in dealing with both the phonetic and semantic aspects of language, the internalist approach adopts as a matter of course a certain form of 'externalism', but one too weak to be of any interest: that observation of usage plays a role in establishing some properties of an expression, its sound and meaning. To be of any significance, externalism must go well beyond that truism.

The two weaker theses seem to me about as far as we can go at this level of generality. The interesting questions, which are questions of empirical science, arise when we pursue them at greater depth. Following this course, we can learn quite a lot, but we arrive at a picture of language and mind that is unlike prevailing orthodoxies.

These are large topics. I will try to indicate why this point of view may be a reasonable one.

The Materialist Orthodoxy

Let's begin with the big question: materialism, the mind-body problem. That was a serious scientific question during the seventeenth century scientific revolution. The reason is that there was a notion of body (matter, the physical, etc.); therefore it made sense to ask what fell within its scope—what fell within 'the mechanical philosophy'. Rejecting occult forces, Descartes and other scientists could meaningfully pose the question whether certain aspects of the world fall within the theory of body, or not. Descartes' major scientific work was the effort to show how far the mechanical philosophy reached, but he also argued that some aspects of the world lie beyond it and cannot be captured by any automaton, notably the ordinary use of language, which was of central importance in Cartesian thought. More generally, an automaton could not accommodate the behaviour of a creature that is only 'incited and inclined' to act in certain ways, but not 'compelled' to do so, as a machine is (apart from probabilistic and random elements, irrelevant here).

These were leading topics of inquiry in the years that followed, alongside the efforts to come to terms with Newton's refutation of the mechanical philosophy. One interesting development led to La Mettrie's thesis that humans are indeed complex machines, and that the Cartesian tests for other minds can be met. The tests primarily had to do with use of language. La Mettrie argued that the incapacity of apes to use language does not reflect a lack of mind, but rather defects in articulatory organs. He proposed that they be given the kinds of training then being used with some success for the deaf. In his *Natural History of the Soul*, he held that 'it is the organisation of the nervous system, from the beginning of the nerves to the end of the cortex, which freely exercises in a healthy state all the properties' of thought, contrary to what Descartes argued—though neither La Mettrie nor anyone else attempted to come to terms with the actual Cartesian arguments, beyond expressing the belief that they could somehow be overcome. So things stand today too, in fact.

Another approach to the problems of materialism explored 'Locke's suggestion': that it is not inconsistent to imagine that the Creator might have chosen to 'superadd to matter a faculty of thinking' just as he had given bodies the capacity to attract without contact, as Newton had shown, though 'as far as we can conceive' that cannot be. We cannot exclude by reason alone the possibility that 'God may give to matter thought, reason, and volition, as well as sense and spontaneous motion', Locke concluded.

Newton himself disagreed, even dismissing the possibility that attraction is a property of matter. 'It is inconceivable', he wrote in a famous letter of 1693, 'that inanimate brute Matter should, without the Mediation of something else, which is not material, operate upon and affect other Matter without mutual Contact'. Action at a distance through a vacuum, he wrote, 'is to me so great an Absurdity, that I believe no Man who has in philosophical matters a competent Faculty of thinking, can ever fall into it' (where 'philosophical' means what we call 'scientific'), though elsewhere he did entertain the unwelcome possibility that 'small particles of bodies' might have 'certain powers, virtues or forces, by which they act at a distance', absurd as it seems. To the end of his life Newton sought some escape from the dilemma. Mature Newtonian physics—the final version of his *Principia*—invokes not dualism but a kind of 'trialism', with passive matter, active forces, and a 'subtle aether' relating them. The active forces are divine, the passive matter lacks any spiritual character, and the aether is semi-divine. Newton thought that he had found empirical support for these conclusions in the experiments with electricity that he witnessed as head of the Royal Society in his later years: electricity is clearly material (its effects are tangible), yet also clearly immaterial (the source of the electrical effluvium loses no weight). This picture, so modern scholarship reveals, was animated by Newton's dedication to the Arian heresy, which rejected the Trinity and considered the Son to be only semi-divine. Recall that Newton was interested in Grand Theory, physics occupying only a small corner of his concerns. Despite the reverence in which Newton was held, the suggestion that Locke offered with much diffidence continued to be pursued. Summarising a long controversy, Hume held that 'we cannot know from any other principle, whether matter, by its structure or arrangement, may not be the cause of thought'. Later, the eminent chemist Joseph Priestley, who seems to have pursued Locke's suggestion more fully than anyone else, concluded that matter is no more 'incompatible with sensation and thought' than with attraction and repulsion. In the latter case, though it is beyond our powers to conceive, we do accept that matter 'is possessed of powers of attraction and repulsion' that act at a 'real and in general an assignable distance from what we call the body itself'. There is no reason not to take the same stand with regard to the phenomena of mind, concluding—however it may offend common sense—that 'The powers of sensation or perception and thought' are properties of 'a certain organised system of matter'. Properties 'termed mental' are 'the result (whether necessary or not) of such an organical structure as that of the brain'. It is as reasonable to believe 'that the powers of sensation and thought are the necessary result of a particular organisation, as that sound is the necessary result of a particular concussion of the air'. Thought in humans 'is a property of the nervous system, or rather of the brain'—the conclusion that La Mettrie had reached well before, by a somewhat different route.

Despite sharp disagreement, much of the post-Newtonian controversy keeps within crucial shared assumptions. Specifically, both the Newtonians and the advocates of Locke's suggestion, or its continental materialist variant, rejected a distinction between body and mind: the occult principles of attraction and repulsion and those that enter into the workings of the mind are on a par. Either matter is passive, and all lie beyond its scope, as Newton held; or matter is itself active, and all are properties of matter, perhaps in some organised state. The 'subtle spirit' that Newton sought, which 'pervades and lies hid in all gross bodies', was to account for interaction, electrical attraction and repulsion, light, sensation, and the way 'members of animal bodies move at the command of the will'. The 'active matter' of his opponents was to accommodate the same range of phenomena. Whether one follows Newton's path of seeking an explanation in the domain of the divine and semi-divine, or the alternative account in terms of 'active matter', the mind-body distinction dissolves. It is hard to see what the alternative might be, in the wake of Newton's demonstration that the mechanical philosophy is false, and that not only the mental aspects of the world, but all others as well, fall beyond the scope of the material as conceived by common sense and by the scientists who carried forward the Galilean revolution.

These intriguing developments lie at the heart of our scientific tradition, and are also quite relevant to current concerns, I think. Hardly a year passes without some best-selling book setting forth the 'startling' and 'astonishing' idea that thought might be 'superadded' to matter as 'a property of the nervous system, or rather of the brain', as had been concluded centuries earlier. Just what the alternative is supposed to be, or why standard conclusions of two centuries ago should still strike us as shocking and daring hypotheses, is left unsaid. It would be very interesting if some reason were now offered to believe the conclusions of La Mettrie, Priestley and many others. But in this respect, I'm afraid, we remain unenlightened.

Recall that Cartesian dualism was straight science: postulation of something beyond the bounds of body is right or wrong. In fact, right, though not for Descartes' reasons. Rather, for reasons that were considered most distressing, if not outrageous and intolerable, by leading scientists of the day—Leibniz, Huygens, Bernoulli and others, even Newton himself. Newton's 'trialism' is also straight science, right or wrong. And the same is true of the 'man-machine' hypothesis of La Mettrie and others, and the various efforts to develop 'Locke's suggestion'.

The crucial discovery was that bodies do not exist. It is common to ridicule the idea of the 'ghost in the machine' (as in Gilbert Ryle's influential work, for example). But this misses the point. Newton exorcised the machine, leaving the ghost intact. Furthermore, nothing has replaced the machine. Rather, the sciences went on to postulate ever more exotic and occult entities: chemical elements whose 'number and nature' will probably never be known (Lavoisier), fields and waves, curved space-time, the notions of quantum theory, infinite one-dimensional strings in space of high dimensionality, and even stranger notions.

The criterion of conformity to common sense vanished along with contact mechanics. There is also no coherent notion of material, physical, and so on. Hence there is no mind-body problem, no question about reduction of the mental to the physical, or even unification of the two domains. The contemporary orthodoxies seem unintelligible, along with the efforts to refute them. Advocates and critics are in the same (sinking) boat, and no reconciliation is needed, or possible.

It is not that the concepts lack meaning. We can speak of the 'physical world' just as we speak of the 'real truth'—but without implying that the *real* truth stands alongside some *non-real* truth; or that the *physical* world stands alongside some *non-physical* world. Similarly, we can intelligibly speak of 'the real world'. We can say, perfectly intelligibly, that despite much inflated rhetoric, in the real world free trade does not exist; that statement may be true or false, and is surely meaningful, but does not imply that the world has two parts, real and unreal. Similarly, we can say that oceans are real and lines of latitude, though a useful part of some branch of science, are not; but, again, without suggesting that the world is divided into the real and the non-real.

Such terms as 'physical' and 'real' have a semantic function, no doubt, but they do not divide the category they qualify into two subcategories. With regard to 'physical', there has been no meaning to that idea since Newton. The problem is not the vagueness or imprecision of such notions as 'physical' or 'real'. To believe that is to misunderstand the terms and their usage. We do not seek a way to clarify the notion 'real truth' or to sharpen the boundary distinguishing the 'real world' from some 'unreal world'. The quest is equally misguided in the case of 'physical' and 'material'.

Suppose someone were to pose the problem of how to deal with the two kinds of truths or worlds, 'real' and 'non-real', and were to ask whether the second category can be reduced to the former or is a separate and irreducible domain, or whether there is some way to resolve the problem posed by this distinction. The right response is not to evaluate specific proposals put forth to answer the questions, but to suggest a course of Wittgensteinian therapy to overcome the delusion that some question has been raised. The same is true in the case of 'physical world' versus 'non-physical world'—at least, until some new notion of 'physical' is put forth to replace the old, not a very reasonable endeavour, it would seem.

For such reasons, it is hard to make sense of the project of 'naturalisation of philosophy'. The difficulty can also be formulated in somewhat different terms. Recall that the enterprise seeks to show that philosophy is 'continuous with' or 'harmonious with' the natural sciences. These are taken to include the mechanical, chemical, electrical, optical . . . aspects of the world; but not the mental aspects. Why?

The reason cannot be that we just rely on those folks over in the physics department. That would simply be irrational, and, besides, they don't even rely on themselves. Thus the American Physical Society just published a book by the very distinguished physicist John Wheeler, in which he suggests that 'at a very deep bottom', the world consists of nothing but bits of information. Whatever the merits of the proposal, advocates of the 'naturalisation of philosophy' agree, in fact insist, that it is not the province of the philosopher to second-guess their physicist colleagues.

Nor can the reason be that too little is known about the mental aspects the world; the distinction is supposed to be one of principle. Nor is it that the unification problem has not been solved; that was also true of the chemical aspects, pre-Pauling. It is not that the mental aspects raise questions of normativity, morality, and so on, while the others do not. We also ask questions of different kinds about light, gravitational attraction, complex molecules, ant colonies, and so on. Furthermore issues of morality and normative force cross-cut the 'physical–mental' divide: 'physical abilities' enter into determining culpability (say, inability to fly to the tenth floor of a burning building to save a child); having a blue sensation does not relate to morality or normativity, or understanding the meaning of 'water' (I'll return to that).

It may seem offensive to common sense and sound thinking to suppose that certain matters (intentionality and aboutness, consciousness, behaviour that is uncaused but appropriate, or whatever) are among 'the ultimate and irreducible properties of things' that physicists seek to catalogue (Jerry Fodor's formulation). But the stipulation is not very helpful. Why these, but not attraction and repulsion? Newton was no fool, certainly, and it seemed just as absurd to him to suppose that interaction without contact could be among the phenomena of nature.

Until recently it was widely agreed that none of these questions makes much sense: the 'physical world' is beyond our intuitive grasp, whether we include its mental aspects or not. Hume wrote that 'Newton seemed to draw off the veil from some of the mysteries of nature', but 'he shewed at the same time the imperfections of the mechanical philosophy; and thereby restored [Nature's] ultimate secrets to that obscurity in which they ever did and ever will remain'. A century later, in his classic *History of Materialism* (translated into English with an approving introduction by Bertrand Russell), Friedrich Lange put the point as follows, discussing 'the real service rendered by Newton':

> We have in our own days so accustomed ourselves to the abstract notion of forces, or rather to a notion hovering in a mystic obscurity between abstraction and concrete comprehension, that we no longer find any difficulty in making one particle of matter act upon another without immediate contact. We may, indeed, imagine that in the proposition, 'No force without matter', we have uttered something very Materialistic, while all the time we calmly allow particles of matter to act upon each other through void space without any material link. From such ideas the great mathematicians and physicists of the seventeenth century were far removed. They were all in so far still genuine Materialists in the sense of ancient Materialism, that they made immediate contact a condition of influence. The collision of atoms or the attraction by hook shaped particles, a mere modification of collision, were the type of all Mechanism and the whole movement of science tended towards Mechanism.

We may not yet have accustomed ourselves to the conclusions of Priestley and others, but custom is no criterion for imposing any fundamental divide, metaphysical or other, between various aspects of the one and only world.

Modern discussion of these issues has two variants. One inquires into the status of mental entities, asking whether there are such entities (states, properties, etc.) 'over and above ordinary physical entities, entities identifiable in the physical sciences or entities that common sense would regard as physical'. Another variant asks whether (and if so how) 'mentalistic talk' finds 'its place in our attempts to describe and explain the world' (Burge).

We might think of these as metaphysical and epistemological, respectively; or as adopting the material and formal modes, in Rudolf Carnap's terms.

For the metaphysical variant to make sense, we have to have a notion of physical entity; we don't. It is mere stipulation to include gravitational attraction, fields, Kekulé's structural formulas, curved space-time, quarks, superstrings, etc., but not the processes, events, entities, and so on postulated in the study of mental aspects of the world. This highly influential doctrine, of which Quine has long been the most prominent advocate, seems to have no force; the same holds for critics.

As for the epistemological variant, we can be reasonably confident that 'mentalistic talk' will find no place in attempts to describe and explain the world. But that is uninteresting, because the same is true of 'physicalistic talk': such ordinary expressions as 'the rock is rolling down the hill', 'flowers are growing', 'he's getting fat', 'the aeroplane is descending', 'the hawk is swooping down to catch its prey', 'the skies are darkening but the weather is slowly improving', 'the comet is heading towards Jupiter (but will probably miss it)', 'the ant is rebuilding its colony after it was totally destroyed'. None of these—in fact, virtually nothing we say about the 'physical world'—can be translated into the sciences. There is no more reason to expect that some future science of the mental, if it ever develops, will care about translating such statements as 'John speaks Chinese' or 'John took his umbrella because he expected rain'. Scientific inquiry looks at the problems in its own and generally different ways, perhaps using distinct faculties of mind.

The Externalist Orthodoxy

This brings us to the second aspect of the topic of language and nature: How does the use of language relate to the world?

The prevailing picture, established in the modern period particularly by Gottlob Frege, is based on three principles:

I   There is a common store of thoughts.

II   There is a common language that expresses these
     thoughts.

III The language is a set of well-formed expressions,
     and its semantics is based on a relation between
     parts of these expressions and things in the world.

This is the 'representational' thesis I mentioned earlier, and
is also accepted by 'externalist' critics of the Fregean model.

Frege used the German word 'Bedeutung' for the purported
relation between expressions and things, but in an invented technical sense, because German lacks the relevant notion. English translations use such terms as 'reference' or 'denotation', also in a technical sense, for the same reason; the notion does not exist in English, or, it seems, any human language. There are somewhat similar notions: 'talk about', 'ask for', 'refer to', etc. But when we look at all closely at these, we find that they have properties that make them quite unsuited for the representational model. There is nothing wrong with introduction of technical terms for theoretical inquiry. On the contrary, there is no alternative; beyond the most elementary level, rational inquiry departs from the resources of common sense and ordinary language. What we ask about a theoretical framework is something different: Is it the right one, for the purposes at hand?

The Fregean picture is intelligible, perhaps correct, for the inquiry that primarily concerned Frege himself: exploring the nature of mathematics. As for natural language, Frege considered it too 'imperfect' to merit much attention. Keeping to, say, arithmetic, we can say intelligibly that there is a shared thought that two and two is four, and can construct common symbolic systems in which the thought can be expressed (I and II of the model). Turning to III, the symbolic system that is devised can be viewed as an infinite set of well-formed expressions (a certain mathematical object): in standard notation, '$(2+2)=4$' but not some re-

arrangement of these, say ')2=+(4'. Its semantics is based on a
relation between the numeral '2' and the number two, an object
in some Platonic universe, and between '(2+2)=4' and The True,
another such object. And so on.

The picture also seems plausible in a normative sense for scientific inquiry, a rather special human endeavour. Both the history of science and introspection suggest that the scientist may
be aiming intuitively at something like the Fregean picture:
shared symbolic systems with terms that pick out what we hope
are real things in the world: quarks, molecules, ants, human languages and their elements, etc.

But the picture makes no sense at all with regard to human
language—a biological entity, to be investigated by the methods
of the sciences, without arbitrary stipulations drawn from some
other concern. The notion 'common store of thoughts' has no empirical status, and is unlikely to gain one even if the science of the
future discovers a reason, unknown today, to postulate entities
that resemble 'what we think (believe, fear, hope, expect, want,
etc.)'. Principle I seems groundless at best, senseless at worst.

As for II, the notion 'common language' has no place in efforts to understand the phenomena of language and to explain
them. Two people may talk alike, as they may look alike or live
near one another. But it makes no more sense to postulate a
'common language' that they share than a common shape or a
common area. As in the case of 'physical' or 'real', the problem
is not vagueness or unclarity: there is nothing to clarify; the world
does not have shapes and areas, or shared languages. Nor are
the terms devoid of meaning; they are just fine for ordinary
usage. It makes sense for me to tell you that I live near Boston
and far from Sydney, or to tell a Martian that I live near both but
far from the moon. The same holds for looking alike, and speaking alike. I do or do not speak like people in Sydney depending
on the circumstances of the discourse. Some such circum-

stances—pretty complicated ones—pick out what we sometimes call 'places' and 'languages'. From some points of view, the greater Boston area is a place; from others not. Chinese is a 'language' and Romance not, as a result of such matters as colours on maps and stability of empires. But Chinese is no more an element of the world than the area around Boston; arguably much less so, because the conditions of individuation are so vastly more intricate and interest-related.

Similar considerations hold for the norms and conventions of language. If by 'conventions' we mean something like 'regularities in usage', then we can put the matter aside; these are few and scattered, and do not begin to serve the purposes for which the notions are invoked. If we understand the terms in some useful sense, without the air of objectivity, every social grouping has norms and conventions, including the various complex and overlapping communities of linguistic usage to which any person belongs, even in the simplest of societies. Discussion of norms can be perfectly intelligible, whether we are speaking of setting a table or giving a lecture. But the belief that there is something to be found here that has any interesting bearing on the theory of meaning or knowledge of language or following rules is surely mistaken, for reasons amply discussed elsewhere.

These should be truisms. Unfortunately, they serve to render a good part of the most interesting and thoughtful work in philosophy of language and mind virtually unintelligible, something that should trouble people more than it does, in my opinion.

One prop of the externalist thesis rests on the assumption that the notion of 'common language' with its norms and conventions enters crucially into determining the 'content' of expressions and thought—what we mean and what we think. But that part of the thesis rests on sand, unless some questions are answered that have yet to be addressed, even acknowledged, and that seem unanswerable, in that they are wrongly put.

Turning to principle III of the model, human languages differ radically from Fregean symbolic systems in just about every crucial respect. We may call the latter 'languages' if we like, adopting a certain metaphor, but we then have to be careful not to be misled by it. In human language, there is no such category as 'well-formed expression'. For Fregean systems, the notion of 'the true grammar' or 'the right generative procedure' is meaningless; any characterisation of the well-formed expressions will do. For human language, it is the only meaningful notion; in fact, it makes good sense to identify a language, for the purposes of theoretical inquiry as a generative procedure that associates sound and meaning in a specific way. Those who are familiar with the literature of linguistics, philosophy, and cognitive psychology will recognise that these simple facts suffice to undermine a wide range of discussion of alleged problems of extensional equivalence, generative capacity, recursiveness, and much else. Study of such topics can at best be indirectly suggestive; the concepts they use simply have no application in natural language.

Let us turn finally to the relation of Bedeutung-reference allegedly holding between words and things. It is an empirical question whether human language works that way, and the answer seems to be that it does not. This is not a matter of vagueness or 'open texture'. Rather, the system is designed quite differently. As far as is known, it is no more reasonable to seek some thing-in-the-world that is picked out by the word 'river' or 'tree' or 'water' or 'Boston' than to seek some collection of motions of molecules that is picked out by the first syllable or final consonant of the word 'Boston'. With sufficient heroism, one could defend such theses, but they seem to make no sense at all. Each such usage of the words may well pick out, in some sense, specific motions of molecules and things-in-the-world (the world as it is, or is conceived to be); but that is a different and entirely irrelevant matter.

Let us return to the observation that ordinary physicalistic talk finds no place in scientific inquiry. This is agreed for physics, perhaps 'hard science' generally. But it has been argued by contemporary philosophers (who often agree on little else) that the 'special sciences' like geology or biology do use common sense notions. Thus Hilary Putnam holds that the theory of evolution uses the ordinary concept 'human being', and it has been suggested (by Jerry Fodor, if I am interpreting him correctly) that the notion 'river' is used in geology. But such ideas are incorrect.

It is true enough that the theory of evolution is concerned with the thing now producing these words, but not under the description 'person' or 'human being', with their curious properties of individuation in terms of psychic continuity, and the like. Furthermore, as Locke pointed out, these are 'forensic notions', understood within a framework of legal responsibility, moral judgment, and so on, which plays no role in the theory of evolution.

Take 'river'. Long before Locke, Thomas Hobbes recognised that it 'will be the same river which flows from one and the same fountain, whether the same water, or other water, or something else than water, flow from thence'. The identity of a thing depends on the manner of its generation, he concluded, an idea that goes back to Aristotle (and, as Hobbes observed, underlies the famous example of the 'ship of Theseus', which is the same ship even if each plank is replaced over time). No such notion enters into geology. Furthermore, these observations much understate the complexity of the concept *river*. Take the Charles River, which flows past my office. Not only might it remain the same river if it comes to be constituted mostly (perhaps entirely) of chemicals from factories upstream, as Hobbes pointed out, but also if its flow were reversed, or it were directed in a different course, or made to end up in a lake instead of flowing into the sea, or even divided into separate streams of water, possibly converging later on. No concept remotely like this enters into the earth sciences.

The same is true of words generally. From Hobbes to Locke to Hume, a leading topic was the nature of such concepts as *tree*, something individuated in terms of its common life, the sympathy of its parts and their contributions to the same end, and so on. Hume furthermore rejected the idea that 'there is a peculiar nature belonging to this form', as Shaftesbury put it, concluding that the identity is 'fictitious', something that we 'ascribe to the minds of men'—on a par with the phonetic units of mental representations, such as the first syllable of 'Boston' or its final consonant.

I think Hume was right about that, contrary to the second major prop of the externalist orthodoxy that has prevailed for some years: the idea that facts about the world enter into determining the meanings of our words (apart from the trivial respect in which all agree that they do, mentioned earlier). Hume's conclusion seems still more compelling if we look more closely at such concepts as *tree*, which are far more intricate than Locke, Hume, and others supposed. Try the following thought experiment, for example. Suppose you transplant a tree to somewhere else, cut off a branch and plant it in the original place, and find ten years later that the two objects are indistinguishable. Which is the original tree? We know the answer, and it is a curious one—one illustration of many complexities.

What about the water that flows in the river (sometimes). Until well into the late eighteenth century, water was considered the prototypical simple unanalysable substance, though with one qualification. To corpuscularians like Boyle and Newton, it was constituted of minute and undetectable particles, the building blocks of nature, which could be rearranged in various ways to produce anything, so that transmutation was feasible in principle. In fact, a famous experiment of von Helmont's in 1647, which is sometimes taken to have founded the modern science of chemistry, showed that pure water could be converted into a tree, a highly organised form. The demonstration was quite convincing, not really refuted until Lavoisier. But, before that, water was taken to be as simple a substance as there could be.

We know very little about 'folk psychology' or 'common sense', and, in particular, do not know how to sort out the innate components that lie at its roots from the cultural overlays that shape these in one or another way. But one might speculate that the simplicity of such substances as water is not too remote from genuine 'folk psychology'.

On the other hand, we also know that the untutored mind—each of us, because no one knows enough to do the tutoring, and experience is of only marginal relevance—understands the concept *water* in a far more intricate way. Suppose there are two cups on the table, Cup 1 containing pure H2O and Cup 2 filled from the faucet in the sink. Suppose I dip a tea bag in Cup 1. It is now tea, not water. Suppose that what comes from the reservoir is pure H2O that has passed through a filter at the reservoir to kill bacteria, and suppose further that it is a tea filter; someone discovered that tea kills bacteria. Cup 2, filled from the faucet, contains H2O with some tea as an 'impurity'. But it is water, not tea, unlike the contents of Cup 1, which is tea. One cup contains water, the other tea, though the two might be chemically identical.

The facts are obvious on introspection, and have been confirmed by empirical inquiry. Experiments by Barbara Malt show that *water*—even *prototypical water*—correlates quite weakly with H2O content, even for people who know the relevant chemistry. Rather, what is water depends on a complex array of human interests and concerns.

Even the purest water may not be water for human languages, whatever scientists may say in their own symbolic systems (possibly using the same sounds). A recent technical article in the journal *Science* observes that glass is 'a liquid that has lost its ability to flow', lacking a crystalline structure (unlike ice), and structurally 'barely distinguishable from the fluid substance it was before it passed, quite abruptly in some cases, into the glassy state'. Furthermore, it has recently been found that 'most of the universe's water exists in the glassy state (in comets . . .)', that is, as 'naturally occurring glassy water'.

But what is 'most of the universe's water' for the chemist who wrote the article is not water at all for you or me. Returning to Cups 1 and 2, suppose they are made from pure H2O in the glassy state (taken from a comet). Suppose Jones asks for water and I give him one of the cups, having the cup itself in mind, not its contents. Then I am misleading him or worse, though it is pure H2O, 'naturally occurring glassy water'. And, as noted, I am responding to his request properly if I give him what came from the faucet, though it is not pure H2O. But I am not responding properly to his request if I give him the chemically identical substance formed by dipping a tea bag into pure H2O.

Even in the case of the simplest substance, its constitution is only a weak factor in establishing its identity as such-and-such; and the concept 'same substance as this', where 'same' is determined by the truth about the world (which science may or may not know, yet or ever), is not a determinative factor.

Such considerations as these render the externalist thesis highly implausible, in my opinion, and weaken still further much of the argumentation that has been used to support it ('twin earth' thought experiments, and so on). The 'same essence' approach to the meanings of so-called 'natural kind terms' seems at best very dubious, along with the notions 'rigid designator' and the like.

These conclusions are reinforced when we look more closely at those parts of language that seem 'most referential': pronouns and other terms involved in 'dependent reference'. Even here, we find that the actual meanings are 'ascribed to the mind' in complex ways, and that not only the externalist thesis, but the referential thesis as well, are simply untenable. Language just does not work that way, however relevant such ideas may be for the functioning of other human capacities, perhaps the 'science-forming faculty', if indeed that is a distinctive component of the mind, as it may be.

For similar reasons, we cannot assume that statements (let alone sentences) have truth conditions. At most they can have something more complex: 'truth indications', in some sense. The issue is not 'open texture' or 'family resemblance' in the Wittgensteinian sense. Nor does the conclusion lend any weight to the belief that semantics is 'holistic' in the Quinean sense that semantic properties are assigned to the whole array of words, not to each individually. Each of these familiar pictures of the nature of meaning seems partially correct, but only partially. There is good evidence that words have intrinsic properties of sound, form, and meaning; but also open texture, which allows their meanings to be extended and sharpened in certain ways; and also holistic properties that allow some mutual adjustment. The intrinsic properties suffice to establish certain formal relations among expressions, interpreted as rhyme, entailment, and in other ways by the performance systems associated with language faculty. Among the intrinsic semantic relations that seem well established on empirical grounds are analytic connections among expressions, a subclass of no special significance for the study of natural language semantics, though perhaps of independent interest in the different context of the concerns of modern philosophy. Only *perhaps*, because it is not clear that human language has much to do with these, or that they capture what was of traditional interest.

The fixed and rich intrinsic structure of expressions, specifically their semantic properties, must be shared among people and languages to a large extent, because they are known without evidence and thus have their origins in the shared human bio-logical endowment that determines a substantial part of what we know, as recognised across a broad range, including Plato, Descartes, Hume, and others.

Language as a Natural Object

Returning finally to the two aspects of the topic of language and nature with which I began, it seems to me reasonable to draw the following general conclusions.

With regard to the place of language (and mind generally) in nature, there is little to say. The issues of materialism, physicalism, and so on do not arise. There are no coherent questions, hence no answers. We simply study the mental (including the linguistic) as-pects of the world as we do all others. As for human language, it is a biological object with highly intricate and very specific properties, quite unlike the constructed formal systems called 'language' by metaphoric extension that is harmless if not taken seriously, but that has in fact been highly misleading. In particular, there is no question of how human languages represent the world, or the world as it is thought to be. They don't. Expressions function in a quite different way, in their sensorimotor aspects and other prop-erties of language use. There is no reference-based semantics, hence no coherent externalist thesis about language and thought; the latter is untenable for more specific reasons as well. There is a rich and intriguing internalist semantics, really part of syntax, on a par in this respect with phonology. Both systems provide 'instruc-tions' for performance systems, which use them in complex and largely predetermined ways for articulation, interpretation, inquiry, expression of thought, and various forms of human interaction. There are hard and important questions about how the mental ob-jects formed by the operations of the language faculty are used, with regard to both their phonetic and semantic elements.

These are central problems of human biology. We can chip away at some of them, in some cases, with some success and even quite surprising results. Investigation of language and its use in broader social settings relies on what is understood about the biological object, language, even when the fact is denied; there is no coherent alternative. Such inquiry can only benefit from recognition of this reality, instead of denying it on irrational and often ideological grounds. In this respect, at least, the study of human society resembles inquiry into ant, bird, and other non-human communities, though it differs in many other crucial respects, in no small measure because of the unique linguistic capacities of the human species. About that, the Cartesian insights are not challenged by what is understood today, though the framework in which they were expressed has long ago been abandoned.

Many of the classical problems—specifically, the ones that particularly concerned Descartes and underlie his dualist metaphysics—remain immune to any sensible inquiry, for what reason, we can only speculate. Hume could well turn out to be right in his conclusion that Nature's 'ultimate secrets ever will remain in obscurity', including what he called elsewhere 'the secret springs and principles, by which the human mind is actuated in its operations'. It is not impossible that we will someday understand why this is true, insofar as it is, even without being able to penetrate the mysteries. However that may be, it is improper to pretend to understand what we know nothing of, though there is great merit in pressing to the limits the intellectual capacities that we so far only barely understand.

3

Writers and Intellectual Responsibility

I've been asked to comment on a question that I find, frankly, rather puzzling every time it is posed, which is quite often. I should tell you in advance that I have little to say about it beyond truisms. The only justification I can think of for subjecting you to these is that they are so commonly denied, if not in words, then in consistent practice.

Questions come in many varieties. Some, one can try to say something about. Others, one can only stare at in bewilderment. Perhaps they are too hard, the kind that come up constantly in scientific inquiry, which, at its most serious, is pressing the boundaries of always limited understanding. Perhaps they are too easy; the answers can be put in a phrase. These are the questions that are perplexing. The one I've been asked to discuss is among them, at least for me.

At one level, the answer is too easy: the intellectual responsibility of the writer, or any decent person, is to tell the truth. Incidentally, I'm interpreting the phrase 'intellectual responsibility' narrowly; there are many dimensions that I'll put aside, aesthetic dimensions, for example.

Though at this level of generality there is an easy answer, qualifications and complexities quickly arise. To add a few of these, it is a moral imperative to find out and tell the truth as *best one can*, about things *that matter*, to *the right audience*. The questions become harder, sometimes verging on unanswerability, when we try to spell out the meaning of the qualifications.

About the responsibility to try to find out and tell the truth, there is nothing much to say, except that it is often hard, and can be personally costly, particularly for those who are more vulnerable. That is true even in societies that are very free; in others, the costs can be severe indeed.

Let's turn to the second part, determining what matters. Here there are many factors. Some questions are important because of intellectual interest. To mention one raised regularly in best-selling books these days: do the brain sciences have anything to tell us about consciousness or other phenomena of mind? But these are not the factors that concern us here. Rather, the moral dimension, which has to do with likely consequences, particularly for human life.

The responsibility of the writer as a *moral agent* is to try to bring the truth about *matters of human significance* to *an audience that can do something about them*. That is part of what it means to be a moral agent rather than a monster. It's hard to think of a less contentious proposal than this truism. Or so one might think. Unfortunately, that is not quite the case, for a simple reason: the standard practice of the intellectual communities to which we (more or less) belong rejects this elementary moral principle, with considerable fervor and passion, in fact. We may even have sunk to historical lower depths, in this regard, by the natural measure: comparison of standard practice to opportunities available.

I'll return to that unpleasant possibility, but just to illustrate what I have in mind, take the issue that actually brought me to Australia. The visit has been in the works for many years, but the immediate occasion was an invitation to speak on the issue of East Timor.

In 1978, I testified about the matter at the UN. The testimony was published in the right-wing libertarian journal *Inquiry*. Concluding the testimony, I made an observation that was hard to miss, though it is scrupulously missed, so let me make it again. There were two major atrocities in process at that time, in the same part of the world, and of roughly the same scale and character: Cambodia and East Timor. These two atrocities differed, however, in several other respects, which shed no little light on the topic we are considering. Let's list a few, each easily demonstrated and not controversial among people with a shred of rationality and integrity.

Let's begin with Khmer Rouge atrocities:

1 They were crimes against humanity, if the concept has meaning.

2 They were attributable to an official enemy.

3 They were ideologically serviceable, offering justification for US crimes in Indochina for 25 years and for others in process and in the works. And they were exploited quite deliberately for those purposes, both for reconstruction of the faith and as a weapon to implement further atrocities (we must torture and kill 'to prevent another Pol Pot', the doctrine held).

4 No one had any suggestion as to how to mitigate the crimes of the KR, let alone to end them.

5 They elicited a huge outcry and show of indignation, remarkable by comparative standards, and with a record of deceit that would have impressed Stalin (which is no exaggeration). Fabrications were also uncorrectable; exposure led only to more passionate reiteration and applause for the authors of the deceit, however childish and absurd, and the mildest suggestion that one might try to keep to

the truth, which was awful enough, aroused virtual hysteria, and renewed deceit.

6 These crimes became the very symbol of evil, placed alongside those of Hitler and Stalin, where they remain in the approved list of twentieth century horrors.

Let's turn next to the atrocities in East Timor, comparing them with the KR atrocities in these respects, point by point:

1 They were crimes against humanity but, furthermore, crimes carried out in the process of outright aggression, war crimes, hence clearly within the purview of international law.

2 Responsibility for them traced directly back to Washington and its allies.

3 They were ideologically dysfunctional, given the locus of responsibility.

4 To terminate them has always been very easy, given the locus of responsibility. This is not Bosnia, or Rwanda, or Chechnya. There has been no need to send troops, bomb Jakarta, impose sanctions, even issue warnings. It would have been enough to turn off the tap.

5 The reaction (I'll keep here to North America, though the observations generalise rather broadly) was almost total silence, apart from reiteration of lies of the State Department and Indonesian Generals, reported as fact—again, at a level of deceit that Stalin would have admired, though this time in the opposite direction.

6 The Western-backed crimes are no symbol of evil, and no blot on our record.

The pattern is rather striking. It takes considerable talent not to notice it, and to avoid drawing certain conclusions from it. It is a tribute to our educational systems that they have conferred the required talents with such impressive success.

It's worth elaborating a bit on the two last points. In fact, my article was the first in the US (or, to my knowledge, Canada) devoted specifically to East Timor, only the second that dealt with the topic at all, after three years of huge atrocities, perhaps the worst relative to population since the Holocaust, funded mainly by the American taxpayer. Meanwhile Washington and the intellectual community basked in self-adulation about how 'human rights is the Soul of our foreign policy', in the words of the man who at that very moment was accelerating the weapons flow to Indonesia as atrocities peaked and the perpetrators were running short because of the ferocity of their assault. All in silence, though it was all public. In that year, 1978, media coverage in the US and Canada, quite high before the Indonesian invasion, reduced to flat zero.

It was later conceded that what had happened was problematic, perhaps even 'the shaming of Indonesia' (as the New York Times described it). In contrast, there was no 'shaming of the United States' (or of the New York Times). At worst we failed to attend closely enough to the unpleasant acts of people who lack our civilised standards, and may not have done enough to stop the acts for which we were eagerly providing the decisive military and diplomatic support; understandable, since our minds were elsewhere at the time. As for the atrocities that we inadvertently missed, these were the unfortunate errors of a leader whose human rights record is 'checkered', the New York Times Asia correspondent explained. He remained, however, a 'moderate' (Christian Science Monitor) who is 'at heart benign', unfairly criticised by 'propagandists for the guerrillas' in East Timor who 'talk of the army's savagery and use of torture' (Economist).

When meagre recognition was finally given to the (continuing) crimes in East Timor—always absolving ourselves from any responsibility for our deliberate and decisive role—no one was so vulgar as to recall some earlier history. Its most revealing feature is surely the display of utter euphoria at the 'staggering mass slaughter' conducted by the 'Indonesian moderates' in 1965, in the words of the editors of the Newspaper of Record, who joined their colleagues in unrestrained joy at the news of 'the boiling bloodbath' (*Time*), 'a gleam of light in Asia' as the leading liberal pundit of the *Times* described it with approval. Respectable commentators praised Washington for keeping a low public posture, refraining from expressing pride in its contribution to the achievements of the moderates, and its pleasure in the outcome. That was wise, the *Times* editors observed, since too public an embrace of the country's new rulers 'could well hurt them', though it was fine to offer 'generous pledges of rice, cotton and machinery' and to resume the aid that had been held back before the 'staggering mass slaughter' set matters right.

The episode, which tells us quite a lot about our actual standards, is deeply buried in the memory hole. I've reviewed it in a recent book (*Year 501*). The texts have to be read to be believed, but there is little reason for concern; the affair is destined to remain in proper obscurity

As every literate person knows, there was also another example, in the same place and the same years, that could be used to make exactly the same point as the Cambodia–Timor comparison: namely, the two halves of the 'decade of genocide', as the years 1969–1979 were described by the only independent governmental inquiry (Finland)—another topic that has been deleted from history (not that it ever really passed through those august portals), and that tells us more about Western civilisation, if we choose to look.

I've barely scratched the surface. The truth is much worse, and we ought to know on what page of history it belongs. Furthermore, the examples are not unique, even unusual. The story continues as we meet; pick some part of the world at random, and you are likely to find examples. Take Latin America, the traditional domain of US power, hence the natural place to look if one wants to understand the values that dominate the contemporary world. Half of US military aid goes to Colombia, increasing under Clinton. Colombia is also the worst human rights violator in the hemisphere. The awesome atrocities of the leading beneficiaries of US military aid and training are regularly documented by human rights monitors, the Church, and others, in gruesome detail. But the facts are rarely reported, and apart from the small solidarity organisations and fringe publications, all of this passes virtually without comment. What makes its way through the filter is official fairy tales about the war against drugs, dismissed as an absurdity by the human rights groups and all other knowledgeable observers, but religiously repeated as fact in the Free Press.

That this is a standard pattern has been shown beyond reasonable doubt, in thousands of pages of detailed documentation that are usually ignored. Or, if noticed, dismissed with ritual sneers: 'tirade', 'routine', 'conspiracy theory', 'anti-American' (an interesting term, borrowed from the lexicon of totalitarianism), and other devices the culture provides to avoid the dangers of thought and to protect the faithful from inappropriate fact.

It's rather interesting to compare contemporary defenders of doctrinal purity with medieval thinkers, who took heresy seriously and felt the need to confront it with careful argument. That level of integrity is rare today, an honest inquiry will show. The fact—and fact it is—is perhaps worth pondering.

Applying the opening truism to the few cases just reviewed, it reads as follows: The responsibility of Western intellectuals has been to tell the truth about the 'shaming of the West' to a Western audience, who can act to terminate the crimes effectively, easily, and quickly. Simple, unambiguous, and plainly correct. If they chose to condemn KR atrocities, well and good, as long as they tried to keep to the truth. But it was a matter of limited importance, unless they had some proposal about what to do; no one did. One should also tell the truth about Genghis Khan, but the task hardly ranks high on the moral scale.

Actual behaviour has consistently been exactly the opposite, and remains so, which again tells us something about ourselves, if we choose to learn.

Let's consider more closely the third part of the moral imperative: the audience. The audience is properly chosen if it should know the truth: for enlightenment, but primarily for action that will be of human significance, that will help to relieve suffering and distress. We are now back to truism, though there are disagreements, in this case even among people who see eye-to-eye on the fundamental issues.

Let me give a personal example. For much of my life, I've been closely involved with pacifist groups in direct action and resistance, and educational and organising projects. We've spent days in jail together, and it is a freakish accident that they did not extend to many years, as we realistically expected 30 years ago (an interesting tale, but a different one). That creates bonds of loyalty and friendship, but also brings out some disagreements. So, my Quaker friends and colleagues in disrupting illegitimate authority adopt the slogan: 'Speak truth to power'. I strongly disagree. The audience is entirely wrong, and the effort hardly more than a form of self-indulgence. It is a waste of time and a pointless pursuit to speak truth to Henry Kissinger, or the CEO of General Motors, or others who exercise power in coercive institutions—truths that they already know well enough, for the most part.

Again, a qualification is in order. Insofar as such people dissociate themselves from their institutional setting and become human beings, moral agents, then they join everyone else. But in their institutional roles, as people who wield power, they are hardly worth addressing, any more than the worst tyrants and criminals, who are also human beings, however terrible their actions. To speak truth to power is not a particularly honourable vocation. One should seek out an audience that matters—and furthermore (another important qualification), it should not be seen as an audience, but as a community of common concern in which one hopes to participate constructively. We should not be speaking *to*, but *with*. That is second nature to any good teacher, and should be to any writer and intellectual as well.

Perhaps this is enough to suggest that even the question of choice of audience is not entirely trivial.

Let's return to the more crucial aspects of the question: seeking and telling the truth about things that are important. The obligation to do so may seem transparent, but it is not, at least in certain cultures—including ours, as examples I gave illustrate. But Western intellectuals nevertheless understand the point very well, and have no trouble applying elementary moral principles in at least one case: official enemies, say, Stalinist Russia.

Within that society, the value system imposed by authority held that the responsibility of the intellectual is to serve power interests: to record with a show of horror the terrible deeds (real or alleged) of designated enemies, and to conceal or prettify the crimes of the state and its agents. Russian intellectuals who fulfilled these responsibilities were praised and honoured; those who rejected these demands were treated rather differently, as we know.

Here, the judgments were reversed. Russian intellectuals who kept to what was expected of them were regarded with contempt, dismissed as commissars and apparatchiks. Those who rejected these demands, we honoured as dissidents, people who tried to tell the truth about things that mattered—for *them*, in *their circumstances*. If they failed to condemn Western crimes, or even denied them, it was a matter of no interest to decent people, though the commissars were of course outraged. All of that, again, is trivially obvious, and aroused no controversy, properly. These distinctions between commissar and dissident go back to the origins of recorded history. Take the Platonic *Dialogues*, or even more dramatically, the Bible. The intellectuals who gained respect and honour were those who were condemned centuries later as the false prophets— the courtiers, the commissars. Those who came to be honoured much later as the Prophets received rather different treatment at the time. They told the truth about things that matter, ranging from geopolitical analysis to moral values, and suffered the punishment that is meted out with no slight consistency to those who commit the sin of honesty and integrity.

The punishment varies, depending on the nature of the society. In Brezhnev's Russia, it could be exile or expulsion. In a typical US dependency like El Salvador, the miscreant might be left in pieces in a ditch after hideous torture, or have his brains blown out by US-trained elite battalions. In a Black ghetto in the US, punishment can be ugly—in one recent case, even Gestapo-style assassination of two Black organisers with the collaboration of the national political police; the facts are known and not denied, but considered a matter of no concern, given the targets. They are assigned to the same category as the endless atrocities that we tolerate, fund, supervise, or carry out directly elsewhere. That's not hard to demonstrate, if it is not already obvious, and tells us more about prevailing values.

Let's take a step back. We have no difficulty distinguishing commissar from dissident in enemy states, or even in the distant past. But when we turn to truths that matter in the moral realm, looking at ourselves, judgments again reverse, and we fall right back into the near- universal pattern: the commissars are honoured, the dissidents berated for their iniquity. It's again all too easy to demonstrate.

The principles that we apply with increasing facility as our own responsibility declines are the merest truisms. But since they are so commonly denied, often with great outrage, perhaps I might restate them, beginning with the case that is uncontroversial.

1   If Soviet intellectuals told the truth about American crimes, well and good, but they won no praise from us. There are plenty of commissars around to do that, and Soviet citizens had more important things to do. Soviet crimes in Poland and Czechoslovakia did not come within shouting distance of those of the US in Central America, to pick the obvious parallel, but it was nevertheless the moral duty of the Russian intellectual to focus attention on the former, even to the exclusion of far worse crimes beyond the reach of Russian power.

2   If a Soviet intellectual exaggerated or fabricated American crimes, then he became an object of contempt.

3   If a Soviet intellectual ignored American crimes, it was a matter of no consequence. Our admiration for dissidents was in no way diminished if they refused comment on these atrocities.

4   If Soviet intellectuals denied or minimised American crimes, as many did, it was also a matter of minor or even null significance. Their responsibilities lay at home.

5   If Soviet intellectuals ignored or justified Soviet crimes, that was criminal.

Note that there was no lack of information about Western crimes, at least if we can believe the government-funded studies carried out by Russian research centres in the United States, which found, in 1979, that 96 per cent of the middle elite and 77 per cent of blue-collar workers listened to foreign radio broadcasts. Even through the haze of distortion, ample information was available to react properly to US crimes. But failure do so was a matter of little consequence—as all agree, in this case.

The principles are valid, and apply with little change to our society.

To spell them out:

1   If Western intellectuals told the truth about the crimes of the USSR, Pol Pot, Saddam Hussein (after he was designated an enemy in August 1990), that's fine, but has no moral standing.

2   If they exaggerate or fabricate such crimes, they become objects of contempt.

3   If they ignore such crimes, it is a matter of little significance.

4   If they deny or minimise such crimes, it is also a minor matter.

5   And if they ignore or justify the crimes in which their own state is implicated, that is criminal.

That much is straight logic, but I admit that I don't quite adhere to it. I would not accept the conclusions 3 and 4 with regard to Western intellectuals, and have always regarded such a stance as abhorrent. Perhaps a case can be made for that apparent irrationality, perhaps in terms of the special responsibilities that accrue to privilege. Note that it requires an argument, one that is not so simple to give. But for the rest, there should be not the slightest question, point 5 of course being the most important, by a huge margin.

The logic applies over a broad range, including the examples mentioned before. Or others that are of considerable current relevance as well. Let's try a simple thought experiment. Imagine that the USSR had survived unchanged after the Soviet withdrawal from Afghanistan. Suppose that some Soviet intellectual were then to rage about the terrible atrocities of the victorious

Afghan resistance, particularly the forces of Washington's favourite, the Islamic fundamentalist fanatic Gulbuddin Hekmatyar. Few would be impressed, even if he had protested the Soviet invasion; if he had not, his behaviour would be contemptible. Suppose some journal that had offered critical support for the invasion of Afghanistan, with a call for negotiations with the United States (not the terrorists they directed in Afghanistan) and complaints about the cost, were to ask whether Hekmatyar's atrocities 'warrant a reconsideration of our opposition to the Afghan war'; I happen to be quoting the title of a 1978 symposium in the American journal *Dissent*, with 'Afghan' replacing 'Vietnam'. Suppose that a Soviet intellectual were to have ignored the fate of the Afghan refugees who fled Soviet terror, and then to be overcome with compassion for those fleeing Hekmatyar, forming support groups to provide them aid and help them settle in the Soviet Union. You can surely fill in the blanks.

We know what to think about the invented Soviet example, and an honest person will have no difficulty applying the reasoning to the actual case in our own free societies.

We also know how to apply the same valid reasoning to correspondents in Phnom Penh, or earlier in Vientiane, who had no time for the huge flow of victims of US terror bombings, refusing even to cross the street to interview them, but later were trekking courageously through the jungle to find refugees from Pol Pot's terror. Not Timorese refugees, however. They were invisible even when brought to the doors of editorial offices in New York and Washington, as was finally done in desperation. An honest person will also know how to react to the 'structurally serious explanation' for the differential treatment of victims of Indonesian aggression and Khmer Rouge terror offered by British Southeast Asia correspondent William Shawcross: the reason was a 'comparative lack of sources' in the Timorese case, and lack of access to refugees—Lisbon and Darwin being so much harder to reach from London than the Thai–Cambodian border, putting aside, out of charity, the claim about sources.

It is all too easy to spin out case after case, and to see just what they imply. Still more revealing is the fact that it is virtually never done, as is the reaction if someone dares to say that two and two is four.

It could be argued that it is unfair to compare Western and Soviet intellectuals. That is in fact correct. It is quite unfair to compare Soviet intellectuals who pretended that the invasion of Afghanistan was the *defence* of Afghanistan from terrorists supported by the CIA, and Western intellectuals who pretended (and still do) that the US invasion of South Vietnam from 1961 was the *defence* of South Vietnam from terrorists supported by Hanoi (or Moscow, or Beijing). Throughout, the comparison is grossly unfair—to the commissars, who could at least plead fear, not mere servility and cowardice.

The observation generalises. The moral culpability of those who ignore the crimes that matter by moral standards is greater to the extent that the society is free and open, so that they can speak more freely, and act more effectively to bring those crimes to an end. And it is greater for those who have a measure of privilege within the more free and open societies, those who have the resources, the training, the facilities and opportunities to speak and act effectively: the intellectuals, in short. Again, that is simple logic. It is easy enough to see how the principles apply in case after case, and how the simple moral imperatives compare with consistent practice. The conclusions are instructive, once again.

Let's proceed. Soviet commissars, however corrupt, generally *were* able to recognise that the invasion of Afghanistan was just that: an invasion of Afghanistan. They might have justified it, perhaps out of fear, but few were so depraved as to deny the fact. Western intellectual culture is very different. I can't speak of Australia, but in the United States, I've been searching for over 30 years to see if I can find even one accurate reference in the mainstream to John F. Kennedy's escalation of US intervention in Indochina from support for a standard Latin America-style terror state to outright aggression against South Vietnam, which bore the brunt of US aggression in Indochina throughout. I don't read everything, of course, but I do my share. And I have yet to find a single reference, apart from the far-out margins. The event certainly took place, but it is unmentionable, unthinkable within the intellectual culture—which cannot even plead fear in self-justification.

The reality is much worse. Not only are properly educated people immune from the bare facts, but they have even succeeded in shifting the responsibility to the victims. Vietnam was the guilty party according to the standard version, though, admittedly, there is a spectrum. Keeping to high office for illustration, at the dovish extreme we find Jimmy Carter, who explained, in the course of one of his sermons on human rights, that we owe Vietnam no debt, because 'the destruction was mutual', as a walk through Quang Ngai province and San Francisco quickly reveals. There was no reaction, apart from margins of the usual margins. At the other extreme, we find Ronald Reagan—or more accurately, those who handed him his note cards—and the Senators who demand that we continue to punish Vietnam for the crimes it committed against us. And in the middle there are the moderates, like George Bush, who explained that 'Hanoi knows today that we seek only answers without the threat of retribution for the past'. We can never forgive them for what they have done to us, but we are willing to 'begin writing the last chapter of the Vietnam war' if they dedicate all their efforts to locating the remains of American pilots who they viciously shot down from the skies. The magnanimity happens to be a response to the demands of the business community, who recognise that torture is fun, but profits more so.

The President's thoughtful comments, as usual eliciting no reaction, were reported in a front-page story in the *New York Times*. The adjacent column reports the failure of the Japanese 'unambiguously' to accept the blame for their 'wartime aggression', revealing again the flaw in the Japanese character that has so puzzled American commentators.

It is worth mentioning the effects of education and privilege. Among intellectuals, even at the height of protest against the war, the harshest criticism—with the usual marginal exceptions—was that the war was a 'mistake', a case of good intentions that went awry because of ignorance, naivety, and failure to understand Vietnamese culture and history. In contrast, since the question has been asked in polls from the mid-1970s, about 70 per cent of the general population has taken the position that the war was 'fundamentally wrong and immoral', not 'a mistake'. The figure is remarkable, not only because it is unusually high for an open question on a poll with many choices, but because those who expressed that view had very likely come to it on their own. They are unlikely to have seen or heard it in the media and journals of opinion. It is not the only case, and again merits some thought.

To be sure, the US political class is following a worthy tradition in placing the blame upon the victims of its villainy. Distinguished precedents include the huge indemnities imposed on Haiti in 1825 in punishment for the crime of having liberated itself from France, and the similar treatment of Indonesia by its longtime Dutch benefactors after it had committed the same crime. These are among the prerogatives of power, along with the lack of reaction to them.

Still more remarkable is the fact that the Western stance inspires great acclaim, notably self-acclaim. The sordid spectacle is only made more vivid by the fact that the penalties for honesty and integrity are so slight, at least for people who enjoy the protections accorded to wealth and privilege in our free societies.

Often our mawkish exercises of self-flagellation are too much to bear. Thus the editors of the *Wall Street Journal* (15 September 1994) berate the State Department for succumbing to the 'political correctness' that has been 'the bane of campus life', referring to its endorsement of 'the Brezhnev view' of America in 'a technical document mandated by a UN treaty' that obligates all signers to comment on their own human rights records—on 'human rights abuses *within* the United States', the editors proclaim with horror over this colossal absurdity. They present the excerpts that so shock them, which observe that the 'American struggle for justice' has been marred by such violations as 'the enslavement and disenfranchisement of African Americans and the virtual destruction of many Native American civilizations'. What an outrage to parrot such lies of Soviet propaganda! The editors' reaction to the scandal tells us a good deal more than they realise about the function of the idiotic concept of 'political correctness', devised as an ideological weapon in the course of the extraordinary right-wing assault on the residual independence of the universities and other institutions. Reactions were in part the same, though mixed in this case with praise, when Robert McNamara, the chief architect of a war that left some four million dead in Indochina, issued his apology for what he had done: his apology to *Americans*, for the suffering and disruption of their society that had been caused by the errors of people seeking to do good, but failing.

There is nothing new about these observations. Witnessing 'the triumphal march of civilization across the desert', De Tocqueville marvelled at the ability of the American colonists to destroy the native population with complete 'respect for the laws of humanity', 'with singular felicity, tranquilly, legally, philanthropically, without shedding blood, and without violating a single great principle of morality in the eyes of the world'. In 1880, Helen Jackson wrote a remarkable account of a 'Century of Dishonour', in many respects still unsurpassed, recording the treatment of 'that hapless race of native Americans, which we are exterminating with such merciless and perfidious cruelty', as John Quincy Adams described the process in a rare moment of honesty years after his own signal contribution had been completed. Jackson's wonderful book was virtually ignored, as it was when reprinted in a limited edition of 2000 copies in 1964; it is scarcely known today, and unavailable. To be sure, her name was known. She was bitterly denounced for her treachery in the widely read celebration of 'the Winning of the West' by the much-admired racist historian Theodore Roosevelt, later President, who proclaimed that: 'As a nation, our Indian policy is to be blamed, because of the weakness it displayed, because of its shortsightedness, and its occasional leaning to the policy of sentimental humanitarians; and we have often promised what was impossible to perform; but there has been no wilful wrong-doing'.

And so the triumphal march of civilisation goes on, until the present.

Also not new is the comparison of free and totalitarian societies. In expounding his First Principles of Government, David Hume observed that the rulers must ultimately rely on controlling thought: 'Tis therefore, on opinion only that government is founded; and this maxim extends to the most despotic and most military governments, as well as to the most free and most popular'. Half a century ago, George Orwell devoted his introduction to *Animal Farm* to free and democratic England, noting that outcomes there are not all that different from the totalitarian state he was satirising, though the methods were different—no compliment to British intellectuals, he made clear. 'The sinister fact about literary censorship in England', he wrote, 'is that it is largely voluntary. Unpopular ideas can be silenced, and inconvenient facts kept dark, without any need for any official ban'.

Without the exercise of force, 'Anyone who challenges the prevailing orthodoxy finds himself silenced with surprising effectiveness', thanks to the internalisation of the values of subordination and conformity and the control of the press by 'wealthy men who have every motive to be dishonest on certain important topics'. Orwell's analysis was thin and his examples skimpy but there has been a good deal of water under the bridge since. The analysis has been much extended, and there is now an extensive record demonstrating the accuracy of his perceptions about the free societies—which remained unpublished, discovered in his papers only 30 years later, perhaps illustrating his point.

For reasons too obvious to review, the topic of Orwell's unpublished introduction is far more important for Westerners than yet another exposure of the crimes of the hated enemy in his most famous work, a few years later. And of much greater intellectual interest as well. The methods of control used in the 'most despotic' governments are transparent; those of 'the most free and most popular' societies are far more interesting to unravel. Had Orwell's work focused on these vastly more important and intellectually challenging issues, he would be no hero in the West. Rather, he would have been another Helen Jackson, or would have endured the scandalous abuse that was Bertrand Russell's penalty for integrity and honesty. The likely outcome is indicated by the case of the man who pioneered the study of corporate propaganda, the prime contemporary instrument for waging 'the everlasting battle for the minds of men', in the words of a leading figure in the public relations industry: the Australian social scientist Alex Carey, whose insightful and revealing work has circulated privately for years among people interested in understanding the modern world, but has only just now begun to be published in accessible form (*Taking the Risk Out of Democracy*, 1995). He, too, greatly to his credit, has been the target of obloquy and vilification by the 'voluntary' commissars, as readers of the local press know well.

At this point we begin, barely begin, to approach the real questions of the intellectual and moral responsibility of the writer. And we discover that there is, after all, quite a bit to say, and many answers to give. The answers are not exactly flattering to ourselves and the milieu in which we live and work, but should be at the very core of our concerns and activities, in our schools, our journals, and our communities.

If that were to take place, we could claim to be entering the civilised world.

4

Goals and Visions

In referring to goals and visions, I have in mind a practical rather than a very principled distinction. As is usual in human affairs, it is the practical perspective that matters most. Such theoretical understanding as we have is far too thin to carry much weight.

By visions, I mean the conception of a future society that animates what we actually do, a society in which a decent human being might want to live. By goals, I mean the choices and tasks that are within reach, that we will pursue one way or another guided by a vision that may be distant and hazy.

An animating vision must rest on some conception of human nature, of what's good for people, of their needs and rights, of the aspects of their nature that should be nurtured, encouraged and permitted to flourish for their benefit and that of others. The concept of human nature that underlies our visions is usually tacit and inchoate, but it is always there, perhaps implicitly, whether one chooses to leave things as they are and cultivate one's own garden, or to work for small changes, or for revolutionary ones.

This much, at least, is true of people who regard themselves as moral agents, not monsters—who care about the effects of what they do or fail to do.

On all such matters, our knowledge and understanding are shallow; as in virtually every area of human life, we proceed on the basis of intuition and experience, hopes and fears. Goals involve hard choices with very serious human consequences. We adopt them on the basis of imperfect evidence and limited understanding, and though our visions can and should be a guide, they are at best a very partial one. They are not clear, nor are they stable, at least for people who care about the consequences of their acts. Sensible people will look forward to a clearer articulation of their animating visions and to the critical evaluation of them in the light of reason and experience. So far, the substance is pretty meagre, and there are no signs of any change in that state of affairs. Slogans are easy, but not very helpful when real choices have to be made.

Goals versus Visions

Goals and visions can appear to be in conflict, and often are. There's no contradiction in that, as I think we all know from ordinary experience. Let me take my own case, to illustrate what I have in mind.

My personal visions are fairly traditional anarchist ones, with origins in the Enlightenment and classical liberalism. Before proceeding, I have to clarify what I mean by that. I do not mean the version of classical liberalism that has been reconstructed for ideological purposes, but the original, before it was broken on the rocks of rising industrial capitalism, as Rudolf Rocker put it in his work on anarchosyndicalism 60 years ago—rather accurately, I think.[1]

As state capitalism developed into the modern era, economic, political and ideological systems have increasingly been taken over by vast institutions of private tyranny that are about as close to the totalitarian ideal as any that humans have so far constructed. 'Within the corporation,' political economist Robert Brady wrote half a century ago, 'all policies emanate from the control above. In the union of this power to determine policy with the execution thereof, all authority necessarily proceeds from the top to the bottom and all responsibility from the bottom to the top. This is, of course, the inverse of "democratic" control; it follows the structural conditions of dictatorial power'. 'What in political circles would be called legislative, executive, and judicial powers' is gathered in 'controlling hands' which, 'so far as policy formulation and execution are concerned, are found at the peak of the pyramid and are manipulated without significant check from its base'. As private power 'grows and expands', it is transformed 'into a community force ever more politically potent and politically conscious', ever more dedicated to a 'propaganda program' that 'becomes a matter of converting the public . . . to the point of view of the control pyramid'. That project, already substantial in the period Brady reviewed, reached an awesome scale a few years later as American business sought to beat back the social democratic currents of the postwar world, which reached the United States as well, and to win what its leaders called 'the everlasting battle for the minds of men', using the huge resources of the public relations industry, the entertainment industry, the corporate media, and whatever else could be mobilised by the 'control pyramids' of the social and economic order. These are crucially important features of the modern world, as is dramatically revealed by the few careful studies.[2]

The 'banking institutions and moneyed incorporations' of which Thomas Jefferson warned in his later years—predicting that, if not curbed, they would become a form of absolutism that would destroy the promise of the democratic revolution—have since more than fulfilled his most dire expectations. They have become largely unaccountable and increasingly immune from popular interference and public inspection while gaining great and expanding control over the global order. Those inside their hierarchical command structure take orders from above and send orders down below. Those outside may try to rent themselves to the system of power, but have little other relation to it (except by purchasing what it offers, if they can). The world is more complex than any simple description, but Brady's is pretty close, even more so today than when he wrote.

It should be added that the extraordinary power that corporations and financial institutions enjoy was not the result of popular choices. It was crafted by courts and lawyers in the course of the construction of a developmental state that serves the interests of private power, and extended by playing one state against another to seek special privileges, not hard for large private institutions. That is the major reason why the current Congress, business-run to an unusual degree, seeks to devolve federal authority to the states, more easily threatened and manipulated. I'm speaking of the United States, where the process has been rather well studied in academic scholarship. I'll keep to that case; as far as I know, it is much the same elsewhere.

We tend to think of the resulting structures of power as immutable, virtually a part of nature. They are anything but that. These forms of private tyranny only reached something like their current form, with the rights of immortal persons, early in this century. The grants of rights and the legal theory that lay behind them are rooted in much the same intellectual soil as nourished the other two major forms of twentieth century totalitarianism, Fascism and Bolshevism. There is no reason to consider this tendency in human affairs to be more permanent than its ignoble brethren.[3]

Conventional practice is to restrict such terms as 'totalitarian' and 'dictatorship' to political power. Brady is unusual in not keeping to this convention, a natural one, which helps to remove centres of decision- making from the public eye. The effort to do so is expected in any society based on illegitimate authority— any actual society, that is. That is why, for example, accounts in terms of personal characteristics and failings, vague and unspecific cultural practices, and the like, are much preferred to the study of the structure and function of powerful institutions.

When I speak of classical liberalism, I mean the ideas that were swept away, in considerable measure, by the rising tides of state capitalist autocracy. These ideas survived (or were reinvented) in various forms in the culture of resistance to the new forms of oppression, serving as an animating vision for popular struggles that have considerably expanded the scope of freedom, justice, and rights. They were also taken up, adapted, and developed within libertarian left currents. According to this anarchist vision, any structure of hierarchy and authority carries a heavy burden of justification, whether it involves personal relations or a larger social order. If it cannot bear that burden— sometimes it can—then it is illegitimate and should be dismantled. When honestly posed and squarely faced, that challenge can rarely be sustained. Genuine libertarians have their work cut out for them.

State power and private tyranny are prime examples at the outerlimits, but the issues arise pretty much across the board: in relations among parents and children, teachers and students, men and women, those now alive and the future generations that will be compelled to live with the results of what we do, indeed just about everywhere. In particular, the anarchist vision, in almost every variety has looked forward to the dismantling of state power. Personally, I share that vision, though it runs directly counter to my goals. Hence the tension to which I referred.

My short-term goals are to defend and even strengthen elements of state authority which, though illegitimate in fundamental ways, are critically necessary right now to impede the dedicated efforts to 'roll back' the progress that has been achieved in extending democracy and human rights. State authority is now under severe attack in the more democratic societies, but not because it conflicts with the libertarian vision. Rather the opposite: because it offers (weak) protection to some aspects of that vision. Governments have a fatal flaw: unlike the private tyrannies, the institutions of state power and authority offer to the despised public an opportunity to play some role, however limited, in managing their own affairs. That defect is intolerable to the masters, who now feel, with some justification, that changes in the international economic and political order offer the prospects of creating a kind of 'utopia for the masters', with dismal prospects for most of the rest. It should be unnecessary to spell out here what I mean. The effects are all too obvious even in the rich societies, from the corridors of power to the streets, countryside, and prisons. For reasons that merit attention but that lie beyond the scope of these remarks, the rollback campaign is currently spearheaded by dominant sectors of societies in which the values under attack have been realised in some of their most advanced forms, the English-speaking world; no small irony but no contradiction either.

It is worth bearing in mind that fulfilment of the utopian dream has been celebrated as an imminent prospect from early in the nineteenth century (I'll return briefly to that period). By the 1880s, the revolutionary socialist artist William Morris could write:

> I know it is at present the received opinion that the competitive or 'Devil take the hindmost' system is the last system of economy which the world will see; that it is perfection, and therefore finality has been reached in it; and it is doubtless a bold thing to fly in the face of this opinion, which I am told is held even by the most learned men.

If history is really at an end, as confidently proclaimed, then 'civilisation will die', but all of history says it is not so, he added. The hope that 'perfection' was in sight flourished again in the 1920s. With the strong support of liberal opinion generally, and of course the business world, Woodrow Wilson's Red Scare had successfully undermined unions and independent thought, helping to establish an era of business dominance that was expected to be permanent. With the collapse of unions, working people had no power and little hope at the peak of the automobile boom.

The crushing of unions and workers' rights, often by violence, shocked even the right-wing British press. An Australian visitor, astounded by the weakness of American unions, observed in 1928 that 'Labour organisation exists only by the tolerance of employers . . . It has no real part in determining industrial conditions'. Again, the next few years showed that the hopes were premature. But these recurrent dreams provide a model that the 'control pyramids' and their political agents seek to reconstitute today.[4]

In today's world, I think, the goals of a committed anarchist should be to defend some state institutions from the attack against them, while trying at the same time to pry them open to more meaningful public participation—and ultimately, to dismantle them in a much more free society, if the appropriate circumstances can be achieved.

Right or wrong—and that's a matter of uncertain judgment—this stand is not undermined by the apparent conflict between goals and visions. Such conflict is a normal feature of everyday life, which we somehow try to live with but cannot escape.

The 'Humanistic Conception'

With this in mind, I'd like to turn to the broader question of visions. It is particularly pertinent today against the background of the intensifying attempt to reverse, undermine, and dismantle the gains that have been won by long and often bitter popular struggle. The issues are of historic importance, and are often veiled in distortion and deceit in campaigns to 'convert the public to the point of view of the control pyramid'. There could hardly be a better moment to consider the ideals and visions that have been articulated, modified, reshaped, and often turned into their opposite as industrial society has developed to its current stage, with a massive assault against democracy, human rights, and even markets, while the triumph of these values is being hailed by those who are leading the attack against them—a process that will win nods of recognition from those familiar with what used to be called 'propaganda' in more honest days. It is a moment in human affairs that is as interesting intellectually as it is ominous from a human point of view.

Let me begin by sketching a point of view that was articulated by two leading twentieth century thinkers, Bertrand Russell and John Dewey, who disagreed on a great many things, but shared a vision that Russell called 'the humanistic conception'—to quote Dewey, the belief that the 'ultimate aim' of production is not production of goods, but 'of free human beings associated with one another on terms of equality'. The goal of education, as Russell put it, is 'to give a sense of the value of things other than domination', to help create 'wise citizens of a free community' in which both liberty and 'individual creativeness' will flourish, and working people will be the masters of their fate, not tools of production. Illegitimate structures of coercion must be unravelled; crucially, domination by 'business for private profit through private control of banking, land, industry, reinforced by command of the press, press agents and other means of publicity and propaganda' (Dewey). Unless that is done, Dewey continued, talk of democracy is largely beside the point. Politics will remain 'the shadow cast on society by big business, [and] the attenuation of the shadow will not change the substance'. Democratic forms will lack real content, and people will work 'not freely and intelligently but for the sake of the work earned', a condition that is 'illiberal and immoral'. Accordingly, industry must be changed 'from a feudalistic to a democratic social order' based on workers' control, free association, and federal organisation, in the general style of a range of thought that includes, along with many anarchists, G.D.H. Cole's guild socialism and such left Marxists as Anton Pannekoek, Rosa Luxemburg, Paul Mattick, and others. Russell's views were rather similar, in this regard.[5]

Problems of democracy were the primary focus of Dewey's thought and direct engagement. He was straight out of mainstream America, 'as American as apple pie', in the standard phrase. It is therefore of interest that the ideas he expressed not many years ago would be regarded today in much of the intellectual culture as outlandish or worse, if known, even denounced as 'anti-American' in influential sectors.

The latter phrase, incidentally, is interesting and revealing, as is its recent currency. We expect such notions in totalitarian societies. Thus in Stalinist days, dissidents and critics were condemned as 'anti-Soviet', an intolerable crime; Brazilian neo-Nazi generals and others like them had similar categories. But their appearance in much more free societies, in which subordination to power is voluntary, not coerced, is a far more significant phenomenon. In any milieu that retains even the memory of a democratic culture, such concepts would merely elicit ridicule. Imagine the reaction on the streets of Milan or Oslo to a book entitled *Anti-Italianism* or *The Anti-Norwegians*, denouncing the real or fabricated deeds of those who do not show proper respect for the doctrines of the secular faith. In the Anglo-American societies, however—including Australia, so I've noticed—such performances are treated with solemnity and respect in respectable circles, one of the signs of a serious deterioration of ordinary democratic values.

The ideas expressed in the not very distant past by such outstanding figures as Russell and Dewey are rooted in the Enlightenment and classical liberalism, and retain their revolutionary character: in education, the workplace, and every other sphere of life. If implemented, they would help clear the way to the free development of human beings whose values are not accumulation and domination, but independence of mind and action, free association on terms of equality, and cooperation to achieve common goals. Such people would share Adam Smith's contempt for the 'mean' and 'sordid pursuits' of 'the masters of mankind' and their 'vile maxim': 'All for ourselves, and nothing for other people', the guiding principles we are taught to admire and revere, as traditional values are eroded under unremitting attack. They would readily understand what led a pre-capitalist figure like Smith to warn of the grim consequences of division of labour, and to base his rather nuanced advocacy of markets in part on the belief that under conditions of 'perfect liberty' there would be a natural tendency towards equality, an obvious desideratum on elementary moral grounds.

The 'humanistic conception' that was expressed by Russell and Dewey in a more civilised period, and that is familiar to the libertarian left, is radically at odds with the leading currents of contemporary thought: the guiding ideas of the totalitarian order crafted by Lenin and Trotsky, and of the state capitalist industrial societies of the West. One of these systems has fortunately collapsed, but the other is on a march backwards to what could be a very ugly future.

'The New Spirit of the Age'

It is important to recognise how sharp and dramatic is the clash of values between this humanistic conception and what reigns today, the ideals denounced by the working class press of the mid-nineteenth century as 'the New Spirit of the Age: Gain Wealth, forgetting all but Self', Smith's 'vile maxim', a demeaning and shameful doctrine that no decent person could tolerate. It is remarkable to trace the evolution of values from a pre-capitalist figure like Smith, with his stress on sympathy, the goal of liberty with equality, and the basic human right to creative and fulfilling work, to those who celebrate 'the New Spirit of the Age', often shamelessly invoking Smith's name. Let's put aside the vulgar performances that regularly deface the ideological institutions. Consider instead someone who can at least be taken seriously, say, Nobel Prize-winning economist James Buchanan, who tells us that 'the ideal society is anarchy, in which no one man or group of men coerces another'. He then offers the following gloss, stated authoritatively as fact:

> any person's ideal situation is one that allows him full freedom of action and inhibits the behaviour of others so as to force adherence to his own desires. That is to say, each person seeks mastery over a world of slaves,[6]

a thought that Adam Smith would have considered pathological, as would Wilhelm von Humboldt, John Stuart Mill, or anyone even close to the classical liberal tradition—but that is your fondest dream, in case you hadn't noticed.

One intriguing illustration of the state of the intellectual culture and its prevailing values is the commentary on the difficult problems we face in uplifting the people of Eastern Europe, now at last liberated, so that we can extend to them the loving care we have lavished on our wards elsewhere for several hundred years. The consequences seem rather clear in an impressive array of horror chambers around the world, but miraculously—and most fortunately—they teach no lessons about the values of our civilisation and the principles that guide its noble leaders; only 'anti-Americans' and their ilk could be so demented as to suggest that the consistent record of history might merit a side glance, perhaps. Now there are new opportunities for our beneficence. We can help the people released from Communist tyranny to reach, or at least approach, the blessed state of Bengalis, Haitians, Brazilians, Guatemalans, Filipinos, indigenous peoples everywhere, African slaves, and on, and on.

In late 1994, the *New York Times* ran a series of articles on how our pupils are doing. The one on East Germany opens by quoting a priest who was a leader of the popular protests against the Communist regime. He describes his growing concerns about what is happening in his society: 'brutal competition and the lust for money are destroying our sense of community. Almost everyone feels a level of fear or depression or insecurity', as they master the lessons we provide to the backward peoples of the world. But their reaction carries no lessons for us.[7]

The showcase that everyone is proud of is Poland, where 'capitalism has been kinder' than elsewhere, Jane Perlez reports under the headline 'Fast and Slow Lanes on the Capitalist Road': some Poles are getting the point, but others are slow learners.[8]

Perlez gives examples of both types. The good student is the owner of a small factory that is a 'thriving example' of the best in modern capitalist Poland. Thanks to interest-free government loans in this now- flourishing free market society, her factory produces 'glamorous beaded dresses' and 'intricately designed wedding gowns', sold mostly to rich Germans, but to wealthy Poles as well. Meanwhile, the World Bank reports, poverty has more than doubled since the reforms were instituted while real wages dropped 30 per cent, and by the end of 1994 the Polish economy was expected to recover to 90 per cent of its pre-1989 gross domestic product. But 'capitalism has been kinder': hungry people can appreciate the 'signs of sudden consumption', admiring the wedding gowns in the windows of elegant shops, the 'foreign cars with Polish license plates' roaring down the Warsaw–Berlin road, and the 'nouveau riche women with $1300 cellular telephones tucked in their pocketbooks'.

'People have to be taught to understand they must fight for themselves and can't rely on others', a job counsellor in the Czech Republic explains. Concerned about 'the creation of an entrenched underclass', she is running a training class to teach proper attitudes to people who had 'egalitarian values drilled into their minds' in the days when 'the proud slogan used to be: "I am a miner, who else is better?"'. The fast learners now know the answer to that question: the ex- Nomenklatura, rich beyond their wildest dreams as they become the agents of foreign enterprises, which naturally favour them because of their skills and experience; the bankers set up in business through the 'old boy network'; the Polish women enjoying consumer delights; the government-assisted manufacturers of elegant dresses for export to other rich women. In brief, the right kind of people.

Those are the successes of American values. Then there are the failures, still on the slow lane. Perlez selects as her example a 43-year-old coal miner, who 'sits in his wood-paneled living room admiring the fruits of his labor under Communism—a television set, comfortable furniture, a shiny, modern kitchen', now unemployed after 27 years in the mines and thinking about the years before 1989. They 'were great', he says, and 'life was secure and comfortable'. A slow learner, he finds the new values 'unfathomable', and cannot understand 'why he is at home, jobless and dependent on welfare payments', worrying about his ten children, lacking the skill to 'Gain Wealth, forgetting all but Self'.

It is understandable, then, that Poland should find its place on the shelf alongside the other trophies, inspiring further pride and self- acclaim.

The region is plagued with other slow learners, a problem reviewed in a 'global report' of *Christian Science Monitor* correspondents in the former Communist world. One entrepreneur complained that 'he offered a fellow Ukrainian $100 a month to help him grow roses in a private plot' (in translation: to work for him). 'Compared with the $4 that the man earned on a collective farm, it was a fortune. But the offer was rejected.' The fast learner attributes the irrationality to 'a certain mentality' that lingers on even after the victory of freedom: 'He thinks, "Nyet, I'm not going to leave the collective and be your slave"'. American workers had long been infected with the same unwillingness to become someone's slave, until properly civilised; I'll return to that.

Tenants in an apartment building in Warsaw suffer from the same malady. They do not want to hand over their apartments

to an industrialist who claims ownership of the building from before World War II, asking 'Why should people profit from something they don't have a right to?' There has been 'significant
reform progress' in overcoming such retrograde attitudes, the report continues, though 'there is still great reluctance to let foreigners buy and sell land'. The coordinator of US-sponsored
agricultural initiatives in Ukraine explains that 'You'll never have
a situation where 100 per cent of the land is in private hands.
They've never had democracy'. True, anti-democratic passions
do not run as high as in Vietnam, where a February 1995 decree
'set the clock back': 'In a tribute to Marx, the decree aims to help
Vietnamese by squeezing rent from the privileged few who have
land certificates for businesses', granted in an effort to attract
foreign investment. If only foreign investors and a tiny domestic
elite were allowed to buy up the country, the natives could work
for them (if they are lucky), and we'd have freedom and 'democracy' at last, as in Central America, the Philippines, and other
paradises liberated long ago.[9]

Cubans have long been berated for the same kinds of back-
wardness. Outrage peaked during the Pan-American games held
in the United States, when Cuban athletes failed to succumb to
a huge propaganda campaign to induce them to defect, including
lavish financial offers to become professionals; they felt a commitment to their country and its people, they told reporters. Fury
knew few bounds over the devastating impact of Communist
brainwashing and Marxist doctrine.

Fortunately, Americans are protected from the fact that even
under the conditions of poverty imposed by US economic warfare, Cubans still refuse to accept dollars for domestic service, so
visitors report, not wanting to be 'your slave'. Nor are they likely
to be subjected to the results of a 1994 Gallup poll, considered
to be the first independent and scientific survey, published in the
Miami Spanish-language press but apparently not elsewhere: that

88 per cent said they were 'proud of being Cuban' and 58 per cent that 'the revolution's successes outstrip its failures', 69 per cent identified themselves as 'revolutionaries' (but only 21 per cent as 'Communist' or 'socialist'), 76 per cent said they were 'satisfied with their personal life', and 3 per cent said that 'political problems' were the key problems facing the country.

If such Communist atrocities were to be known, it might be aecessary to nuke Havana instead of simply trying to kill as many people as possible from starvation and disease to bring 'democracy'. That became the new pretext for strangling Cuba after the fall of the Berlin wall, the ideological institutions not missing a beat as they shifted gears. No longer was Cuba an agent of the Kremlin, bent on taking over Latin America and conquering the United States, trembling in terror. The lies of 30 years can be quietly shelved: terror and economic warfare have always been an attempt to bring democracy, in the revised standard version. Therefore we must tighten the embargo that 'has contributed to an increase in hunger, illness, death and to one of the world's largest neurological epidemics in the past century', according to health experts writing in US medical journals in October 1994. The author of one says, 'Well, the fact is that we are killing people', by denying them food and medicines, and equipment for manufacturing their own medical products.

Clinton's 'Cuban Democracy Act'—which President Bush at first vetoed because it was so transparently in violation of international law, and then signed when he was outflanked from the right by Clinton during the election campaign—cut off trade by US subsidiaries abroad, 90 per cent of it food, medicine and medical equipment. That contribution to democracy helped to bring about a considerable decline in Cuban health standards, an increase in mortality rates, and 'the most alarming public health crisis in Cuba in recent memory', a neurological disease that had last been observed in tropical prison camps in Southeast

Asia in World War II, according to the former chief of neuro-epidemiology at the National Institute of Health, the author of one of the articles. To illustrate the effects, a Columbia University Professor of Medicine cites the case of a Swedish water filtration system that Cuba had purchased to produce vaccines, barred because some parts are produced by an American-owned company, so life-saving vaccines can be denied to bring 'democracy' to the survivors.[10]

The successes in 'killing people' and making them suffer are important. In the real world, Castro's Cuba was a concern not because of a military threat, human rights abuses, or dictatorship; rather, for reasons deeply rooted in American history. In the 1820s, as the takeover of the continent was proceeding apace, Cuba was regarded by the political and economic leadership as the next prize to be won. That is 'an object of transcendent importance to the commercial and political interests of our Union', the author of the Monroe Doctrine, John Quincy Adams, advised, agreeing with Jefferson and others that Spain should keep sovereignty until the British deterrent faded, and Cuba would fall into US hands by 'the laws of political . . . gravitation', a 'ripe fruit' for harvest, as it did a century ago. By mid-twentieth century, the ripe fruit was highly valued by US agricultural and gambling interests, among others. Castro's robbery of this US possession was not taken lightly. Worse still, there was a danger of a 'domino effect' of development in terms that might be meaningful to suffering people elsewhere—the most successful health services in Latin America, for example. It was feared that Cuba might be one of those 'rotten apples' that 'spoil the barrel', a 'virus' that might 'infect' others, in the terminology favoured by planners, who care nothing about crimes, but a lot about demonstration effects.

But respectable people do not dwell on such matters or even the elementary facts about the campaign to restore the ripe fruit to its rightful owner since 1959, including its current phase. Few

Americans were exposed to the subversive material in the October 1994 medical journals, or even the fact that, in the same month, the UN General Assembly passed a resolution calling for an end to the illegal embargo by a vote of 101 to 2, the US able to rely only on Israel, now abandoned even by Albania, Romania, and Paraguay, which had briefly joined Washington in its crusade for democracy in earlier years.

The standard story is that Eastern Europe, liberated at last, can now join the wealthy societies of the West. Perhaps, but then one wonders why that hadn't happened during the preceding half millennium, as much of Eastern Europe steadily declined relative to the West, well into this century, becoming its original 'Third World'. A different prospect that might be imagined is that the status quo ante will be more or less restored: parts of the Communist empire that had belonged to the industrial West—western Poland, the Czech Republic, some others—will gradually rejoin it, while others revert to something like their earlier status as service areas for the rich industrial world, which, of course, did not get that way merely because of its unique virtue. As Winston Churchill observed in a paper submitted to his Cabinet colleagues in January 1914,

> we are not a young people with *an innocent record and* a scanty inheritance. We have engrossed to ourselves . . . an *altogether disproportionate* share of the wealth and traffic of the world. We have got all we want in territory, and our claim to be left in the unmolested enjoyment of vast and splendid possessions, *mainly acquired by violence, largely maintained by force*, often seems less reasonable to others than to us.

To be sure, such honesty is rare in respectable society, though the passage would be acceptable without the italicised phrases, as Churchill understood. He did make the paper public in the 1920s, in *The World Crisis*, but with the offending phrases removed.[11]

It is also instructive to observe the framework in which the disaster of Communism is portrayed. That it was a monstrosity has never been in doubt, as was evident from the first moment to anarchists, people of independent mind like Russell and Dewey, and left Marxists—indeed predicted by many of them in advance. Nor could the collapse of the tyranny be anything but an occasion for rejoicing for anyone who values freedom and human dignity. But consider a narrower question: the standard proof that the command economy was a catastrophic failure, demonstrating the superior merits of capitalism: Simply compare West Germany, France, England, and the United States to the Soviet Union and its satellites. QED. The argument is scarcely more than an intellectual reflex, considered so obviously valid as to pass unnoticed, the presupposition of all further inquiry.

It is an interesting argument, with broad applicability. By the same logic, one can, for example, demonstrate the colossal failure of the kindergartens in Cambridge, Massachusetts, and the grand success of MIT: Simply ask how well children entering first grade understand quantum physics as compared with MIT PhDs. QED.

Someone who put forth that argument might be offered psychiatric treatment. The fallacy is trivially obvious. To conduct a sane evaluation, one would have to compare the graduates of the Cambridge kindergartens with children who entered the system at the same level. The same elementary rationality dictates that to evaluate the Soviet command economy as compared with the capitalist alternative, we must compare Eastern European countries to others that were like them when the 'experiment' with the two development models began. Obviously not the West; one has to go back half a millennium to a find a time when it was similar to Eastern Europe. A proper comparison might be Russia and Brazil, or Bulgaria and Guatemala, though that would be unfair to the Communist model, which never had anything remotely like the advantages of the US satellites. If we undertake the rational comparison, we conclude, indeed, that the Communist economic model was a disaster; and the Western one an even more catastrophic failure. There are nuances and complexities, but the basic conclusions are rather solid.

It is intriguing to see how such elementary points cannot be understood, and to observe the reaction to attempts to explore the issue, which also cannot be understood. The exercise offers some useful lessons about the ideological systems of the free societies.[12]

What is happening now in much of Eastern Europe in part recapitulates the general record of regions of the world that were driven to a service role, in which many remain, with exceptions that are instructive. It also falls into place alongside of a long, interesting, and important strand of the history of the industrial societies themselves. Modern America was 'created over its workers' protests', Yale University labour historian David Montgomery points out, protests that were vigorous and outspoken, along with 'fierce struggles'. There were some hard-won victories, interspersed with forced accommodation to 'a most undemocratic America', notably in the 1920s, he observes, when it seemed that 'the house of labor' had 'fallen'.

The voice of working people was clearly and vividly articulated in the labour and community press that flourished from the mid-nineteenth century until World War II, and even beyond, finally destroyed by state and private power. As recently as the 1950s, 800 labour newspapers were still reaching 20–30 million people, seeking—in their words—to combat the corporate offensive to 'sell the American people on the virtues of big business'; to expose racial hatred and 'all kinds of antidemocratic words and deeds'; and to provide 'antidotes for the worst poisons of the kept press', the commercial media, which had the task of 'damning labor at every opportunity while carefully glossing over the sins of the banking and industrial magnates who really control the nation'.[13]

Voices of Resistance

The popular movements of resistance to state capitalist autocracy, and their eloquent voices, have a good deal to teach us about the goals and visions of ordinary people, their understanding and aspirations. The first major study of the mid-nineteenth century labour press (and to my knowledge still the only one) was published 70 years ago by Norman Ware. It makes illuminating reading today, or would, if it were known. Ware focuses on the journals established and run by mechanics and 'factory girls' in industrial towns near Boston, 'the Athens of America' and home of its greatest universities. The towns are still there, largely demoralised and in decay, but no more so than the animating visions of the people who built them and laid the foundation for American wealth and power.

The journals reveal how alien and intolerable the value systems demanded by private power were to working people, who stubbornly refused to abandon normal human sentiments. 'The New Spirit of the Age' that they bitterly condemned 'was repugnant to an astonishingly large section of the earlier American community', Ware writes. The primary reason was 'the decline of the industrial worker as a person', the 'psychological change', the 'loss of dignity and independence' and of democratic rights and freedoms, as the values of industrial capitalism were imposed by state and private power, by violence when necessary.

Workers deplored the 'degradation and the loss of that self-respect which had made the mechanics and laborers the pride of the world', the decline of culture, skill and attainment and even simple human dignity, as they were subjected to what they called 'wage slavery', not very different from the chattel slavery of southern plantations, they felt, as they were forced to sell *themselves*, not what they produced, becoming 'menials' and 'humble subjects' of 'despots'. They described the destruction of 'the spirit of free institutions', with working people reduced to a 'state of servitude' in which they 'see a moneyed aristocracy hanging over us like a mighty avalanche threatening annihilation to every man who dares to question their right to enslave and oppress the poor and unfortunate'. And they could hardly be unaware of the material conditions at home or in nearby Boston, where life expectancy for Irish was estimated at fourteen years in 1849.

Particularly dramatic, and again relevant to the current onslaught against democracy and human rights, was the sharp decline in high culture. The 'factory girls' from the farms of Massachusetts had been accustomed to spend their time reading classics and contemporary literature, and the independent craftsmen, if they had a little money, would hire a boy to read to them while they were working. It has been no small task to drive such thoughts from people's minds, so that today, a respected commentator can dismiss with derision ideas about democratising the Internet to allow access by the less privileged:

> One would imagine that the poor get about all the information they want as things stand now and in many cases, even resist the efforts of schools, libraries and the information media to make them better informed. Indeed, that resistance often helps explain why they are poor

—along with their defective genes, no doubt. The insight was considered so profound that it was highlighted in a special box by the editors.[14]

The labour press also condemned what it called the 'bought priesthood' of the media, the universities, and the intellectual class, apologists for power who sought to justify the despotism that was strengthening its grip and to instil its demeaning values. 'They who work in the mills ought to own them', working people wrote without the benefit of radical intellectuals. In that way they would overcome the 'monarchical principles' that were taking root 'on democratic soil'. Years later, that became a rallying cry for the organised labour movement, even its more conservative sectors.

In a widely circulated address at a trade union picnic, Henry De-
marest Lloyd declared that the 'mission of the labour movement
is to free mankind from the superstitions and sins of the market,
and to abolish the poverty which is the fruit of those sins. That
goal can be attained by extending to the direction of the economy
the principles of democratic politics'. 'It is by the people who do
the work that the hours of labour, the conditions of employment,
the division of the produce is to be determined', he urged in what
David Montgomery calls 'a clarion call to the 1893 AFL convention'. It is by the workers themselves, Lloyd continued, that 'the
captains of industry are to be chosen, and chosen to be servants,
not masters. It is for the welfare of all that the coordinated labour
of all must be directed . . . This is democracy'.[15]

These ideas are, of course, familiar to the libertarian left,
though radically counter to the doctrines of the dominant systems of power, whether called 'left', 'right', or 'centre' in the
largely meaningless terms of contemporary discourse. They have
only recently been suppressed, not for the first time, and can be
recovered, as often before.

Such values would also have been intelligible to the founders
of classical liberalism. As in England earlier, reactions of workers
in the industrial towns of New England illustrate the acuity of
Adam Smith's critique of division of labour. Adopting standard
Enlightenment ideas about freedom and creativity, Smith recognised that 'The understandings of the greater part of men are
necessarily formed by their ordinary employments'. Hence:

> the man whose life is spent in performing a few simple opera-
> tions, of which the effects too are, perhaps, always the same,
> or very nearly the same, has no occasion to exert his under-
> standing . . . and generally becomes as stupid and ignorant as
> it is possible for a human creature to be . . . But in every im-
> proved and civilised society this is the state into which the
> labouring poor, that is, the great body of the people, must nec-
> essarily fall, unless government takes pains to prevent it,

as must be done to bar the destructive impact of economic forces, he felt. If an artisan produces a beautiful object on command, Wilhelm von Humboldt wrote in classic work that inspired Mill, we may admire what he does, but we despise what he is': not a free human being, but a mere device in the hands of others. For similar reasons, 'the labourer who tends a garden is perhaps in a truer sense its owner than the listless voluptuary who enjoys its fruits'. Genuine conservatives continued to recognise that market forces will destroy what is of value in human life, unless sharply constrained. Alexis de Tocqueville, echoing Smith and von Humboldt half a century earlier, asked rhetorically what 'can be expected of a man who has spent twenty years of his life in making heads for pins?'. 'The art advances, the artisan recedes', he commented. Like Smith, he valued equality of condition, recognising it to be the foundation of American democracy, and warning that if 'permanent inequality of conditions' ever becomes established, 'the manufacturing aristocracy which is growing up under our eyes', and which 'is one of the harshest that has ever existed in the world', might escape its confines, spelling the end of democracy. Jefferson also took it as a fundamental proposition that 'widespread poverty and concentrated wealth cannot exist side by side in a democracy'.[16]

It was only in the early nineteenth century that the destructive and inhuman market forces that the founders of classical liberalism condemned were elevated to objects of veneration, their sanctity established with the certainty of 'the principles of gravitation' by Ricardo and other classical economists as their contribution to the class war that was being fought in industrialising England—doctrines now being resurrected as 'the everlasting battle for the minds of men' is waged with renewed intensity and cruelty.

It should be noted that, in the real world, these economic counterparts to Newton's laws were heeded in practice much as they are today. The rare studies of the topic by economic historians estimate that about half the industrial sector of New England would have closed down had the economy been opened to the much cheaper products of British industry, itself established and sustained with ample resort to state power. Much the same is true today, as will quickly be discovered by anyone who sweeps aside the fog of rhetoric and looks at the reality of 'economic liberalism' and the 'entrepreneurial values' it fosters.

John Dewey and Bertrand Russell are two of the twentieth century inheritors of this tradition, with its roots in the Enlightenment and classical liberalism, captured most vividly, I think, in the inspiring record of the struggle, organisation and thinking of working men and women as they sought to maintain and expand the sphere of freedom and justice in the face of the new despotism of state-supported private power.

One basic issue was formulated by Thomas Jefferson in his later years, as he observed the growth of the new 'manufacturing aristocracy' that alarmed de Tocqueville. Much concerned with the fate of the democratic experiment, he drew a distinction between 'aristocrats' and 'democrats'. The 'aristocrats' are 'those who fear and distrust the people, and wish to draw all powers from them into the hands of the higher classes'. The democrats, in contrast, 'identify with the people, have confidence in them, cherish and consider them as the honest & safe . . . depository of the public interest', if not always 'the most wise'. The aristocrats of his day were the advocates of the rising capitalist state, which Jefferson regarded with dismay, recognising the obvious contradiction between democracy and capitalism—or, more accurately, 'really existing capitalism', linked closely to state power.

Jefferson's description of the 'aristocrats' was developed further by Bakunin, who predicted that the 'new class' of intellectuals would follow one of two parallel paths. They might seek to exploit popular struggles to take state power into their own hands, becoming a 'Red bureaucracy' that will impose the most cruel and vicious regime of history. Or they might perceive that power lies elsewhere and offer themselves as its 'bought priesthood', serving the real masters either as managers or apologists, who ' eat the people with the people's stick' in the state capitalist democracies.

That must be one of the few predictions of the social sciences to have come true so dramatically. It deserves a place of honour in the famous canon for that reason alone, though we will wait a long time for that.

'Tough Love'

There is, I think, an eerie similarity between the present period and the days when contemporary ideology—what is now called 'neoliberalism' or 'economic rationalism'—was being fashioned by Ricardo, Malthus, and others. Their task was to demonstrate to people that they have no rights, contrary to what they foolishly believe. Indeed, that is proven by 'science'. The grave intellectual error of pre-capitalist culture was the belief that people have a place in the society and a right to it, perhaps a rotten place, but at least something. The new science demonstrated that the concept of a 'right to live' was a simple fallacy. It had to be patiently explained to misguided people that they have no rights, other than the right to try their luck in the market. A person lacking independent wealth who cannot survive in the labour market 'has no claim of right to the smallest portion of food, and, in fact, has no business to be where he is', Malthus proclaimed in influential work. It is a 'great evil' and violation of 'natural liberty' to mislead the poor into believing that they have further rights, Ricardo held, outraged at this assault against the principles of economic science and elementary rationality, and the moral principles that are no less exalted. The message is simple. You have a free choice: the labour market, the workhouse prison, death, or go somewhere else—as was possible when vast spaces were opening thanks to the extermination and expulsion of indigenous populations, not exactly by market principles.

The founders of the science were surpassed by none in their devotion to the 'happiness of the people', and even advocated some extension of the franchise to this end: 'not indeed, universally to all people, but to that part of them which cannot be supposed to have any interest in overturning the right of property', Ricardo explained, adding that still heavier restrictions would be appropriate if it were shown that 'limiting the elective franchise to the very narrowest bounds' would guarantee more 'security for a good choice of representatives'. There is an ample record of similar thoughts to the present day.[17]

It is useful to remember what happened when the laws of economic rationalism were formulated and imposed—in the familiar dual manner: market discipline for the weak, but the ministrations of the nanny state, when needed, to protect the wealthy and privileged. By the 1830s, the victory of the new ideology was substantial, and it was established more fully a few years later. There was a slight problem, however. People couldn't seem to get it into their heads that they had no intrinsic rights. Being foolish and ignorant, they found it hard to grasp the simple truth that they have no right to live, and they reacted in all sorts of irrational ways. For some time, the British army was spending a good part of its energies putting down riots. Later things took a more ominous turn. People began to organise. The Chartist movement and later the labour movement became significant forces. At that point, the masters began to be a bit frightened, recognising that *we* can deny them the right to live, but *they* can deny us the right to rule. Something had to be done.

Fortunately, there was a solution. The 'science', which is somewhat more flexible than Newton's, began to change. By mid-century, it had been substantially reshaped in the hands of John Stuart Mill and even such solid characters as Nassau Senior, formerly a pillar of orthodoxy. It turned out that the principles of gravitation now included the rudiments of what slowly became the capitalist welfare state, with some kind of social contract, established through long and hard struggle, with many reverses, but significant successes as well.

Now there is an attempt to reverse the history, to go back to the happy days when the principles of economic rationalism briefly reigned, gravely demonstrating that people have no rights beyond what they can gain in the labour market. And since now the injunction to 'go somewhere else' won't work, the choices are narrowed to the workhouse prison or starvation, as a matter of natural law, which reveals that any attempt to help the poor only harms them—the poor, that is; the rich are miraculously helped thereby, as when state power intervenes to bail out investors after the collapse of the highly touted Mexican 'economic miracle', or to save failing banks and industries, or to bar Japan from American markets to allow domestic corporations to reconstruct the steel, automotive, and electronics industry in the 1980s (amidst impressive rhetoric about free markets by the most protectionist administration in the postwar era and its acolytes). And far more; this is the merest icing on the cake. But the rest are subject to the iron principles of economic rationalism, now sometimes called 'tough love' by those who allocate the benefits.

Unfortunately, this is no caricature. In fact, caricature is scarcely possible. One recalls Mark Twain's despairing comment, in his (long-ignored) anti-imperialist essays, on his inability to satirise one of the admired heroes of the slaughter of Filipinos: 'No satire of Funston could reach perfection, because Funston occupies that summit himself . . . [he is] satire incarnated'.

What is being reported blandly on the front pages would elicit ridicule and horror in a society with a genuinely free and democratic intellectual culture. Take just one example. Consider the economic capital of the richest country in the world: New York City. Its Mayor, Rudolph Giuliani, finally came clean about his fiscal policies, including the radically regressive shift in the tax burden: reduction in taxes on the rich ('all of the Mayor's tax cuts benefit business', the *New York Times* noted in the small print) and increase in taxes on the poor (concealed as rise in transit fares for school children and working people, higher tuition at city schools, etc.). Coupled with severe cutbacks in public funds that serve public needs, these policies should help the poor go somewhere else, the Mayor explained. These measures would 'enable them to move freely around the country', the report in the *Times* elaborated, under the headline: 'Giuliani Sees Welfare Cuts Providing a Chance to Move'.[18]

In short, those who were bound by the welfare system and public services are at last liberated from their chains, much as the founders of the doctrines of classical liberalism advised in their rigorously demonstrated theorems. And it is all for their benefit, the newly reconstituted science proves. As we admire the imposing edifice of rationality incarnated, the compassion for the poor brings tears to the eyes.

Where will the liberated masses go? Perhaps to *favelas* on the outskirts, so they can be 'free' to find their way back somehow to do the dirty work for those who are entitled to enjoy the richest city in the world, with inequality greater than Guatemala and 40 per cent of children already below the poverty line before these new measures of 'tough love' are instituted.

Bleeding hearts who cannot comprehend the favours being lavished on the poor should at least be able to see that there is no alternative. 'The lesson of the next few years may be that New York is simply not wealthy or economically vital enough to afford the extensive public sector that it has created over the post great Depression period', we learn from an expert opinion featured in another *Times* front-page story.

The loss of economic vitality is real enough, in part a result of 'urban development' programs that eliminated a flourishing manufacturing base in favour of the expanding financial sector. The city's wealth is another matter. The expert opinion to which the *Times* turned is the report to investors of the J.P. Morgan investment firm, fifth in the ranking of commercial banks in the 1995 *Fortune* 500 listing, suffering from a mere US$1.2 billion in profits in 1994. To be sure, it was not a great year for J.P. Morgan as compared with the 'stunning' profit increase of 54 per cent for the 500 with a mere 2.6 per cent increase of employment and 8.2 per cent sales gain in 'one of the most profitable years ever for American business', as *Fortune* reported exultantly. The business press hailed another 'banner year for U.S. corporate profits', while 'U.S. household wealth seems to have actually fallen' in this fourth straight year of double-digit profit growth and fourteenth straight year of decline in real wages. The *Fortune* 500 have attained new heights of 'economic might', with revenues close to two-thirds of gross domestic product, a good bit more than Germany or Britain, not to speak of their power over the global economy—an impressive concentration of power in unaccountable private tyrannies, and another welcome blow against democracy and markets.[19]

We live in 'lean and mean times', and everyone has to tighten their belts; so the mantra goes. In reality, the country is awash in capital, with 'surging profits' that are 'overflowing the coffers of Corporate America', *Business Week* exulted even before the grand news came in about the record-breaking final quarter of 1994, with a 'phenomenal 71 per cent advance' for the 900 companies in *BW*'s 'Corporate Scoreboard'. And, with times so tough all over, what choice is there but to 'provide a chance to move' to the now-liberated masses?[20]

'Tough love' is just the right phrase: love for the rich and privileged, tough for everyone else.

The rollback campaign on the social, economic, political, and ideological fronts exploits opportunities afforded by significant shifts of power in the past 20 years, into the hands of the masters. The intellectual level of prevailing discourse is beneath contempt, and the moral level grotesque. But the assessment of prospects that lies behind them is not unrealistic. That is, I think, the situation in which we now find ourselves, as we consider goals and visions.

As always in the past, one can choose to be a democrat in Jefferson's sense, or an aristocrat. The latter path offers rich rewards, given the locus of wealth, privilege and power, and the ends it naturally seeks. The other path is one of struggle, often defeat, but also rewards that cannot be imagined by those who succumb to 'the New Spirit of the Age: Gain Wealth, forgetting all but Self'.

Today's world is far from that of Thomas Jefferson or mid-nineteenth century workers. The choices it offers, however, have not changed in any fundamental way.

5

Democracy and Markets in the New World Order

'Enduring Truths'

There is a conventional picture of the new era we are entering and the promise it holds. It was formulated clearly by National Security Adviser Anthony Lake when he announced the Clinton Doctrine in September 1993: 'Throughout the Cold War, we contained a global threat to market democracies: now we should seek to enlarge their reach'. The 'new world' opening before us 'presents immense opportunities' to move forward to 'consolidate the victory of democracy and open markets', he expanded a year later.

The issues are much deeper than the Cold War, Lake elaborated. Our defence of freedom and justice against Fascism and Communism was only a phase in a history of dedication to 'a tolerant society, in which leaders and governments exist not to use or abuse people but to provide them with freedom and opportunity'. That is the 'constant face' of everything the US has done in the world, and 'the idea' that 'we are defending' again today. It is the 'enduring truth about this new world' in which we can more effectively pursue our historic mission, confronting the remaining 'enemies of the tolerant society' to which we have always been dedicated, moving from 'containment' to 'enlargement'.

Fortunately for the world, the sole superpower 'of course' is unique in history in that 'we do not seek to expand the reach of our institutions by force, subversion or repression', keeping to persuasion, compassion, and peaceful means.[1]

Commentators were duly impressed by this enlightened vision and lucid restatement of conventional truths. A year earlier, Thomas Friedman, the chief diplomatic correspondent of the *New York Times*, had written that 'America's victory in the Cold War was a victory for a set of political and economic principles: democracy and the free market'. At last others too are coming to understand that 'the free market is the wave of the future—a future for which America is both the gatekeeper and the model'. The world is lucky to have such a noble gatekeeper, we are constantly informed. Too noble, many fear, among them Henry Kissinger, who has often warned that the altruism of US policy goes too far for its own good. Sometimes the truths rise from mere empirical fact to pure logic. Thus the Eaton Professor of the Science of Government at Harvard, Samuel Huntington, writes that the United States must maintain its 'international primacy' for the benefit of the world because, alone among nations, its 'national identity is defined by a set of universal political and economic values', namely 'liberty, democracy, equality, private property, and markets'; accordingly, 'the promotion of democracy, human rights, and markets are [*sic*] far more central to American policy than to the policy of any other country'.[2]

Since this is a matter of *definition*, the Science of Government teaches, we may dispense with the tedious work of empirical confirmation. A wise decision. Otherwise someone looking just at the recent past might ask, for example, how our principled rejection of 'force, subversion or repression' is illustrated by the terrorist wars of the Reagan years in Central America, which left three countries in ruins, strewn with tens of thousands of tortured and mutilated corpses. Or how the Kennedy Administration, at the other extreme of the political spectrum, was demonstrating the same commitment with its international terrorist campaign against Cuba and its escalation of the attack against South Vietnam, moving from support for the standard Latin American-style terror state that Eisenhower had instituted to outright aggression, including bombing of civilian targets by the US Air Force, the use of napalm, crop destruction to starve out the indigenous resistance, and other such means.

Or some deluded person might ask how the same Administration, at the peak period of American liberalism, was 'containing a global threat to market democracies' when it prepared the overthrow of the parliamentary government of Brazil, paving the way to a regime of killers and torturers, with a domino effect that left neo-Nazi regimes in control of much of the hemisphere, always with firm US support if not initiative. The resulting plague of repression was something new even in the bloody history of 'our little region over here which has never bothered anybody', as Secretary of War Henry Stimson described the hemisphere in May 1945 while explaining that regional systems must be disbanded apart from our own, which were to be extended—'as part of our obligation to the security of the world', the influential liberal Democrat Abe Fortas added, explaining that 'what was good for us was good for the world'.

If facts are indeed irrelevant, we may overlook the conclusion of the leading academic specialist on the US and human rights in Latin America, Lars Schoultz, in his standard scholarly work on the topic: the goal of the National Security States was 'to destroy permanently a perceived threat to the existing structure of socioeconomic privilege by eliminating the political participation of the numerical majority . . .'. Their establishment, their goals, and their accomplishments are traceable in large measure to a historic 1962 decision of the Kennedy Administration: to shift the mission of the Latin American military from 'hemispheric defence' to 'internal security', while providing enhanced military aid and training to ensure that the task would be properly performed. 'Hemispheric defence' was a relic from World War II, but 'internal security'—a euphemism for war against the domestic population—is a serious matter. The change of mission ordered by the liberals of Camelot changed the US stance from toleration 'of the rapacity and cruelty of the Latin American military' to 'direct complicity' in 'the methods of Heinrich Himmler's extermination squads', in the words of Charles Maechling, who led counterinsurgency and internal defence planning from 1961 to 1966.[3]

All of this—only a pea on a mountain—has no bearing on the 'enduring truths' about the 'political and economic principles' to which the 'tolerant society' is dedicated, so we are instructed. Or perhaps the record even reveals its dedication to the idea that 'leaders and governments exist not to use or abuse people but to provide them with freedom and opportunity'.

The actions are indeed seen much that way as they proceed, with startling uniformity; the occasional shafts of light should not mislead. At the dissident extreme, Asia scholar John King Fairbank criticised the Vietnam War in his presidential address to the American Historical Association in December 1968, explaining that the US became involved 'mainly through an excess of righteousness and disinterested benevolence'. Years later, when the record was known in even more shameful detail, Anthony Lewis of the *New York Times*, at the outer reaches of media dissidence, criticised our 'bungling efforts to do good' which, *by 1969*, had become 'a disaster'. At the other end of the spectrum, critics of the war were accused of turning what all regard as a 'noble cause' into a costly failure.

As for the military coup in Brazil, it was 'a great victory for free world', Kennedy's Ambassador Lincoln Gordon reported, undertaken 'to preserve and not destroy Brazil's democracy'. It was 'the single most decisive victory of freedom in the mid-twentieth century', which should 'create a greatly improved climate for private investments'—so in that sense, at least, it did contain a threat to market democracy.

Given that the enduring truths are the very 'definition of our national identity', we also do not have to evaluate other cases, in fact the whole historical record, which reveals that the US has acted to destroy democracy and undermine human rights with some consistency, the pretexts shifting to satisfy contingent doctrinal requirements. For many years, the reflexive justification for any horror was the Cold War, a tale that regularly collapses, case by case, on inspection. One general indication of its significance is the continuity of policies before and after. The Czar was firmly on his throne when Woodrow Wilson, keeping to a long tradition, launched his murderous invasions of Haiti and the Dominican Republic. This exercise of 'Wilsonian idealism' killed thousands, restored virtually slavery in Haiti, and dismantled its parliamentary system because legislators refused to accept a 'progressive' Constitution written in Washington that allowed US investors to turn the country into their private plantation; and, perhaps most important, left both countries in the hands of terrorist armies dedicated to 'internal security', and trained and armed for the task. With no Bolsheviks in sight, the US was defending itself against the Huns.

In earlier years, conquest and terror were acts of self-defence against (among others) Spain, England, and the 'merciless Indian savages' whose crimes are denounced in the Declaration of Independence in a remarkable inversion of the facts that is scarcely noticed after 200 years. Innocent Americans were even under attack by 'hordes of lawless Indians' and 'runaway negroes' waging 'savage, servile, exterminating war against the United States' in 1818; Secretary of State John Quincy Adams's official justification for the conquest of Florida in 1818 in which General Andrew Jackson was exterminating indigenous people and runaway slaves in the conquered territory, an important and much admired state paper that established the doctrine of executive war without the congressional approval required by the Constitution. So the ugly story continues.

Sometimes the enemy is the entire world. President Lyndon Johnson warned in November 1966 that the people out there outnumber us 15 to 1, and 'If might did make right they would sweep over the United States and take what we have'. The grave dangers were underscored by the corruption of the United Nations, then falling under 'the tyranny of the majority' as decolonisation and recovery from the war weakened the ability of the US to impose discipline. By the 1960s, diplomatic correspondent Barbara Crossette of the *New York Times* writes in retrospect, 'Moscow and many newly independent nations were isolating and vilifying the United States'. It is hardly surprising, then, that the US was forced, in self-defence, to take a commanding lead in vetoing Security Council resolutions, blocking the General Assembly, and refusing to provide legally obligated funding. Sober commentators probed the causes of the world's moral decline. *Times* cultural commentator Richard Bernstein, famous more recently for his condemnation of 'political correctness', attributed it to 'the very structure and political culture' of the UN and the lack of diplomatic skills among naive Americans. The title was 'The U.N. vs. the U.S.', not 'The U.S. vs. the U.N.'; it is the world that is out of step when the US stands alone. Though the UN's reputation for integrity revived as it followed US orders once again during the Gulf War, and for once Washington did not have to veto resolutions condemning aggression and atrocities, this 'wondrous sea change', as the *Times* editors called it, did not last long. Throughout these grim years, 'There were times when only the United States and Israel voted together, and people questioned whether we had any friends there', the Chairman of the

House Committee on International Relations, moderate New York Republican Benjamin Gilman, commented recently. Many times, in fact, though the US has sometimes been able to mobilise El Salvador, Romania, and a few others to the cause of justice and freedom; and in the Security Council, Britain is fairly reliable, taking second place in vetoes (France a distant third) since the 1960s, when Moscow's dominance became intolerable to true democrats.[4]

As Kennedy's 'monolithic and ruthless conspiracy' engaged in world conquest faded from the scene in the 1980s, the search was on for new aggressors threatening our borders and our lives. Libya, disliked and defenceless, served as a particularly useful punching bag for courageous Reaganites. Other candidates include crazed Arabs generally, international terrorists, or whoever else can be conjured up. When George Bush celebrated the fall of the Berlin Wall by invading Panama, it was not in defence against Communism; rather, the demon Noriega, captured, tried, and condemned for his crimes, almost all committed while he was on the CIA payroll. At this moment, half of US military aid goes to Colombia, the hemisphere's leading human rights violator, with a shocking record of atrocities. The pattern is typical, but the pretext is not; this time, it is defence against narcotraffickers. US military aid and training go almost entirely to military forces that are not involved in the 'drug war', except in one respect: as reported by the international human rights monitors and all other competent observers, the recipients of US aid and training and their paramilitary associates are at the heart of the racket, a global enterprise that has been abetted by US policy in most remarkable ways, for half a century.

Various devices are at hand to demonstrate the irrelevance of a morbid fascination with fact. Realist scholars explain that appeal to the historical record 'confound[s] the abuse of reality with reality itself'. Reality is the unachieved 'national purpose' revealed by 'the evidence of history as our minds reflect it'; the actual historical record is a mere artefact, which tells us nothing about 'the Purpose of America'. To think otherwise is to fall into 'the error of atheism, which denies the validity of religion on similar grounds'.[5]

Also ready on the shelf is the doctrine of 'change of course'. True, we made errors in the past, a result of our innocence and excessive good will. But that is behind us, and we can therefore keep to the grand vistas that lie ahead, ignoring all of history and what it might suggest about the functioning and behaviour of institutional structures that remain unchanged. The doctrine is invoked with impressive regularity, always with sober nods of approval for the profundity of the insight.

Suppose then that we adopt the doctrine and keep just to 'our little region over here' right now, in 1995, before the next change of course takes effect—somehow always leaving us on the same track.

In May 1995, the Bishop and priests of the Diocese of Apartado in the northwest region of Colombia issued a 'Communique to Public Opinion' about 'the moment of terror' in which the people are living, 'caused by homicides and disappearances'. 'The paramilitary groups have mercilessly decimated entire towns', they charge, while the authorities, 'facing the tragedy of the people, . . . remain indifferent without opposing the advance of this macabre plan of death and destruction'. Their charges are backed by the Mayor of Apartado, who alleges that the paramilitary groups are 'virtually running wild with an escalation of murders and horrible mutilations' while the tens of thousands of military and police watch in silence.

As does the world, in particular, the country that is providing the arms and training. The Communique may reach a few people in the solidarity groups, but will not find its way through the usual filters, for the usual reasons. It is the wrong story: the responsibility lies in the wrong hands, and the atrocities could readily be stopped if the public were alerted. So far, all efforts to expose the use of half of US military aid have been successfully deflected, but if that proves impossible, they can be dismissed with yawns and sneers about 'old stories' and 'routine America-bashing', or by appeal to the doctrine of 'change of course'; this was a few weeks ago, after all.

The current upsurge of military–paramilitary atrocities in Colombia seems to be part of land-grab efforts related to a multi-billion dollar development project in the region. The paramilitaries are closely linked to the landowners, ranchers, and narcotraffickers, one of the most important of whom recently became supreme commander of the paramilitary units of the Magdalena Medio region, long known for the close cooperation of the military, drug lords, landowners, and paramilitary forces. The agents of this 'macabre plan of death and destruction' are the usual ones, as are the targets: grassroots civic and popular organisations and their leaders, peasants, indigenous people and the Black population, in fact anyone who gets in the way of the alliance of the government, drug rackets, and 'legitimate' economic powers. All of this continues a regular pattern, including the silence.

Markets in the Real World

Since the enduring truths lie beyond the reach of trivial fact, we may cheerfully put aside other qualms. Take the dedication to markets. If that is part of the 'national identity' by definition, it would be plain silly to bring up the fact that, from its origins, the US has been 'the mother country and bastion of modern protectionism'. I am quoting the eminent economic historian Paul Bairoch, who proceeds to document his more general conclusion that 'it is difficult to find another case where the facts so contradict a dominant theory' as the doctrine that free markets were the engine of growth;[6] or, for that matter, that great powers adhered to them except for temporary advantage. That 'late developers' have departed from these principles has been familiar since the work of Alexander Gerschenkron, at least. The same is true of their predecessors. The United States, in particular, has always been extreme in rejecting market discipline. That is how it developed from the beginning, including textiles, steel, energy, chemicals, computers and electronics, pharmaceuticals and biotechnology, agribusiness, and so on, gaining enormous wealth and power instead of pursuing its comparative advantage in exporting furs, in accord with the stern principles of economic rationality.

Nor did the American developmental state break new ground. Britain had followed a similar course, only turning to free trade after 150 years of protectionism had given it such enormous advantages that a 'level playing field' seemed a fairly safe bet, even then relying on the fact that 40 per cent of its exports could go to the Third World (1800–1938). It is not easy to find an exception, from the origins of Europe's industrial revolution, when Daniel Defoe, expressing the common perception in 1728, warned that England faced an uphill struggle in attempting to compete with 'China, India and other Eastern countries'. The problem was that they have 'the most extended Manufacture, and the greatest variety in the World; and their Manufactures push themselves upon the World, by the meer Stress of their Cheapness'. They also may have had the highest real wages in the world at the time and the best conditions for working class organisation, so the most detailed recent scholarship indicates, contrary to long-standing beliefs. 'Britain itself would have been deindustrialized by the cheapness of Indian calicoes if protectionist policies had not been adopted', the same work concludes.[7]

Contemporaries saw matters much in that light. A century after Defoe, liberal historian Horace Wilson observed ruefully that without protection, 'the mills of Paisley and Manchester would have been stopped in their outset, and could scarcely have been again set in motion, even by the power of steam. They were created by the sacrifice of Indian manufacturers'. It was India, not Britain, that was deindustrialised, including steel, ship-building, and other manufactures.

Britain showed the same 'constant face' when Egypt tried to undertake an industrial revolution under Mohammed Ali; with rich agricultural resources and domestic cotton, Egyptian development might have succeeded, as France and Britain feared, had it not been for British financial and military power, which intervened to bar unwanted competition and interference with British imperial strategy. Unlike the US at the same time, Egypt was unable to attempt a course of independent development in radical violation of the principles of economic science.[8]

Serious comparative studies are few, but what they suggest has much contemporary relevance. It can hardly escape notice that one part of the South resisted colonisation: Japan, the one part that developed, with its colonies in tow; a brutal colonial power, Japan nevertheless industrialised and developed its colonies, unlike the West. Or that the earliest colony happens to be the one part of northern Europe to retain Third World characteristics: Ireland. One of the leading historians of Africa, Basil Davidson, observes that modernising reforms in West Africa's Fanti Confederation and Asante kingdom were similar to those implemented by Japan at the same time, and indeed were seen in that light by African commentators and historians, one of whom wrote bitterly a few years later that 'The same laudable object was before them both, [but] the African's attempt was ruthlessly crushed and his plans frustrated' by British force. Davidson's own view is that the potential 'was in substance no different from the potential realised by the Japanese after 1867'. But West Africa joins Egypt and India, not Japan and the United States, which were able to pursue an independent path, free from colonial rule and the strictures of economic rationality.[9]

By the 1920s, England could not compete with more efficient Japanese industry. It therefore called the game off, returning to the practices that allowed it to develop in the first place. The empire was effectively closed to Japanese trade; Dutch and Americans followed suit. These were among the steps on the road to the Pacific phase of World War II, and among those ignored in the 50th anniversary commemorations.

The Reaganites followed much the same course in the face of Japanese competition half a century later. Had they permitted the market forces they worshipped in public to function, there would be no steel or automobile manufacturing in the United States today; nor semiconductors, massively parallel computing, and much else. The Reagan Administration simply closed the market to Japanese competition while pouring in public funds, measures expanded under Clinton. No such measures were needed to safeguard the leading civilian export industry, aircraft, or the huge and profitable tourism industry, based on aircraft and government-funded infrastructure. These are hardly more than an off-shoot of the major component of the welfare state: the Pentagon system (even the 'defense highway system' that was part of the state–corporate social engineering project that changed the face of America).

It was entirely natural for Clinton to select the Boeing corporation as the model for the 'grand vision of a free market future' that he proclaimed at the Seattle meeting of the Asia–Pacific Economic Conference (APEC) in 1993, to much acclaim. One could hardly find a finer prototype of the publicly subsidised private-profit economy that is proudly called 'free enterprise'. The triumph of the free market was further underscored by Clinton's announcement of his one APEC achievement: contracts with China for aircraft, nuclear power generators, supercomputers, and satellites, produced by Boeing, GE, Cray and Hughes Aircraft, all paragons of free enterprise (the sales were illegal because of China's alleged involvement in nuclear and missile proliferation, but the State Department explained that Washington would 'interpret' the laws as inapplicable).

Equally appropriate was Clinton's selection at the Jakarta APEC session a year later: Exxon, another prime example of independent entrepreneurial values unhampered by the nanny state. Once again, Clinton was praised not only for the grand vision, but also for the successes of 'the Administration's campaign of commercial diplomacy', which 'will mean jobs for Americans', *Times* political correspondent Elaine Sciolino reported. She was referring to Clinton's announcement of a new US$35 billion contract for Exxon to cooperate with Indonesia's Pertamina oil company to develop a natural gas field for the benefit of other US corporations and Indonesia's state-owned electrical company. That should provide lots of 'jobs for Americans'—at least lawyers, bankers, executives and managers, maybe a handful of skilled workers for a short period. The good news for American workers led to a rapid increase in Exxon's stock.[10]

It is perhaps worth mentioning that the word 'profits' has largely disappeared from respectable discourse. In contemporary Newspeak, the word is to be pronounced 'jobs'. Understanding the conventions, we appreciate the accuracy of the praise for Clinton's success in gaining 'jobs for Americans'. The same conventions allow recognition of the fact that the Pentagon is not *only* for defence against foreign hordes; it also provides 'jobs'. 'Politicians of both parties see the defense budget as a jobs program', Lawrence Korb of the Brookings Institution writes in a criticism of the inflated military budget. Profits for investors and higher salaries for top executives? Perish the thought.

The business press, however, has laxer standards. As the US pressured Japan to accept more car parts from US manufacturers in mid-1995, the respectable media featured the official theme: 'This is just being hard-nosed and understanding the interests of the American people', unfairly deprived of jobs (US trade representative Mickey Kantor). But the *Wall Street Journal* could lift the veil. US parts-makers were indeed hoping that state power would pry open the Japanese market, which they intended to supply from their plants in China, Southeast Asia, and Japan itself. There would be few jobs for Americans in the literal sense of the word, but plenty of 'jobs' for US-based transnationals in the Orwellian sense.[11]

No resort to this device is too ludicrous to elicit even a raised eyebrow, so conventional has it become.

Defiance of market principles and state violence have been significant factors in economic development, including postwar Europe, Japan, and the NICs in its periphery, all of which received a crucial economic stimulus from US military adventures. Today's First and Third Worlds were far more similar in the eighteenth century. One reason for the enormous difference since is that the rulers were able to avoid the market discipline rammed down the throats of their dependencies. 'There is no doubt', Bairoch concludes in his detailed refutation of the leading 'myth of economic science', 'that the Third World's compulsory economic liberalism in the nineteenth century is a major element in explaining the delay in its industrialisation', in fact, its 'de-industrialisation', a story that continues to the present under various guises. Bairoch in fact considerably understates the role of state intervention for the wealthy, because he limits himself in conventional manner to a narrow category of market interferences: protection. But that is only a small part of the story. To mention only one omission, the early industrial revolution in England and the US was fuelled by cotton, which was cheap and accessible thanks to the expulsion or extermination of the native population of the southeast United States and the import of slaves, departures from market orthodoxy that do not enter the odes to its wonders. So the story continues to the present.

Keeping to protectionist measures, Bairoch concludes that after World War II, the US at last moved towards liberal internationalism after a long history of violating these principles, including its most rapid period of growth, when tariffs were far higher than competitors. But that belief can be sustained only by ignoring the huge state component of the economy, which undergirded all of high-technology industry during the 'golden age of free market capitalism'. In the 1950s, virtually all funds for research and development of computers came from the taxpayer, along with 85 per cent of R&D for electronics generally. I'll return to the matter; ignoring it, we can understand little about the contemporary economy or 'really existing free markets'. Similarly, the huge social engineering project that led to the 'suburbanization of America', with enormous consequences, relied on extensive state intervention, from the local to national level, along with major corporate crime that received a tap on the wrist in the courts; consumer choices were a slight factor.[12]

There are fluctuations, to be sure. The statist reactionaries of the Reagan years broke new records in protectionism and public subsidy, boasting about it quite openly to their business audience. Secretary of the Treasury James Baker 'proudly proclaimed that Mr Ronald Reagan had "granted more import relief to US industry than any of his predecessors in more than half a century"', international economist Fred Bergsten writes, adding that the Reaganites specialised in 'the most insidious form of protectionism': 'managed trade' that most 'restricts trade and closes markets', and 'raises prices, reduces competition and reinforces cartel behaviour'. Baker was much too modest. The free trade enthusiasts and fiscal conservatives imposed more protectionist measures than all postwar administrations combined, virtually doubling import restrictions to 23 per cent, while rapidly increasing deficits as well, burdening the taxpayer with huge interest payments.[13]

Though the Reaganites generally led the pack, almost all industrial societies have become more protectionist in recent years. The effects on the South have been severe. Protectionist measures of the rich have been a significant factor in doubling the already huge gap between the poorest and richest countries in the past generation. The 1992 UN Development Report estimates that protectionist and financial measures of the rich countries deprived the South of US$1/2 trillion a year, about 12 times total 'aid'—most of it publicly subsidised export promotion. This behaviour is 'virtually criminal', the distinguished Irish diplomat and author Erskine Childers observed recently. He also notes that the West, under US lead, blocked a 1991 resolution tabled at the General Assembly by the South against 'economic measures as a means of political and economic coercion against developing countries', the favoured technique, apart from terror, by which Washington has sought to destroy such independent upstarts as Cuba and Nicaragua—while never ceasing to chant odes to the free market. The facts are 'very little known', Childers writes, 'because of course such things do not get reported by the dominant Northern media'. He hopes that some day this 'wholesale moral abdication by Northern countries' will lead to 'their utter shame before their own citizens'.[14]

No one familiar with the 'enduring truths' is holding their breath.

Childers couldn't be more right about the 'utter shame'. Two years ago, WHO director-general Hiroshi Nakajima reported that 11 million children die every year from easily treatable diseases because the developed world lacks the will to provide the meagre resources needed to overcome this 'preventable tragedy'—a 'silent genocide' that should shame all of us. In June 1995, UNICEF released its annual report, estimating at 13 million the number of children who die because the rich countries deny them pennies of aid. That too evaded the 'dominant Northern media', at least in the United States, though the national press did report on the same day that Congress planned to reduce by a third the princely sum of US$425 million that had been proposed for UNICEF for the coming year, also slashing foreign aid by US$3 billion over two years (while leaving intact the US$3 billion that goes to a rich country that serves US interests, Israel, along with US$2.1 billion to Egypt, for similar reasons; that amounts to almost half the total). The US already had the most miserly aid record of OECD countries, but not miserly enough, Congress has determined.

Shortly after, Washington informed the UN Industrial Development Organisation (UNIDO) that it would provide only half of its US$26 million pledge (legally binding under UN treaties), forcing a large curtailment of UNIDO's operations. The Group of 77 was 'deeply shocked and dismayed' at this further illegal action by the leading debtor, already US$8 million in arrears. Only the most diligent could discover the facts, once again.

The actions that would 'utterly shame' any decent person have little to do with public opinion. On the contrary, recent studies again show that 'a strong majority' of the public favour maintaining or even increasing aid, and directing it to the poor rather than to strategic allies and military purposes. A 'strong majority' would also be willing to pay more taxes if aid went to people who need it, and an 'overwhelming majority rejects the idea that the United States should only give when it promotes the U.S. national interest'. All exactly the opposite of the policies executed by the political leadership, who never cease to proclaim their service to the public will.[15]

The regularity of the pattern is instructive. Thus President Clinton agrees that the US must lower its contributions to UN peacekeeping operations while his right-wing adversaries want to go much further, shackling or even ending them. In contrast, they are favoured by over 80 per cent of the public. Half consistently support US participation, 88 per cent if there are fair prospects of success. Only 5–10 per cent consistently oppose such operations, the remainder varying with circumstances. The effect of fatalities in Somalia was slight, contrary to much pretence. Two-thirds favour contributing US troops to a UN operation to protect 'safe havens' or to stop atrocities in Bosnia; 80 per cent take the same position with regard to Rwanda, if the UN were to conclude that genocide is underway.

Nevertheless, 60 per cent of the population think the US has 'done enough to stop the war in Bosnia'—namely, nothing. But not because of cruelty or indifference, as other studies reveal. There is also opposition to foreign aid, particularly on the part of the 25 per cent of the population who believe it to be the biggest item on the federal budget. In fact, about half of discretionary spending goes to the Pentagon, a fact known to under one-third of the population, while foreign aid is undetectable (putting aside its purposes).[16]

Such apparently contradictory results are not hard to explain. People would like to do the right thing, but have been drowned in 'enduring truths' about our altruism and awesome benevolence, and the ingratitude of a hostile world. For similar reasons, overwhelming majorities support more help for the poor but call for cutting welfare: why spend our hard-earned money for Black mothers in Cadillacs who breed like rabbits to get more welfare cheques? And having been deluged with these and other fairy tales—sometimes related by figures like Ronald Reagan, who may even have believed his famous anecdotes—they also much overestimate the share of the Federal budget that goes to welfare, and are quite unaware that it has fallen radically over the past 20 years from a level that was low to begin with by comparative standards. A similar barrage leads the public to feel crushed by an overwhelming tax burden; only Turkey and Australia are lower, relative to GDP, among the OECD countries (1991).

Also hidden in the shadows is the fact that the tax system is unusually regressive. A particularly telling measure is the effect of taxes and transfers (benefits, etc.) on alleviating poverty. The most careful study of the topic, by economists Lawrence Mishel and Jared Bernstein, concludes that 'the U.S. system of taxes and transfers is much less effective in reducing poverty than that of any other [industrialised] country', and is becoming 'even *less* effective over time', particularly in the Reagan years, while it has grown more effective elsewhere. Children suffer particularly under the US system. In the average comparable country, such measures reduced child poverty by over half from 1979 into the 1980s, while in the US they reduced it by less than a quarter in 1979, down to 8.5 per cent in 1986 as Reaganite policies took effect.

Currently fashionable 'flat tax' proposals call for excluding financial gains (dividends, capital gains, interest), which constitute almost half of income for the top 1 per cent of families, a proportion that declines very rapidly as we move to lower income levels. 'It's hard to find a definition of "fairness" more compelling than the idea that every citizen is treated equally', *Fortune* magazine declares in an upbeat cover story on 'the beginning of the end of the American income tax system', quoting an economist for a right-wing research institute.[17]

What business leaders call their 'everlasting battle for the minds of men' may not have changed attitudes very much, but it has left the population mired in confusion, which is just as good for the fundamental purpose: driving the 'great beast', as Alexander Hamilton called the people, out of the public arena, where it does not belong, sentiments echoed across the spectrum throughout American history—again, not an innovation or exception.

But once again, such matters have no bearing on the state of American democracy, if indeed the enduring truths are beyond the reach of evidence.

Democracy: 'Containing the People'

It would be unfair to imply that everyone considers facts irrelevant. I've already mentioned a few examples to the contrary and there are others. Take democracy according to the canon, the principle that guides and inspires the political leadership above any other. To evaluate the theory we naturally turn to the place where policy makers had a relatively free hand: 'our little region over here', rich in resources and potential, and one of the world's worst horror chambers—another fact from which we are to learn nothing. But what about the 1980s, when there was yet another 'change of course' as the Reagan Administration led a grand crusade to bring the benefits of democracy to oppressed people? Perhaps the most serious studies of the topic within the mainstream are by Thomas Carothers, who combines the view of a historian with that of an insider, having been involved in the Reagan Administration programs to 'assist democracy' in Latin America. These programs were 'sincere', he writes, but largely a failure—though an oddly systematic one. Where US influence was least, progress was greatest: in the southern cone, where there was real progress, opposed by the Reaganites at every step although they took credit for it when the tide could not be stemmed. Where US influence was greatest—in Central America—progress was least. Here Washington 'inevitably sought only limited, top-down forms of democratic change that did not risk upsetting the traditional structures of power with which the United States has long been allied', Carothers writes. The US sought to maintain 'the basic order of . . . quite undemocratic societies' and to avoid 'populist-based change' that might upset 'established economic and political orders' and open 'a leftist direction'.[18] As, indeed, quite generally.

It is only by looking closely at individual cases that one can appreciate the depth of the fear and hatred of democracy in elite circles. One of the most instructive examples is Nicaragua, also well studied, but in work that is far from the public eye.

Nicaragua had elections in 1984, widely praised by even hostile international observers and by the professional organisation of Latin American scholars, which studied them in unusual depth. But they could not be controlled, so they did not take place. Period. The first elections, by official fiat and near universal practice, were in 1990—we need not tarry on the official tale that the elections always scheduled for 1990 took place only because of US pressures, standard apologetics for the terrorist war. As the electoral campaign opened, the White House announced that US terror and economic warfare would continue unless Washington's candidate were elected; that is considered no interference with the 'democratic process' in the United States, or the West generally. When the elections came out 'the right way', the Latin American press, largely hostile to the Sandinistas, generally interpreted it as a victory for George Bush. The US reaction was different. The Newspaper of Record was typical, with its headlines hailing the 'Victory for U.S. Fair Play' as Americans were 'United in Joy' in the style of Albania and North Korea. At the outer limits, columnist Anthony Lewis could scarcely contain his admiration for Washington's 'experiment in peace and democracy', which gave 'fresh testimony to the power of Jefferson's idea: government with the consent of the governed . . . To say so seems romantic, but then we live in a romantic age'.

Few had any doubts as to how 'Jefferson's idea' was realised. Thus *Time* magazine rejoiced as 'democracy burst forth' in Nicaragua, outlining the methods of 'U.S. Fair Play': to 'wreck the economy and prosecute a long and deadly proxy war until the exhausted natives overthrow the unwanted government themselves', with a cost to us that is 'minimal', leaving the victim 'with wrecked bridges, sabotaged power stations, and ruined farms', and providing Washington's candidate with 'a winning issue', ending the 'impoverishment of the people of Nicaragua'.[19]

But that's all down the memory hole, along with the rest of the sordid story. Also best avoided is what happened to the shattered society after 'democracy burst forth'. For the overwhelming majority the outcome has been a disaster, so much so that the UN Food and Agriculture Organisation (FAO) predicts that 'Nicaragua's next generation will be smaller, weaker, and less intelligent than today's population'—those who survive, that is. Deaths from malnutrition of children under four have increased by 35 per cent since the 'romantic age' began. Homeless waifs beg for pennies on the streets, or sniff glue to 'take away the hunger'. Creatures that scarcely resemble humans scour the Managua dump for scraps of food. There has been massive starvation on the Atlantic Coast and a huge drug epidemic. The facts are reported by relief organisations and at the usual margins, but are of no interest to the perpetrators of the crimes, including those who shed bitter tears over the sad fate of the coastal people subjected to 'genocide' by the cruel Sandinistas; abuses were real, though undetectable by comparison to what the same people fervently supported, as the international human rights monitors vainly reported.[20]

Of all of these crimes, the most cruel is the destruction of hope in a demoralised society, sinking into helplessness, misery, and despair. The facts filed away out of sight tell us a lot about the passion for democracy and human rights, in case after shameful case.

What Carothers describes is exactly what we are seeing right now in the prize model of the Clinton Doctrine offered by National Security Adviser Lake: Haiti. Its elected President was allowed to return after the popular organisations had been subjected to a sufficient dose of terror, but only after he too had been educated—given 'a crash course in democracy and capitalism', as his leading supporter in Washington described the process of civilising the troublesome priest, in terms far more sympathetic to the 'radical extremist' than the norm. President Aristide was compelled to accept a US-dictated economic program stipulating that 'The renovated state must focus on an economic strategy centered on the energy and initiative of Civil Society, especially the private sector, both national and foreign'. US investors are the core of Haitian Civil Society, along with the super-rich coup backers, but not the Haitian peasants and slum-dwellers who scandalised Washington by creating a civil society so lively and vibrant that they were able to elect a President and enter the public arena. That impropriety was overcome in the usual way with ample US complicity; for example, by the decision of the Bush and Clinton administrations to allow the Texaco Oil Company to supply the coup leaders and their wealthy supporters in violation of the sanctions, a crucial fact revealed by Associated Press the day before US troops landed in September 1994, though also kept from the public eye. The 'renovated state' is now back on track, following the policies of Washington's candidate in the 1990 elections, in which he received 14 per cent of the vote.[21]

An honest inquiry will reveal that the conventional picture ranges from dubious to false in every crucial respect, save one: the importance of enduring truths. It is only necessary that we agree to look at the historical record to discover what they are, and why. And surely we should take them quite seriously as we consider the likely future, with institutional structures essentially unchanged and operating with little constraint.

Pursuing this course, we find reason to believe that the 'new world' that is portrayed in such bright and hopeful colours may indeed be marked by a shift away from 'containment', but not to 'enlargement'; rather, to 'rollback', to borrow another term from the lexicon of international affairs. For over a century those whom Adam Smith called 'the principal architects of policy'—in his day the 'merchants and manufacturers' of England, in ours, their inheritors—have sought to contain democracy and human rights, disdaining markets except when they confer advantage. As in Smith's day they naturally try to mobilise state power to ensure that their own interests 'are most peculiarly attended to', however 'grievous' the impact on others. Since the early 1970s, important changes in the global economy have opened the prospect of not just containing but actually rolling back the victories for human rights, freedom, and democracy that have been won in a century of bitter popular struggle—an alluring prospect, as the current scene illustrates vividly. The enduring truths are likely not only to persist, but to become still more grim for much of the world's population; at home as well, as the social contract is unravelled.

These are large topics, and I can only hope to touch on a few of them.[22] But let me try to flesh out the story as I see it with some specific detail.

A good place to start is in Washington, right now. The standard picture is that a 'historic political realignment' took place in the congressional elections of 1994 that swept Newt Gingrich and his army into power in a 'landslide victory', a 'triumph of conservatism' that reflects the continuing 'drift to the right'. With their 'overwhelming popular mandate', the Gingrich army will fulfil the promises of the Contract with America. They will 'get government off our backs' so that we can return to the happy days when the free market reigned and restore 'family values', ridding us of 'the excesses of the welfare state' and the other residues of the failed 'big government' policies of New Deal liberalism and the 'Great Society'. By dismantling the 'nanny state', they will be able to 'create jobs for Americans' and win security and freedom for the 'middle class'. And they will take over and successfully lead the crusade to establish the American Dream of free market democracy, worldwide. That's the basic story. It has a familiar ring. Ten years before, Ronald Reagan was re-elected in the second 'conservative landslide' in four years. In the first, in 1980, Reagan won a bare majority of the popular vote and 28 per cent of the electorate. Exit polls showed that the vote was not 'for Reagan' but 'against Carter'—who had in fact initiated the policies that the Reaganites took up and implemented, with the general support of congressional Democrats: accelerated military spending (the state sector of the economy) and cutbacks in programs that serve the vast majority. Polls in 1980 revealed that 11 per cent of Reagan voters chose him because 'he's a real conservative'—whatever that term is supposed to mean.

In 1984, there were great efforts to get out the vote, and they worked: it increased by 1 per cent. The number of voters who supported Reagan as a 'real conservative' dropped to 4 per cent. A considerable majority of those who voted hoped that Reaganite legislative programs would not be enacted. Public opinion studies showed a continuation of the steady drift towards a kind of New Deal-style welfare state liberalism.

Why the votes? The concerns and desires of the public are not articulated in the political system—one reason why voting so sharply skewed towards privileged sectors.

When the interests of the privileged and powerful are the guiding commitment of both political factions, people who do not share these interests tend to stay home. William Dean Burnham, a leading specialist on electoral politics, pointed out that the class pattern of abstention 'seems inseparably linked to another crucial comparative peculiarity of the American political system: the total absence of a socialist or laborite party as an organized competitor in the electoral market'. That was fifteen years ago, and it has only become more pronounced as civil society has been even more effectively dismantled: unions, political organisations, and so on.

In the United States, 'the interests of the bottom three-fifths of society' are not represented in the political system, political commentator Thomas Edsall of the *Washington Post* pointed out a decade ago, referring to the Reagan elections. There are many consequences apart from the highly skewed voting pattern. One is that half the population thinks that both parties should be disbanded. Over 80 per cent regard the economic system as 'inherently unfair' and the government 'run for the benefit of the few and the special interests, not the people' (up from a steady 50 per cent for a similarly worded question in the pre-Reagan years)—though what people might mean by 'special interests' is another question. The same proportion think that workers have too little influence—though only 20 per cent feel that way about unions and 40 per cent consider them too influential, another sign of the effects of the propaganda system in inducing confusion, if not in changing attitudes.

That brings us to 1994, the next in the series of 'conservative landslides'. Of the 38 per cent of the electorate who took part, a bare majority voted Republican. 'Republicans claimed about 52 percent of all votes cast for candidates in contested House seats, slightly better than a two-point improvement from 1992', when the Democrats won, the polling director of the *Washington Post* reported. One out of six voters described the outcome as 'an affirmation of the Republican agenda'. A 'more conservative Congress' was considered an issue by a rousing 12 per cent of the voters. An overwhelming majority had never heard of Gingrich's Contract with America, which articulated the Republican agenda and has since been relentlessly implemented, with much fanfare about the popular will, and less said about the fact that it is the first contract in history with only one party signing, and the other scarcely knowing of its existence.

When asked about the central components of the Contract, large majorities opposed almost all, notably the central one: large cuts in social spending. Over 60 per cent of the population wanted to see such spending *increased* at the time of the elections. Gingrich himself was highly unpopular, even more than Clinton, whose ratings are very low; and that distaste has only persisted as the program has been implemented.

There was plenty of opposition to Democrats; the election was a 'vote against'. But it was nuanced. Clinton-style 'New Democrats'—in effect, moderate Republicans—lost heavily but not those who kept to the traditional liberal agenda and tried to activate the old Democratic coalition: the majority of the population who see themselves, correctly, as effectively disenfranchised.

Voting was even more heavily skewed toward the wealthy and privileged than before. Democrats were heavily preferred by those who earn less than US$30 000 a year (about the median) and ran even with Republicans in the US$30 000–US$50 000 range. The opinion profiles of non-voters were similar on major issues to those who voted the Democratic ticket. Voters who sensed a decline in their standard of living chose Republicans—or, more accurately, opposed incumbent Democrats—by close to two to one. Most are white males with very uncertain economic futures, just the people who would have been part of a left-populist coalition committed to equitable economic growth and political democracy were such an option to intrude into the business-run political arena. In its absence, many are turning to religious fanaticism, cults of every imaginable kind, paramilitary organisations ('militias'), and other forms of irrationality, an ominous development, with precedents that we remember, and that now concern even the corporate executives who applaud the actions of the Gingrich army in its dedicated service to the most rich and privileged.

Nevertheless, despite the propaganda onslaught of the last half century, the general population has somehow maintained social democratic attitudes. Substantial majorities believe the government should assist people in need, and favour spending for health, education, help for the poor, and protection of the environment. As I've already mentioned, they also approve of foreign aid for the needy and peacekeeping operations. But policy follows a radically different course.

The central doctrine—a balanced budget—is a striking illustration. Business favours it. 'American business has spoken: Balance the federal budget', *Business Week* concludes from a poll of senior business executives. And when business speaks, so does the political class and the press—at least the headlines. Those who look no further will have little sense of a complex reality.

In Australia, Graham Richardson reports from New York that 'Americans are convinced . . . that budgets should be balanced irrespective of prevailing conditions', and support cuts in social spending to that end. His source is Don Hewitt, 'the elder statesman of American current affairs television', with whom he had breakfast in the Edwardian Room of the Plaza Hotel, 'one of New York's finest'. Hewitt is 'a man accustomed to mixing with presidents, billionaires and stars', and 'to have stayed on top in [TV] current affairs for so long means that Hewitt has a real feel for the pulse of middle America'—not the owners of the corporate media and the advertisers to whom they sell their product (audiences), or the billionaires who dine in the Edwardian Room. When Hewitt tells us what Americans want, 'you have to take notice', just as you have to be impressed by 'the huge swing to the Republicans' in the elections, just reviewed.

In England, under the headline 'We're all for balanced budgets now', the commentator on America for the *Financial Times*, Michael Prowse, writes that 'Newt Gingrich and his Republican revolutionaries once again deserve our applause' for pursuing a balanced budget in the face of the 'cynical strategy' of those who oppose big cuts in social programs. And the revolutionaries reflect the will of the people, Prowse writes: 'polls show 80 percent approval for the goal of a balanced budget'.[23]

Richardson no doubt reports what his source believes, or at least prefers to believe; and Prowse is right about the headlines and what he may well hear on the major elite news program on National Public Radio, regularly accused of liberal bias, where a leading commentator, Robert Siegel, reports that 'Americans voted for a balanced budget', detailing the cuts in education and welfare pursuant to the public will. But if we move beyond the Edwardian Room and the headlines, we find a different picture. It is true that most people would prefer a balanced budget, just as they would like to see their household budgets balanced, with all debt magically removed at no cost. But the same polls show that in response to the obvious next question—Do you want the budget balanced if that entails spending reductions for education, health, the environment, and other favoured programs?— support dwindles to a small minority in the 20–30 per cent range. So we learn, for example, from the small print in an article headlined 'Americans Like G.O.P. Agenda But Split on How to Reach Goals', reporting data showing that Americans *dislike* the GOP agenda, overwhelmingly. Other polls give similar results: balanced budget, Fine; with cuts in social spending, No. As the Republicans targeted the Departments of Education and Energy for elimination, 80 per cent wanted to preserve the former, 63 per cent the latter. 'A strong 72 per cent oppose any reduction in education whatsoever', the *Wall Street Journal* reported, and 'solid majorities oppose any substantial cuts in Social Security, the Medicare health program for the elderly and the Medicaid health program for the poor'— all targeted for severe reduction along with many other popular programs, with only Social Security on hold.[24]

The facts, however, are unwelcome, apart from one: business has spoken, and that's really all we have to know. Furthermore, with little in the way of a counterforce within the doctrinal system, wish will become reality over time, very likely.

The same holds pretty much across the board. Polls show consistently that the public is opposed to more Pentagon spending. But the voice of business again says the opposite; business leaders are well aware that the Pentagon is the core of the welfare state for the rich. Accordingly, Clinton's first reaction to the Republican 'landslide' was to announce a substantial increase in Pentagon spending; his right-wing opponents quickly upped the ante. In real dollars, the Pentagon budget is at about 85 per cent of the Cold War average, US$30 billion a year higher than under Nixon. The Cold War enemy is, of course, now an ally even in military production: thus its advanced research programs enabled the US to regain the world lead in pulsed power and microwave weaponry, *Jane's Defence Weekly* reported. The figures give some indication of how large 'the threat to market democracy' posed by the Great Satan loomed in the eyes of planners who sought to 'contain' it and 'roll it back'.

In April 1995, the far-right Heritage Foundation submitted its budget proposal, basically adopted by Congress. It called for an increase in the Pentagon budget in accord with the wishes of one out of six taxpayers, while sharply cutting funds for education, drug addiction programs, the environment, and other social spending favoured by two-thirds of the public. 'The issue [is] philosophical', a policy analyst at the Heritage Foundation explains: 'Taxpayers should not be forced to support activities they may not agree with'; certain taxpayers, that is. 'The issue', in this case, was specifically the Foundation's call for 'defunding the left', defined as Catholic Charities, the American Association of Retired Persons, and others who try to help the wrong sorts of people, sometimes with minuscule Federal grants—a rather flattering image of 'the left', incidentally.[25]

The increase in Pentagon spending was opposed not only by the population, but even by the Joint Chiefs of Staff, who warned that it would cause problems for the military down the road. But no matter: business has spoken, and the statist reactionaries know how to listen.

For 'the principal architects of policy' to flout public opinion is neither surprising nor particularly unusual, though it is an indication of how democracy is understood by those who sing its praises. But the pattern has become so consistent and dramatic as to call forth some commentary, which is unusual. The respected political commentator of the *Christian Science Monitor*, Brad Knickerbocker, mused that 'It's almost as if lawmakers looked at what Americans want . . .—and then marched off in the opposite direction'. He happened to be referring to energy and environmental policies, but the conclusions hold dramatically, well beyond even the norm.[26]

Those truly concerned about democracy would do well to attend closely to the founding principles of the first modern democracy 200 years ago, still in many ways the model. In the debates in 1787 on the Federal Constitution, James Madison observed that 'In England, at this day if elections were open to all classes of people, the property of landed proprietors would be insecure. An agrarian law would soon take place'. To ward off such injustice, 'our government ought to secure the permanent interests of the country against innovation', establishing checks and balances so 'as to protect the minority of the opulent against the majority'.

The constitutional framework adhered closely to Madison's design. The 'permanent interest' he identified has remained the 'Purpose of America' at home, in the eyes of the powerful, and 'the tolerant society' they manage has always insisted on upholding the same principle abroad—'multilaterally when we can and unilaterally as we must', as Clinton's UN Ambassador instructed the UN Security Council in October 1994 just as Anthony Lake was lauding our historic commitment to pacifist principles.[27]

There are two 'cardinal objects of government', Madison held: 'the rights of persons, and the rights of property'. It is the latter that must have priority, because the rights of property will constantly be under threat from 'the will of the majority', who may, by their power in a democracy, 'trespass on the rights of a minority'. Madison's more vague formulations have often been misread as expressing a general concern that 'the tyranny of the majority' might trample individual rights: say to freedom of speech and conscience. But that reading mistakes Madison's concern, which was much more restricted, as he made quite clear. The primary threat was to 'the rights of property'. The rights of the 'opulent minority' that government must protect as its primary duty are, furthermore, quite unlike 'the rights of persons'; the latter are to be granted uniformly under the Constitutional system, whereas 'the rights of property' are narrowly held in the hands of the 'opulent minority'. The majority are denied these rights, and must be prevented from infringing on them.

The Madisonian rhetoric, which has largely dominated subsequent discussion, is misleading in other ways. It is senseless to compare rights of persons and rights of property. The pen in my hand is my property but it has no rights, though perhaps I have a right to own it. The rights of property are rights of persons—certain persons, always to be a minority, it was held. The Madisonian framework, then, concerns only rights of persons, and assigns to an opulent minority among them extra rights in addition to the rights theoretically shared by all; indeed it privileges these additional rights, holding that they must take precedence over the rights that are shared. The issues are obscured—rather seriously in fact—by the rhetoric in which they are formulated, and in much subsequent discussion.

To ensure that the rights of the opulent minority are privileged, they must hold the reins of government, Madison held. He added that this is only fair, because property 'chiefly bears the burden of government', and 'In a certain sense the Country may be said to belong to [the owners of the soil]'—a notion that generalised in the obvious way as the society shifted from an agricultural to a manufacturing and financial power base. As Jennifer Nedelsky points out in the most careful analysis of 'the Madisonian framework and its legacy', his primary focus on 'the protection of property' cast '"the people", the future majority, in the role of a problem to be contained'. This conception was accepted as a matter of course by almost all of the Framers, she notes, citing James Wilson as 'the only one who declared that property was not the main object of government' and who 'gave priority to what was seen by his colleagues as the major threat to property: the political liberty of the people'.

Thomas Jefferson took a position like Wilson's, but he had no direct role in these deliberations. As for Madison, some years later he did come to recognise—apparently with some shock— that the 'opulent minority' would abuse its power, not acting in the enlightened manner he had rather naively anticipated. Madison deplored 'the daring depravity of the times' as the wealthy came to use their control of government much in the way that Adam Smith had described, with the 'stock jobber' coming to be 'the pretorian [sic] band of the Government, at once its tool and its tyrant; bribed by its largesses and overawing it by its clamours and combinations'.[28]

A central theme of American history is the implementation of the original Madisonian framework, basically preserved through many social changes. Nedelsky observes that this legacy, though attenuated, helps explain 'the weaknesses of the democratic tradition' in the United States, and its failure to deal with 'the interpenetration of economic and political power'—or, more accurately, its success in dealing with the problem in a specific way: by sanctifying privileging the rights of those who own the country. These rights have come virtually to define the concept of democracy.

Thus it was in the service of democracy that radio, later television, was kept from the public domain and handed over to a few huge corporations; private tyranny equals freedom. That is second nature. Few detect a problem when a well-known journalist writes in the *New York Times*: 'As every schoolchild must know, a free press—which means a press free of government—is essential to a democratic system' (David Shipler). In contrast, a press free of Murdoch or Berlusconi, or huge corporations, is not essential.

As Madison's praetorian band tightened its grip, politics became ever more 'the shadow cast on society by big business', as Adam Smith's truism was formulated by America's leading twentieth century philosopher, John Dewey. The system that developed did not simply protect property, Nedelsky adds, but 'inequality of property', in accord with its basic design, subordinating the rights of the great majority of the population in all other spheres of life as well. The only serious challenge to these ideas has been from labour and other popular movements, which have certainly won victories, though they have been marginalised to an extent unusual in industrial democracies, and are now losing the gains that they had won.[29]

The 'top-down' structures of power that Carothers describes as a 'failure' of American efforts to enhance democracy are anything but that. They are not only another success in the project of undermining democracy in US domains—which is why the 'failure' is so systematic— but also reflect the nature of the domestic society. The facts are not hard to discover in history and doctrine, if we lift the veils of rhetoric that conceal them.

'Free Market Conservatism'

Following the same course, we can come to understand the concept of 'free market conservatism'. Its real meaning is revealed by a closer look at the most passionate enthusiasts for 'getting the government off our backs' and letting the market reign undisturbed. Speaker of the House Newt Gingrich is perhaps the most striking example. He represents Cobb County, Georgia, which the *New York Times* selected in a front-page story to illustrate the rising tide of 'conservatism' and contempt for the 'nanny state'. The headline reads: 'Conservatism Flowering Among the Malls', in this rich suburb of Atlanta, scrupulously insulated from any urban infection so that the inhabitants can enjoy the fruits of their 'entrepreneurial values' and market enthusiasms, defended in Congress by its leading conservative, Newt Gingrich, who describes his district with pride as a 'Norman Rockwell world with fiber optic computers and jet airplanes'.[30]

There's a small footnote, however. Cobb County receives more Federal subsidies than any other suburban county in the country, with two interesting exceptions: Arlington, Virginia, which is effectively part of the Federal government, and the Florida home of the Kennedy Space Centre, another component of the system of public subsidy, private profit. When we move out of the Federal system itself, Cobb County takes the lead in extorting funds from the taxpayer—who is also responsible for funding the 'jet planes and fiber optic computers' of the Norman Rockwell world. Most jobs in Cobb County, properly high paying, are gained by feeding at the public trough. The wealth of the Atlanta region generally can be traced substantially to the same source. Meanwhile praises to market miracles reach the heavens where 'conservatism is flowering'.

There is also an interesting sidelight. During the congressional campaign, when Gingrich propaganda about the nanny state and welfare excesses was resounding to the rooftops and the New Democrats were on the run, no one was willing to issue a simple rejoinder: Gingrich is the country's leading advocate of the welfare state—for the rich. The reasons for the silence are easy to understand: class interests prevail over narrow electoral ones. It's agreed across the board that the rich must be protected from market discipline by a powerful and interventionist welfare state.

Gingrich's 'Contract with America' neatly exemplifies the ideology of the double-edged 'free market': state protection and public subsidy for the rich, market discipline for the poor. It called for 'cuts in social spending' across the board—for the poor and defenceless, including children and the elderly. And for increasing welfare for the rich, in the classic ways: regressive fiscal measures, and outright subsidy. In the former category are increased tax exemptions for business and the wealthy capital gains cuts, and so on. In the latter are taxpayer subsidies for investment in plants and equipment, more favourable rules for depreciation, dismantling the regulatory apparatus that merely protects people and future generations. The formulations are remarkably brazen. Thus the proposals for business incentives, regressive tax cuts, and other such welfare for the rich appear under the heading 'The Job Creation and Wage Enhancement Act'. The section does indeed include a provision for measures 'to create jobs and raise worker wages'—with the added word: 'unfunded'. But no matter, given prevailing conventions, 'jobs' means 'profits', so it is indeed a 'job creation' proposal, which will continue to 'enhance' wages downwards.

The contract also calls for 'strengthening our national defense' so that we can better 'maintain our credibility around the world'—so that anyone who gets funny ideas, like priests and peasant organisers in Latin America, will learn better. The phrase 'national defense' is hardly even a sick joke, which should elicit ridicule among people with any self-respect. The US faces no threats, but spends almost as much on 'defense' as the rest of the world combined. Military expenditures are no joke, however. Apart from ensuring a particular form of 'stability' in the 'permanent interest' of those who matter, the Pentagon is needed to provide for the likes of Gingrich and his rich constituents, so that they can fulminate against the nanny state that is pouring public funds into their pockets.

Here again a look at history is instructive. As already mentioned, illusions about the viability of free market capitalism have been the domain of ideologists, not actors in the political and economic system. What illusions might have remained about the matter dissipated after the Great Depression and the success of the government-managed World War II economy in overcoming it, with vast growth of production and profits. The lessons were taught to the corporate managers who flocked to Washington 'to carry out one of the most complex pieces of economic planning in history', an experience that 'lessened the ideological fears over the government's role in stabilizing the economy', the leading business historian, Alfred Chandler, points out. They and others anticipated a return to depression unless such measures were retained, in some way. The business world recognised that advanced industry 'cannot satisfactorily exist in a pure, competitive, unsubsidized, "free enterprise" economy' and that 'the government is their only possible savior' (*Fortune, Business Week*). The remarks refer specifically to the aircraft industry established by public funds and wartime profiteering, but they were understood to generalise. For well-known reasons, the Pentagon system was preferred to alternatives and revitalised as the 'savior', sustaining and expanding the aircraft industry and its by-products, along with steel and metals generally, electronics, chemicals, machine tools, automation and robotics, and other central components of the industrial economy.

As long as the fable could be sustained, the Cold War provided the pretext, often as conscious fraud. The first Secretary of the Air Force, Stuart Symington, put the matter plainly in January 1948: 'The word to talk was not "subsidy"; the word to talk was "security"'. As industry representative in Washington, Symington regularly demanded that the military budget 'meet the requirements of the aircraft industry', as he put it. The story continues without essential change until today in just about every functioning sector of the economy, and surely in Cobb County. There, as elsewhere, the 'private sector' relies extensively on welfare payments, subsidies often called 'security'. Dramatically again in the Reagan years, industry has relied on advanced technology that is readily transferred from military to commercial use. This crucial factor in modern industrial development and economic progress has long been understood in the business world, and had been discussed on the left as well, though the debate has been confused by anti-militarist literature that concentrates on the fact that the military path is harmful to the economy as compared with civilian alternates. That is correct, but irrelevant to business leaders, who explained 50 years ago why they preferred the military alternative: primarily reasons of domestic power, not economic health. Some of these topics are at last being investigated even in mainstream academic work, which is useful, though misunderstanding persists in the belief that what is found is 'contrary to the beliefs of analysts from both the right and the left'; it has long been clear in the business press and among left critics. The same studies conclude that the 'defense industrial base' should be maintained— appropriately, on the understanding that the wealthy must be protected from market discipline and the population tricked into subsidising them.[31]

These are major reasons why military spending is increased while anything that might benefit the 'great beast' that threatens 'the opulent minority' must be sharply cut.

The general principles are clear and explicit: free markets are fine for the Third World and its growing counterpart at home. Mothers with dependent children can be sternly lectured on the need for self-reliance, but not dependent executives and investors, please. For them, the welfare state must flourish.

A closer look at particulars again brings out the real meaning of what is happening. Not content with Clinton's increase in the Pentagon budget in radical opposition to the public will, Speaker of the House Gingrich, who represents Lockheed-Martin and other high tech industries, led the House in approving even more public funds for his wealthy constituents. Under his leadership, the House approved a US$3.2 billion 'emergency' supplement for the starving Pentagon, the funds to be drawn from programs for the vast majority. In a vain and pallid gesture that highlights what is at issue, House Democrat David Obey proposed in committee to replace a planned US$5 billion–US$7 billion of cuts in child nutrition, housing, and job training by a five-year delay in deployment of Lockheed F-22 advanced fighters, a (surely underestimated) welfare program of US$72 billion: *delay*, not discontinuation of the taxpayer giveaway. The suggestion was summarily rejected, and scarcely reported.

The word to use remains 'security', not 'subsidy'. And, as often in the past, current plans for 'defense' are designed so as to foster security threats. A minor one is Russia; though now an ally it remains a potential threat to US 'preponderance', the currently fashionable term for global rule. But the primary threat is 'Third World weapons proliferation', Air Force Director of Science and Technology General Richard Paul informed *Jane's*. We must maintain military spending and strengthen the 'defense industrial base' because of 'the growing technological sophistication of Third World conflicts', the Bush Administration had explained to Congress while watching the Berlin Wall collapse, taking with it the most efficient pretext for 'subsidy'. No one who has kept their eyes on the 'security system' will be surprised to learn that both threats are to be enhanced.

Some of the funding for the emergency Pentagon supplement is to be drawn from programs to help dismantle and safeguard the nuclear arsenals of the former USSR. To protect ourselves from the resulting threat, we will have to 'increase the Defense Department's budget', Florida Democratic Representative Pete Peterson commented. Furthermore, 'Third World

weapons proliferation' is to be stimulated, with new contributions to its 'growing technological sophistication'. The US share
in arms sales to Third World countries has reached almost three-
quarters. We must therefore provide them with even more advanced weaponry so that we can tremble in proper fear. The sale
of F-16 aircraft with taxpayer-subsidised loans allows the Air
Force to pay Lockheed to upgrade the aircraft and to develop
the F-22 to counter the threat they pose. The welfare programs
extend beyond Gingrich country. General Paul emphasised, outlining the commitment 'to spin dual-use [Science & Technology]
outside the military' in 'the national interest', 'enhancing our economic security'. Particularly 'enhanced' is the welfare of corporate America, which is to 'transition our work', General Paul
continued in standard bureaucratese.

Gingrich's favourite government-funded cash cow understands the scam perfectly. Lockheed propaganda warns that it is
a 'dangerous world' in which 'sophisticated fighter airplanes and
air defense systems are being sold'—mostly thanks to its 'savior'.
One of the authors adds: 'We've sold the F-16 all over the world;
what if [a friend or ally] turns against us?' To fend off that threat,
we have to sell potential adversaries still more advanced weapons,
and to transfer still more public funds to the shrinking sectors of
the population that bear the burden of 'dazzling' profits. Quite
simple, really.

Arms sales to undemocratic countries—most of the recipients—are opposed by a mere 96 per cent of the population, so
these programs reflect the 'popular mandate' as well as their
companions.[32]

The National Security State is a natural favourite of the advocates of private tyrannies. The device facilitates the transfer of
public funds to advanced industry and to wealthy sectors generally,
with the public cowering in fear of foreign enemies so that planners can operate in 'technocratic insulation', in World Bank lingo.

Furthermore, the 'great beast' has to be dealt with somehow, and the easiest way is to frighten them. With internal enemies as well. Engendering fear and hatred is a standard method of population control, whether the devil is Jews, homosexuals, Arab terrorists, welfare queens (Black, by implication), or criminals lurking in dark corners (ditto). While crime rates have been stable for decades, perception and fear of crime has sharply increased, in large part artificially stimulated, criminologist William Chambliss concludes from the timing of inflamed public rhetoric and polls; the same was true, very dramatically, with regard to drugs.[33]

It is therefore only reasonable that the new 'conservatives' should expand further the domestic security system organised and conducted by the powerful state they wish to nurture. Along with the Pentagon, the rapid growth of the prison system is to be accelerated while constitutional protections are dismantled—for example, by legislation permitting warrantless searches (considered a 'bad idea' by 69 per cent of those who conferred 'the mandate'). The harsh measures of the new crime bills make little sense for a 'war against crime', as experts have regularly pointed out. But they make good sense for a war against the population, with two aspects: frightening into submission the large majority targeted for reduction of quality of life and opportunity; and removal of the growing mass of people who are superfluous but must somehow be controlled as the Third World model is brought home.

Under Reaganite enthusiasts for state power, the number of prisoners in the US almost tripled, leaving the main competitors, South Africa and Russia, well behind—though Russia has just caught up, having begun to grasp the values of its American tutors. The largely fraudulent 'drug war' has served as a leading device to imprison the unwanted population. New crime bills are expected to facilitate the process, with their much harsher sentencing procedures. The vast new expenditures for prisons are also welcomed as another Keynesian stimulus to the economy. 'Businesses Cash In', the *Wall Street Journal* reports, recognising a new way to milk the public. Among the beneficiaries are the construction industry, law firms, the booming and profitable private prison complex, 'the loftiest names in finance' such as Goldman Sachs, Prudential, and others, 'competing to underwrite prison construction with private, tax- exempt bonds. Also standing in line is the 'defense establishment, . . . scenting a new line of business' in high-tech surveillance and control systems of a sort that Big Brother would have admired.[34]

These are the basic reasons, it seems, for the growth of what Chambliss calls 'the crime control industry'. Not that crime isn't a real threat to safety and survival—it is, and has been for a long time. But the causes are not being addressed. Rather, it is being exploited as a method of population control, in various ways.

In general, it is the more vulnerable sectors that are under attack. Children are another natural target. The matter has been addressed in important work, including a UNICEF study by a well-known US economist, Sylvia Ann Hewlett.[35] Reviewing the past fifteen years, Hewlett finds a sharp split between Anglo-American societies and Continental Europe–Japan. The Anglo-American model, Hewlett writes, is a 'disaster' for children and families; the European–Japanese model, in contrast, has improved their situation considerably. Like others, Hewlett attributes the Anglo-American 'disaster' to the ideological preference for 'free markets'. But that is only half true. Whatever one wants to call the reigning ideology it is unfair to tarnish the good name of 'conservatism' by applying it to this form of violent, lawless, reactionary statism, with its contempt for democracy and human rights, and markets as well.

Causes aside, there isn't much doubt about the effects of what Hewlett calls the 'anti-child spirit that is loose in these lands', primarily the US and Britain. The 'neglect-filled Anglo-American model' has largely privatised child-rearing while placing it out of reach of most of the population. The result is a disaster for children and families, while in the 'much more supportive European model', social policy has strengthened support systems for them.

A Blue-Ribbon Commission of the State Boards of Education and the American Medical Association pointed out that 'Never before has one generation of children been less healthy, less cared for or less prepared for life than their parents were at the same age'—though only in the Anglo-American societies, where an 'anti-child, anti-family spirit' has reigned for fifteen years under the guise of 'conservatism' and 'family values'—a doctrinal triumph that any dictator would admire.

In part, the disaster is a simple result of falling wages. For much of the population, both parents have to work overtime merely to provide necessities. And the elimination of 'market rigidities' means that you work extra hours at lower wages—OR ELSE. The consequences are predictable. Contact time between parents and children has declined radically. There is sharp increase in reliance on TV for child supervision, 'latchkey children', child alcoholism and drug use, criminality, violence by and against children, and other obvious effects on health, education, and ability to participate in a democratic society—even survival.

Hunger is most severe among children, with effects that are permanent. Hunger among the elderly is also 'surging', the *Wall Street Journal* reports: 'several million older Americans are going hungry—and their numbers are growing steadily', while some 5 million, about 16 per cent of the population over 60, 'are either hungry or malnourished to some degree'—again, phenomena unknown in other developed societies.[36]

To comprehend what all this means, one has to bear in mind the unparalleled advantages of the United States. To give only one indication, health and life expectancy levels of mid-eighteenth century Americans were not reached until this century by the *upper classes in Britain*. The social and economic catastrophe of state capitalism is an extraordinary phenomenon—for the 'great beast', that is—not to speak of what it has wrought elsewhere. An even more vulnerable target is future generations, who have no 'votes' in the market so that costs can be freely transferred to them in the wealth-concentration frenzy. That is the long-term effect of dismantling the regulatory system, which the Gingrich army hope to achieve across the board by imposing cost–benefit assessment conditions on all environmental and health regulations. The huge Federal bureaucracy required to administer the system can be undercut by refusal to fund it, and any corporate lawyer should be able to tie up proceedings for long periods in this domain of guesses and uncertainties. Related changes in the legal system are designed to protect corporate crime by imposing onerous conditions on victims who seek redress and compensation, eliminating protection for consumers and small time investors, and reducing enforcement powers. That will be a boon for the 'unscrupulous people' who 'steal tens of billions of dollars, maybe hundreds of billions', in financial and insurance frauds, business law professor Benjamin Stein observes, the costs falling on the vulnerable, including the taxpayer, who is expected to pick up the tab when things go sour, as in the savings and loan fiasco, which added many billions to the Federal deficits. It is also an important gift to such corporations as Philip Morris, the biggest corporate donor to the Gingrich army, which needs government protection for marketing its lethal addictive drugs, responsible for far more deaths than the illegal variety, including non- users (unlike hard drugs).[37]

Towards the End of History: the Utopia of the Masters

For most of the population, conditions of life and work are declining, something new in the history of industrial society. The latest edition of the annual scholarly study of 'the state of working America' concludes that during the recovery from the deep Reagan recession of 1982, 'the vast majority of families lost wealth as the economy grew'; all but the top 20 per cent, the authors estimate. As the economy stagnated and fell into recession in 1988–91, 'wealth declined among nearly every income group', and, through the Clinton recovery, median wages have continued their steady decline since 1980. Wages for entry-level jobs—a predictor for the future—fell 30 per cent for male and 18 per cent for female high school graduates (3/4 of the work force), and for the college educated, fell 8 per cent for males and rose 4 per cent for females. Hourly wages dropped over 10 per cent, more for high school graduates. For men with high school education, real income fell a 'stunning' 21 per cent from 1979 to 1990, the 1994 *Economic Report of the President* reported, falling further since. Poverty rates reached double the level of other industrial countries; child poverty is particularly high, far beyond any other industrial society, almost three times the average. Meanwhile salaries for CEOs rose 66 per cent, second only to Britain's 123 per cent rise, though the US retains its huge lead in CEO/worker pay ratio. The slow growth in wealth was concentrated in financial assets, overwhelmingly held by the wealthy. There was a 'spectacular redistribution' of wealth, with inequality now far higher than any other country of the developed world. The share of marketable net worth held by the top 1 per cent is now twice that of England and 50 per cent higher than France, the nearest competitor in the Mishel–Bernstein list. In 1980, differences among these countries were slight, but Reaganite programs directed 60 per cent of marketable wealth gain to the top 1 per cent of income recipients, while the bottom 40 per cent suffered an absolute loss of net worth in real terms; other measures are still more stark.[38]

Mishel and Bernstein identify several factors in the wage decline: primarily a severe drop in the minimum wage and deunionisation, rapid expansion of low-wage service jobs (80 per cent of new jobs created were in the lowest-paying service sector industries), and globalisation of the economy. They find little if any impact of technology on wage and employment structure. A closer look shows extensive state initiative in each of these developments, favouring some economic forces, undermining others; consistently in ways that serve 'the minority of the opulent'. One indication is that 'the emergence of greater wage disparities has been evident only in the United States and Great Britain, the two countries that have moved fastest to "deregulate" their labor markets', though other factors (technological change, etc.) do not single out these cases.

The general situation is similar in England, less so in continental Europe and Japan, though in an increasingly globalised economy, those who pursue the harshest and most inegalitarian policies will carry others along. The end of the Cold War offers new weapons to private power in its battle against the 'pampered Western workers' who are going to have to face reality and give up their 'luxurious life-styles' in the wondrous new world order, the business press warns. But some are doing fine, as the same sources exult. After four straight years of double-digit profit growth, profits—now at a 45-year high—are expected to continue their 'stunning' growth, while real wages and benefits are expected to continue their steady decline. Earnings per share have more than doubled since 1991 for the top 500 corporations, and are expected to double that growth rate in 1996; return on capital for non-financial corporations has more than doubled since 1980, even surpassing the growth of poverty, though not keeping up with the increasing prison population.[39]

Along with democracy, markets are under attack. Even putting aside massive state intervention, increasing economic concentration and market control offers endless devices to evade and undermine market discipline, a long story that there is no time to go into here; to mention only one aspect, some 40 per cent of 'world trade' is intrafirm, over 50 per cent for the US and Japan. This is not 'trade' in any meaningful sense; rather, operations internal to corporations, centrally managed by a highly visible hand, with all sorts of mechanisms for undermining markets in the interest of profit and power.[40]

In reality, the quasi-mercantilist system of transnational corporate capitalism is rife with the kinds of 'conspiracies' of the masters against the public of which Adam Smith famously warned, not to speak of the traditional reliance on state power and public subsidy. A 1992 OECD study concludes that 'Oligopolistic competition and strategic interaction among firms and governments rather than the invisible hand of market forces condition today's competitive advantage and international division of labor in high-technology industries', as in agriculture, pharmaceuticals, services, and major areas of economic activity generally. The vast majority of the world's population, who are subjected to market discipline and regaled with odes to its wonders, are not supposed to hear such words; and rarely do.

The globalisation of production puts tremendous weapons into the hands of private tyrannies. Another critical factor is the huge explosion of unregulated financial capital since Richard Nixon dismantled the Bretton Woods system in the early 1970s. The consequences of the deregulation of financial markets were quickly understood. In 1978, Nobel Prize laureate in economics James Tobin proposed that foreign exchange transactions be taxed to slow the haemorrhage of capital from the real economy (investment and trade) to financial manipulations that now constitute 95 per cent of foreign exchange transactions (as compared with 10 per cent of a far smaller total in 1970). As Tobin observed at this early stage, these processes would drive the world towards a low- growth, low-wage economy. A study directed by Paul Volcker, formerly head of the Federal Reserve, attributes about half of the substantial slow-down in growth since the early 1970s to this factor.

International economist David Felix makes the interesting observation that even the productive sectors that would benefit from the Tobin tax have joined financial capital in resisting it. The reason, he suggests, is that elites generally are 'bonded by a common objective, . . . to shrink, perhaps even to liquidate, the welfare state'. The instant mobility of huge sums of financial capital is a potent weapon to force governments to follow 'fiscally responsible policies', which can bring home the sharply two-tiered Third World model to the rich societies. By enhancing the shadow cast by big business over society and restricting the capacity of governments to respond to the public will, these processes also undermine the threat of democracy, another welcome consequence. The shared elite interest, Felix suggests, overcomes the narrower self-interest of the owners and managers of productive sectors of the economy.[41]

The suggestion is a reasonable one. The history of business and political economy yields many examples of the subordination of narrow gain to the broader interest of the opulent minority, which is unusually class conscious in a business-run society like the United States. Illustrations include central features of the modern world: the creation and sustenance of the Pentagon system of corporate welfare despite its well-known inefficiencies; the openly proclaimed strategy of diversion of soaring profits to creation of excess capacity abroad as a weapon against the domestic working class; the design of automation within the state system to enhance managerial control and de-skill workers even at the cost of efficiency and profitability; and many other examples, including a large part of the foreign policy.

I'm afraid this barely skims the surface. It's easy to see why the masters see a real hope of rolling back the hated welfare state, driving the great beast to its lair, and at last achieving the 'daring depravity of the times' that so shocked Madison in its very early stages, with private tyrannies, now released from even limited public accountability, assuming their proper role as 'the pretorian [sic] band of the Government, at once its tool and its tyrant; bribed by its largesses and overawing it by its clamours and combinations'. It is also easy to understand the mood of desperation, anxiety, hopelessness and fear that is so prevalent in the world, outside of wealthy and privileged sectors and those who sing their praises.

To stem and reverse this course and restore a modicum of respect for the values of the Enlightenment, for freedom and human rights, will be no simple matter. The first step is to penetrate the clouds of deceit and distortion and learn the truth about the world, then to organise and act to change it. That's never been impossible, and never been easy. It's not impossible now, and not easy either. There has rarely been a time in history when that choice carried such dramatic human consequences.

6

The Middle East Settlement: Its Sources and Contours

'What We Say Goes'

Well over a year has passed since the Israel–Arafat agreement of September 1993, the Declaration of Principles (DOP).[1] The signers have received their Nobel Peace Prizes. The substantive meaning of what they signed has been coming into clearer view, with ambiguities falling away. It is a good moment to reflect on what has happened and why, and where the 'peace process' is likely to lead.

Taken literally, the terms of the DOP adhere closely to US–Israeli positions that have been held consistently and for over 20 years in virtual international isolation. The US and its client-allies, which dominate the region, interpret the terms quite literally, so subsequent developments show—hardly a surprise, since they crafted and imposed these terms. This stand finds its place within a broader US conception of how the region should be organised, which goes back to World War II. Although its principles have been stable for a long period, it is only in recent years that Washington has been able to implement them effectively. That seems to me the essence of the ongoing 'peace process'.

The term 'peace process' itself is a standard Orwellism, used uncritically in the United States, and adopted throughout much of the world, given its enormous influence and power. In practice, the term refers to whatever the US leadership happens to be doing at the moment—often undermining the peace process in the literal sense of the term, as inspection of the facts makes rather clear.

The Gulf War established US domination of the Middle East at a level never before achieved, making it possible for Washington to organise the 'peace process' according to US guidelines, beginning at the Madrid meetings in October 1991. A serious analysis of recent diplomacy should begin right here.

As bombs and missiles were raining on Baghdad and hapless Iraqi conscripts hiding in the sands, George Bush proudly announced the slogan of the New World Order, in four simple words: 'What We Say Goes'. 'What We Say' was soon spelled out with no less clarity as the guns fell silent, and Bush returned to the earlier practice of lending aid and support to Saddam Hussein as he mercilessly crushed the Shi'ite and Kurdish uprisings under the eyes of the victorious allied forces, who refused to lift a finger. Support for Saddam was so extreme that the US command would not even allow rebelling Iraqi generals to use captured Iraqi equipment for defence of the population against Saddam's slaughter. A Saudi plan to support the indigenous Shi'ite uprising was quickly killed by the Bush Administration.[2]

The meaning of the New World Order could not have been more vividly articulated. The state of Western culture is also illuminated by the reaction: mostly applause for the statesmanship of our leaders.

The reasons for Washington's tolerant stance towards the ongoing slaughter were outlined at the time by leading analysts: Saddam's atrocities pained us, of course, but were necessary for 'stability'— another useful term of political discourse, which translates as 'Whatever serves the interests of power'.

Official reasoning was outlined by Thomas Friedman, then chief diplomatic correspondent of the *New York Times*. Washington had hoped for 'the best of all worlds', Friedman explained: 'an iron-fisted Iraqi junta without Saddam Hussein'. That would restore the status quo ante, when Saddam's 'iron fist . . . held Iraq together, much to the satisfaction of the American allies, Turkey and Saudi Arabia'—and, of course, the boss in Washington. But this happy outcome proved unfeasible, so the masters of the region had to settle for second best: the same 'iron fist' they had been fortifying while it was torturing dissidents and gassing Kurds, all quite acceptable as long as the gangster in charge was following orders on important matters. Only a few months before Saddam conquered Kuwait, George Bush took the occasion of his invasion of Panama to announce plans to lift a ban on loans to Iraq, implemented shortly after to achieve the 'goal of increasing U.S. exports and put us in a better position to deal with Iraq regarding its human rights record . . .', the State Department explained with a straight face to the few inquiries from Congress. Media and mainstream journals found the whole matter unworthy of comment, even report.[3]

To be sure, not everyone regarded restoration of the 'Beast of Baghdad' or some suitable clone as the 'best of all worlds': Iraqi dissidents, for example. London-based banker Ahmed Chalabi bitterly condemned Washington's stance: 'the United States, covered by the fig leaf of non-interference in Iraqi affairs, is waiting for Saddam to butcher the insurgents in the hope that he can be overthrown later by a suitable officer', he said, an attitude rooted in the US policy of 'supporting dictatorships to maintain stability'. The population of the United States was spared such discordant notes, as it had been throughout the crisis. The voices of Iraqi dissidents were available only to readers of the marginal dissident press, which publicised what could be discovered from foreign sources, and to participants in public meetings organised by peace and justice groups, which offered visiting Iraqi opposition leaders from Europe a ready forum. These facts too are un-

welcome, hence consigned to their usual place in favour of a
rather audacious version that turns the easily determined facts
on their head, an interesting story that I will not pursue here.

Official US spokespersons confirmed that the Bush Administration would not talk to Iraqi opposition leaders: 'We felt that
political meetings with them . . . would not be appropriate for
our policy at this time', State Department spokesman Richard
Boucher stated on March 14. The information system agreed,
continuing to bar authentic Iraqi dissidents from the mainstream
media. It was only in April, well after the hostilities had ended,
that the *Wall Street Journal*, to its credit, broke ranks and offered
space to a spokesman for the Iraqi democratic opposition, Chalabi, who described the outcome as 'the worst of all possible
worlds' for the Iraqi people, whose tragedy is 'awesome'.

According to the standard version, outlined by *New York Times*
Middle East correspondent Alan Cowell a few days later, the
rebels failed because 'very few people outside Iraq wanted them
to win'. The US and 'its Arab coalition partners' came to 'a strik-
ingly unanimous view', he explained: 'whatever the sins of the Iraqi
leader, he offered the West and the region a better hope for his
country's stability than did those who have suffered his repression'.
The conclusion is tenable if we understand 'people' to exclude
Iraqi dissidents and the population of the 'Arab coalition partners',
at least Egypt, the only one free enough to allow some of their
voices to be heard. It is true, however, that the 'unanimous view'
includes the people who count: Washington, editorial offices and
news columns, and the dictatorships of the region. It also included
Turkey and Israel, the former concerned about its own brutally re-
pressed Kurdish population, the latter fearing that Kurdish autonomy in Iraq might 'create a territorial, military contiguity between
Teheran and Damascus', a potential 'danger for Israel' (Moshe
Zak, senior editor of the mass-circulation daily *Ma'ariv*, explaining
the support for Saddam on the part of the top military command

and a broad range of political opinion, including leading doves). Turkey's concerns received some mention, but not the Israeli reaction, which clashes too sharply with preferred imagery.[4]

It is, incidentally, now conceded that when its disobedient friend invaded Kuwait, the Bush Administration expected that he would quickly withdraw, leaving behind a puppet regime—that is, duplicate what the US had just done in Panama. To be sure, no historical parallel is exact. In a high-level meeting immediately after Saddam's invasion of Kuwait, the Chairman of the Joint Chiefs of Staff, Colin Powell, argued against military intervention on grounds that the American people 'do not want their young dying for $1.50 oil'. 'The next few days Iraq will withdraw', he said, putting 'his puppet in. Everyone in the Arab world will be happy'. In contrast, when Washington withdrew partially from Panama after putting its puppet in, many were far from happy (south of the border). Washington's Panama caper aroused great anger throughout the hemisphere, so much so that the puppet regime was expelled from the Group of Eight Latin American democracies as a country under military occupation. Washington was well aware, Latin Americanist Stephen Ropp observes, 'that removing the mantle of United States protection would quickly result in a civilian or military overthrow of Endara and his supporters'—that is, the puppet regime of bankers, businessmen, and narcotraffickers installed by Bush's invasion. Even that government's own Human Rights Commission charged that the right to self-determination and sovereignty of the Panamanian people continues to be violated by the 'state of occupation by a foreign army', four years after the invasion.[5]

Such (unreported) facts aside, the analogy can stand—or could, if it could be understood, even mentioned, within the mainstream.

Washington's concerns explain why it had to block every initiative that might have led to a negotiated Iraqi withdrawal, as it did; and why the international media had to conceal the facts about the diplomatic options, as they too did—with remarkable efficiency, in fact, though it was sometimes conceded quietly that the facts were known. There is an extensive critical literature on the performance of the media during the war, but it too skirts this issue, clearly the most crucial one. How important it was to keep the facts under wraps becomes particularly clear when we discover that on the eve of the bombing, the American population, by about 2 to 1, supported a settlement based on withdrawal of Iraqi troops in the context of consideration of regional issues, not knowing of an Iraqi proposal to this effect a few weeks earlier, or its summary rejection in Washington. The same standards are upheld by current scholarly work, another interesting story that I will put aside here. Similarly, the record of declassified documents, which reveals a good deal about what was going on, is ignored by the most admired scholarly work as it was by the media throughout. Only at the margins does one find exceptions to the pattern.[6]

On the well-understood principle of Tacitus that 'crime once exposed has no refuge but audacity', this miserable performance is now standardly regarded as an illustration of how the democratic system fosters careful, deliberate, and sober airing of all sides of crucial issues before serious decisions are taken.

The Strategic Conception

The Gulf War took place against the background of important changes in the international economy and global affairs that offered the United States opportunities to organise the world that it had not enjoyed since the end of World War II. In the ashes of that catastrophe, the US was at last able to expel from the hemisphere its main rivals, France and Britain, and to implement the Monroe Doctrine. By the 1990s, the US was able to extend the Monroe Doctrine, in effect, over the Middle East. To understand what this implies for the region, it is necessary to dissipate the fog of ideology and see how the Doctrine has actually been understood by planners. Take just the Woodrow Wilson Administration, at the peak moment of 'idealism' in foreign policy. The Monroe Doctrine is based on 'selfishness alone', Wilson's Secretary of State Robert Lansing explained privately and, in advocating it, the US 'considers its own interests. The integrity of other American nations is an incident, not an end'. The President agreed, adding that it would be 'impolitic' to let the public in on the secret. This application of 'Wilsonian idealism' is only reasonable, the Secretary of the Interior added, because Latin Americans are 'naughty children who are exercising all the privileges and rights of grown ups', behaviour that calls for 'a stiff hand, an authoritative hand'.[7]

To gain unilateral control of the Middle East oil-producing regions is no small achievement. As the US became a true superpower in the 1940s, the political leadership considered the region to be the most 'strategically important area in the world' (Eisenhower), 'a stupendous source of strategic power, and one of the greatest material prizes in world history' as well as 'probably the richest economic prize in the world in the field of foreign investment' (State Department, 1940s)—a prize that the US intended to keep for itself and its British client, in the unfolding New World Order of that day.

Since then, the US has kept to a strategic conception for the region that it inherited from its British predecessor. The great 'material prize' is to be administered by local managers, family dictatorships that are weak and dependent, and will do what they are told. They constitute what British imperialist planners had called the 'Arab facade' that would enable Britain to rule behind various 'constitutional fictions' after a grant of nominal independence. The managers can be as brutal and corrupt as they please, as long as they fulfil their function. In this regard they join an impressive collection of tyrants and killers: a string of Latin American military officers, Suharto, Marcos, Mobutu, Ceaucescu, and a host of others like them. It is hard to imagine a crime that might exclude someone from this club. Even Stalin passed muster. Truman liked and admired the 'honest' Russian leader. His death would be a 'real catastrophe', Truman felt, adding that he could 'deal with' Stalin as long as the US got its way 85 per cent of the time. What Stalin did at home was not his concern. Other respected figures agreed, including Churchill, whose fulsome praise for the bloody tyrant continued into 1945: 'Premier Stalin was a person of great power, in whom he had every confidence', Churchill informed his cabinet after Yalta, expressing his hope that he would stay in command.

There is nothing new in the support offered to Middle East monsters and the irrelevance of the most awful crimes if the higher purposes of 'stability' are served. Unless such persistent features of 'really existing diplomacy' are understood, what is happening in the world will remain a mystery.

The *facade* must be protected from the people of the region, who are backward and uncivilised, and do not seem to grasp the reasons why the 'richest economic prize in the world' must benefit not *them*, but rather Western investors. Accordingly, it is necessary to rely on local gendarmes to keep order; at various times, Iran, Turkey, Pakistan, and others. US and British muscle remain in the background, if needed. Israel falls within the second of these three levels of control.

In the corridors of power, the basic ideas are understood well enough, though it is not considered good form to speak too frankly; thus we do not appropriate resources for ourselves, but rather deny them to potential enemies, in self-defence; independently of the facts, we and our allies are engaged in 'counter-terrorism' or 'reprisal', not 'terrorism'; etc. Still, some clarity emerges from the mists.

Much impressed with Israel's military successes in the 1948 war, the Joint Chiefs of Staff described the new state as the major regional military power after Turkey, offering the US means to 'gain strategic advantage in the Middle East that would offset the effects of the decline of British power in that area'. Ten years later, the National Security Council concluded that a 'logical corollary' of opposition to growing Arab nationalism 'would be to support Israel as the only strong pro-Western power left in the Middle East'. Through the 1960s, US analysts saw Israeli power as a barrier to Nasserite threats to the *facade*, a perception confirmed by Israel's destruction of Egypt's military force in 1967. The thesis that Israel could serve as a 'strategic asset' defending US interests and clients from nationalist forces received further support in 1970, when Israel fended off a perceived Syrian threat to the Kingdom of Jordan and perhaps the oil producers. And increasingly in the years that followed.

The strategic asset thesis found its natural place within the Nixon Doctrine, which recognised that the US could 'no longer play policeman to the world' and would therefore 'expect other nations to provide more cops on the beat in their own neighborhood' (Defense Secretary Melvin Laird). Police headquarters, it was understood, remains in Washington; others must pursue their 'regional interests' within the 'overall framework of order' managed by the United States, as Henry Kissinger framed the general idea, admonishing Europe not to break the rules. The two main cops on the beat in the Middle East precinct were Israel and Iran, secretly allied. Scholarship commonly refers to a 'two pillars' strategy for US control, with Iran and Saudi Arabia in mind; that it has been a 'three pillars strategy' has been clear from the 1970s, at least.[8]

In May 1973, the Senate's leading specialist on oil and the Middle East, Democratic hawk Henry Jackson, observed that US dominance of the region is safeguarded by 'the strength and

Western orientation of Israel on the Mediterranean and Iran on the Persian Gulf', two 'reliable friends of the United States'. These friends 'have served to inhibit and contain those irresponsible and radical elements in certain Arab States, who, were they free to do so, would pose a grave threat indeed to our principal sources of petroleum in the Persian Gulf'. At the time, the US scarcely used these sources. The world's leading oil producer until 1970 was Venezuela, which the Wilson Administration had taken over as a private fiefdom half a century earlier, expelling Britain, another illustration of 'Wilsonian idealism', in this case, its dedication to 'the open door' and the principle of 'self-determination'. Other Western hemisphere reserves were substantial as well. But the world's cheapest and most abundant source of oil, in the Gulf region, was needed as a reserve and a lever for world domination, and for the vast wealth that flowed from it, primarily to the US and Britain.

If archival materials become available, they may have much of interest to say about tacit relations over the years between the Arab facade and the two leading gendarmes, with whom they were officially at war. That is most unlikely in Saudi Arabia and the Gulf Emirates, and unfortunately less likely than it once was in the US after the shift in policy towards much harsher censorship under Reagan, apparently still in effect; recent discoveries by Israeli historian Benny Morris also raise doubts about Israeli archives.[9] The secret relations between Israel and the Shah have been extensively revealed, mostly in Israel.

It should have come as no surprise that, after the fall of the Shah, Israel and Saudi Arabia at once began to cooperate in selling US arms to the Iranian army. There has been a substantial public record since 1982. These are the initial stages of what later became known as the 'arms for hostages' scandal when parts could no longer be concealed. There were no hostages when the US–Israel–Saudi operation began, and high Israeli officials were quite frank in explaining what was happening from the earliest days: an effort to inspire a military coup to restore the old order. Furthermore, that is just 'standard operating procedure'. The routine way to overthrow a civilian government is to establish relations with elements in the military, the folks who will have to do the job. The project sometimes meets with success; Indonesia and Chile were two recent examples. Iran turned out to be a harder nut to crack.[10]

Rights accrue to various actors according to their place within the general strategic conception. The US has rights by definition. The cops on the beat have rights unless they defect, in which case, if too independent, they become enemies. The local managers have rights as long as they keep to their business. If an 'iron fist' is needed to preserve 'stability', so be it.

The people in the slums of Cairo or the villages of Lebanon, and others like them, have neither wealth nor power; hence no rights, by simple logic. Their concerns too are 'an incident, not an end'. As for Palestinians, they not only lack rights but, worse, are a nuisance; their unhappy fate has been an irritant, with disruptive effect on Arab popular opinion. Therefore they have *negative* rights, a fact that explains quite a lot. It has been necessary to lance that boil somehow, by violence or in some other way. The idea is that, if the Palestinian issue can be eliminated, it should be possible to bring the tacit relations among the parties with rights to the surface, and extend them, incorporating others in a US-dominated regional system in the most 'strategically important area in the world'.

That has always been the basic logic of the 'peace process'. The framework, stable and long-lasting, does not permit us literally to deduce what happens and will likely continue to; human affairs are too complex for that. But it comes surprisingly close.

Until recently, it has not been feasible to impose the guiding strategic conception fully, in part because of limitations on US

power, in part as a result of problems that attended the commitment to retain Israel's crucial role as a 'strategic asset'. That role
took on added dimensions through the 1970s and 1980s, reaching well beyond the Middle East. That was one consequence of
congressional initiatives from the early 1970s to impose human
rights conditions on the actions of the executive branch; these
initiatives are one of the important effects of the popular movements of the 1960s, which considerably changed attitudes and
perceptions among the general public on a broad range of issues,
to the considerable distress of elite opinion.[11] It therefore became necessary for planners to turn increasingly to surrogates.
To mention only one striking illustration, when John F. Kennedy
decided to send the US Air Force to bomb South Vietnam, there
wasn't a whisper of protest; but when the Reaganites tried to
conduct similar operations in Central America, there was a public uproar, and they had to retreat to massive clandestine terror
operations.

In this context, Israel took on new functions. Thus when congressional human rights conditions prevented President Carter
from sending jet planes to Indonesia in 1978 as atrocities in East
Timor peaked, he could arrange for Israel to send US jets, to be
resupplied through the open funnel. The major contributions,
however, were in Africa and Latin America, particularly as the
Reagan Administration forged an international terror network of
imposing dimensions, including Argentine neo-Nazis, Taiwan,
South Africa, England, Saudi Arabia, Morocco, and others. Recall that small-time operators like Qaddafi hire terrorists, but the
big fellows prefer terrorist states.

On the matter of Israel's central role in US Middle East policies, there has been some internal debate. But for various reasons, which are not without interest, the strategic asset thesis
has rarely faced a serious challenge. The few attempts to deviate
from it have been quickly shot down, in large part in recognition

of Israel's demonstrations of military prowess, which much impressed not only US leaders but also intellectual opinion across a broad spectrum.

These are among the reasons why the US has consistently undermined or deflected diplomatic efforts to resolve the conflict for over 20 years. Most of these initiatives called for some recognition of Palestinian rights, whereas Washington insists that Palestinians have no rights that might interfere with Israeli power. Furthermore, these initiatives called for some kind of international involvement in a settlement; that too Washington is unwilling to accept, though an exception can be made for its British 'lieutenant', to borrow the phrase of an influential Kennedy adviser, describing the 'special relationship' as understood by the senior partner. It has been necessary 'to ensure that the Europeans and Japanese did not get involved in the diplomacy concerning the Middle East', as Henry Kissinger privately explained.[12]

The fundamental premises are so deeply rooted that they have entered into the very terminology in which the issues are framed. Take the term 'rejectionism', which if used in a neutral sense should refer to the rejection of the right of national self-determination of one or the other of the two groups that claim such rights in the former Palestine: the indigenous population, and the Jewish settlers who have gradually replaced them.[13] But the term is not used that way. Rather, 'rejectionists' are those who reject the rights of *one* contestant, Jews: some elements of the PLO, the government of Iran, and some others. In contrast, those who reject the rights of Palestinians (including both of Israel's major political blocs, both US political parties, all Israeli and US governments, virtually all of articulate US opinion) are 'moderates' or 'pragmatists', even 'doves'. More remarkably yet, quite without shame people and organisations who are considered 'civil libertarian' can denounce as 'outrageous' the 'comparison between those Israelis who oppose the creation of a potentially hostile state on Israel's borders and those Palestinians who still support the destruction of Israel . . .'—that is, the comparison between those who deny the right of self- determination to Palestinians, and those who deny that right to Israeli Jews.[14]

The racist usage is so firmly implanted as to be unnoticed, and unintelligible when pointed out. As Orwell observed in his discussion of 'voluntary . . . censorship in England', the most effective device is the 'general tacit agreement that "it wouldn't do" to mention that particular fact'; it is the task of a decent education to inculcate the talents required. And one of the facts 'it wouldn't do' to mention, even to think, is that the US has long been the leader of the Rejection Front.

It is worth noting that the Cold War has been a secondary consideration for the most part, a fact sometimes recognised in internal discussion. Thus in March 1958, Secretary of State John Foster Dulles informed the National Security Council that neither Communism nor the Soviet Union was involved in the three major world crises of the time, all involving the Islamic world: the Middle East, North Africa, and Indonesia. And when one participant suggested that others might be doing the Russians' work for them, President Eisenhower took 'vigorous exception', the record reveals.[15]

We need hardly argue the point any longer; it is coming to be conceded, even officially, the pretext no longer serving any useful purpose. The transition was rapid. Well into 1989, the US was defending itself against global Communist aggression. By the year's end that was not what it was (or even had been) doing. In March 1990, the White House made its regular presentation to Congress to explain why the Pentagon budget must be kept at its colossal level, the first presentation after the fall of the Berlin Wall in November 1989. The conclusion was the usual one, but the reasons were now different: the threat was not the Kremlin, but the 'growing technological sophistication' of the Third World.

In particular, the US must maintain its intervention forces aimed at the Middle East because of 'the free world's reliance on energy supplies from this pivotal region', where the 'threats to our interests could not be laid at the Kremlin's door' in recent years. Or before, for that matter, a fact sometimes acknowledged, as in 1958. Or in 1980, when the architect of President Carter's Rapid Deployment Force (later Central Command), aimed primarily at the Middle East, testified before Congress that its most likely use was not to resist a (highly implausible) Soviet attack, but to deal with indigenous and regional unrest: the 'radical nationalism' that has always been a primary concern.[16]

Of course, in the Middle East as elsewhere, targets of US attack turned to the Russians for support, which the Kremlin was sometimes willing to offer, for purely cynical and opportunistic reasons. And Soviet power had a deterrent effect, as the record repeatedly shows. But these qualifications aside, it remains true that 'the threats to our interests could not be laid at the Kremlin's door'.

By 1991, Washington was in a position to achieve its strategic goals with little regard for world opinion. It was no longer necessary to undermine all diplomatic initiatives, as Washington had been doing for 20 years. The Soviet Union was gone, and, with it, the space for non- alignment, an important fact about world affairs, given little attention in the West but recognised with no slight concern in the Third World. In a Chilean journal, the well-known author Mario Benedetti wrote that 'the combination of the weakening of the USSR and the [US] victory in the Gulf could turn out to be frightening [for the South] because of the breakdown of international military equilibrium which somehow served to contain US yearnings for domination', and because the shot in the arm to Western racist jingoism 'could stimulate even wilder imperialist adventures'. The general mood in the South was captured by Brazilian Cardinal Paulo Evaristo

Arns, who observed that in the Arab countries 'the rich sided with the US government while the *millions* of poor condemned this military aggression'. Throughout the Third World 'there is hatred and fear: When will they decide to invade us', and on what pretext? Apart from the margins, none of this reaches the West, drowned in triumphalism and self-congratulation.[17]

Most of the Third World was in utter disarray in any event, devastated by the catastrophe of capitalism of the 1980s. Europe basically abdicated any role in Middle East affairs, granting the US the near total control it had long sought. The Gulf War sealed the bargain, establishing that 'What We Say Goes' and setting off a genuine 'peace process'—meaning one firmly under unilateral US control.

'Stalemate'

I'll quickly review the relevant backgrounds, beginning from the June war in 1967.

The outcome of the war was highly welcome to the US, with Nasserite influence in the region removed (to the great relief of the *facade*), and Israel in control of the West Bank, Gaza, the Golan Heights, and the Sinai. But the war had brought the world dangerously close to a superpower confrontation. There were threatening 'hot line' communications between Washington and Moscow. Soviet Premier Kosygin at one point warned President Johnson that 'if you want war, you'll have war', Secretary of Defense Robert McNamara reported years later, adding his own judgment that 'we damn near had war' when the US fleet 'turned around a [Soviet] carrier in the Mediterranean'; he gave no details, but it was probably during Israel's conquest of the Syrian Golan Heights after the cease-fire.

Clearly something had to be done. A diplomatic process ensued, leading to UN Security Council Resolution 242, which has provided the basic framework for diplomacy since. Though it was kept purposely vague in the hope of gaining general adherence, there is little doubt as to how the Resolution was understood by the Security Council, including the United States: it called for full peace in return for full Israeli withdrawal, with perhaps minor and mutual adjustments. That the US supported this international consensus is clear from the records that have been released, and in some cases leaked, including an important State Department history. This interpretation of UN 242 was confirmed publicly in the 1969 Rogers Plan presented by Secretary of State William Rogers and approved by President Nixon, which held that 'any change in the pre-existing lines should not reflect the weight of conquest and should be confined to insubstantial alterations required for mutual security'.

UN 242 was not implemented. Though all signed, the Arab states refused full peace and Israel refused full withdrawal. Note that UN 242 is flatly rejectionist: it offers nothing to the Palestinians, who enter only as a refugee problem.

The impasse was broken in February 1971, when President Sadat of Egypt joined the international consensus, accepting the proposal of UN mediator Gunnar Jarring for full peace with Israel in return for full Israeli withdrawal from Egyptian territory. Israel welcomed Egypt's expression 'of its readiness to enter into a peace agreement with Israel', but rejected it, stating that 'Israel will not withdraw to the pre-June 5, 1967 lines'. That position has since been maintained with no deviation by both political groupings, the Labor-based and Likud coalitions.

Sadat's adoption of the official US position placed Washington in a quandary: Should Washington accept it, thus leaving Israel alone among major actors in opposition? Or should the US shift policy, joining Israel in its so-far unilateral rejection of the withdrawal provisions of UN 242? The latter option was preferred by Henry Kissinger, who advocated 'stalemate', on grounds so outlandish that it has been necessary to ignore them, probably out of embarrassment; it is not the only such case.[18] His primary motivation might have been to undermine his rival William Rogers and take over the State Department, as he was soon to do. Kissinger's position prevailed. Since then the US has not only rejected Palestinian rights (at the time, along with the international consensus), but also the withdrawal provisions of UN 242 as understood by its authors—including the United States, contrary to subsequent inventions.[19]

These again are things 'it wouldn't do' to say. Therefore, the whole story is rated 'X'—out of history.

In his memoirs, Israeli Prime Minister Yitzhak Rabin, then Israel's Ambassador in Washington, describes Sadat's acceptance of the 'famous' Jarring proposal as a 'bombshell', a 'milestone' on the path to peace, though unacceptable because 'Sadat's evasive imprint' remained, implying a 'conditional link' between the peace agreement and Israel's withdrawal to the pre-June 1967 borders (in accord with UN 242, as understood at the time outside of Israel). In the US, in contrast, the facts have disappeared. They are invariably ignored in mainstream journalism and commentary, and even in the scholarly record quite often. The most recent example is Mark Tessler's history, which is more balanced than most. In his extensive review of the diplomacy, Sadat's official peace offer and Israel's rejection of it are nowhere mentioned, but a footnote does refer to a 1971 interview in which Sadat informed *Newsweek* editor Arnaud de Borchgrave 'that Egypt was ready to recognize and make peace with Israel'. De Borchgrave informed Israeli Prime Minister Golda Meir 'that Sadat would soon repeat his offer of peace to UN envoy Gunnar Jarring', Tessler continues, but Meir 'dismissed Sadat's overture'.[20]

So much for the 'famous milestone'. Few come even this close to reality.

US rejection of UN 242 under Kissinger's initiative eliminated the matter of withdrawal from the 'peace process'. The issue of rejectionism arose a few years later, as the international consensus shifted to a non- rejectionist position, including the major Arab states and the PLO. That matter came to a head in January 1976, when the Security Council debated a resolution incorporating the wording of UN 242, but adding a provision for a Palestinian state in the West Bank and Gaza Strip. The resolution was supported by the Arab 'confrontation states' (Egypt, Jordan, Syria) and the PLO, the Soviet Union, Europe, and most of the rest of the world. It was vetoed by the United States, now firmly established as the leader of the most extreme fringe of the Rejection Front. Washington vetoed a similar resolution in 1980. The matter then shifted to the General Assembly, which had annual votes in which the US and Israel stood alone in opposition (once with Dominica joining); a negative US vote in the Assembly amounts to a veto, even if the US is completely alone, or virtually so, as is commonly the case. The last of the regular annual votes was in December 1990, 144–2. Another resolution endorsing 'The right of the Palestinian people to self- determination' was considered in November 1994 (124–2).[21]

All of this is banned from history, rarely even reported, displaced from the record in favour of inspiring tales about American efforts to achieve peace, thwarted by Arab rejectionists and other bad characters, perhaps part of a cosmic 'clash of civilisations'.

The 1990 UN vote was just before the Gulf War, which placed the US in a position to impose, at last, its own extreme brand of rejectionism. The Bush Administration had restated these principles well before, in the December 1989 Baker Plan, which simply endorsed the Shamir–Peres Plan proposed by Israel's coalition government in May 1989. According to the Shamir–Peres–Baker Plan, the US and Israel would select certain Palestinians, who would be permitted to discuss 'Israel's initiative', but nothing else. The plan was public in theory, and reported at once in the dissident press, but not elsewhere, and is ignored or misrepresented in much of the best scholarship as well. Only one of its provisions, for elections, receives mention, illustrating what the press sometimes calls the 'yearning for democracy' of American leaders—to be realised by elections under Israeli military control with a good part of the educated sector of the population in prison without charge.

The crucial terms of the Shamir–Peres–Baker Plan were: 1 that there can be no 'additional Palestinian state in the Gaza district and in the area between Israel and Jordan' (Jordan already being a 'Palestinian state'); and 2 that 'There will be no change in the status of Judea, Samaria and Gaza [the West Bank and Gaza Strip] other than in accordance with the basic guidelines of the [Israeli] Government', which exclude Palestinian self-determination.

It is important to bear in mind that this was the official position of the Bush Administration, which is regularly condemned for its bitter anti-Israel stance. It is consistent with the extreme US rejectionism of the preceding years, and is the framework of the 'peace process' the Administration was finally able to impose after the Gulf War.

All of this is doctrinally unacceptable, hence inexpressible if even thinkable in the highly disciplined intellectual culture. The facts are not in dispute, but they are subversive to power, so it is necessary to 'murder history', to borrow the apt term that is used for the regular practice of the commissars. In the media, one can hardly find an exception—though some of the events were reported as they occurred, including the January 1976 events that have completely disappeared from respectable history.

From the early 1980s, the story simply becomes a comic opera, as the elite media and the intellectual community strove with ever greater desperation 'not to see' the increasingly obvious attempts by the PLO to move towards a negotiated settlement—even suppressing the fact, extensively discussed in Israel, that the main purpose of Israel's devastating attack on Lebanon in 1982 was to undermine the threat of PLO efforts to negotiate a political settlement.[22]

'Victor's Peace': the Oslo Agreements

The DOP and subsequent agreements incorporate the extremist version of US–Israeli rejectionism. The final settlement is to be based solely on UN 242, with no recognition of Palestinian national rights. Out the window is the position of most of the world: that UN resolutions calling for Palestinian rights should also be considered alongside of UN 242, which recognises only the rights of existing states. As for the second major issue, withdrawal, the US and Israel have been clear and explicit in affirming that withdrawal will be partial, as they unilaterally determine.

The outcome is fully in accord with the invariant US position on rejectionism and withdrawal (the latter, since 1971). It also falls within the range of the various Israeli proposals over the years, from the Allon Plan of 1968 at the dovish extreme, to the Shamir–Peres–Baker Plan of 1989, and the plans proposed by the ultra-right Ariel Sharon and by the Labor Party in 1992, which scarcely differ. All of this too is well documented and regularly reported accurately in Israel, and in marginal dissident publications in the US, but few Americans could have even an inkling of the facts. By now, with Europe having abandoned the field, the same appears to be true there as well, though, without having attempted a careful review, I am reluctant to say. In this context, it is not very surprising that Norway agreed to be the intermediary for the Israel–Arafat agreement, which kept strictly to traditional US–Israel rejectionism.

As to why Israel decided to shift to the Oslo negotiating channel, excluding the US until it came time for the flourishes (and the money), it may be that the reason was fear that a Clinton-mediated agreement would have no credibility in the Arab world in the light of the Administration's drift towards the hawkish end of the spectrum. This departure from a long history of supporting the less extreme Labor form of rejectionism astonished Israeli commentators. The policies appear to have been crafted by Australian Middle East hawk Martin Indyk and the Washington Institute for Near East Policy that he founded after leaving Israel's Washington lobby AIPAC; the Institute has played an interesting role in US journalism, allowing journalists to present Israeli propaganda while 'merely reporting the facts' in the words of 'experts' supplied by the Institute.

An agreement, of course, has two partners, so it is necessary also to ask why Arafat agreed to what amounted to a complete capitulation to US–Israeli demands. The likely answer is that he saw this as the last chance to hold on to his position of power within the Palestinian movement. The PLO had come to be despised by much of the population of the territories for its corruption and absurd posturing, and, by 1993, opposition to Arafat and calls for democratisation of the organisation had reached dramatic levels, reported in the Israeli press and surely known to Israeli authorities, who saw the chance for the kind of agreement they had always wanted. As a virtual Israeli agent, Arafat could maintain his fiefdom, even with access to substantial funds. From what information is available, this appears to be what led him to Oslo.

The Sharon and Labor plans of 1992, now effectively established in the DOP, are based on the principle to which Israel has adhered steadily since its 1968 Allon Plan: Israel should control as much of the territories as it finds useful, including usable land and resources (particularly West Bank water supplies, on which Israel relies heavily). The modalities of control have been the subject of tactical debate over the years, the intended boundaries of 'Greater Israel' as well. On the matter of modalities, the major issue has been whether authority will be divided in territorial or 'functional' terms, the latter meaning in practice that Israel will continue to control the territory and the Palestinian authority will be responsible for Palestinians within it. As of mid-1995, Israel's position continues to be that there can be at most a 'functional' division of authority at least into 1999: there will be no 'fundamental transfer of sovereignty' to the Palestinians, Foreign Minister Shimon Peres announced over Israeli radio, and most West Bank land will remain under Israeli army control during this period.[23] As for boundaries, current programs indicate an intention to include within 'Greater Israel' the Jordan Valley, about one-third of the Gaza Strip, the area around the nebulous and rapidly expanding entity of 'Greater Jerusalem', which reaches by now almost as far east as Jericho, and whatever else Israel chooses to incorporate, with the blessing (and financing) of its superpower patron. The 'Greater Jerusalem' expansion effectively splits the West Bank into 'cantons' in accord with the Sharon Plan; a separate access corridor to Jordan settled by Israelis cantonises the region further.

When the DOP was announced, knowledgeable observers recognised that it did not offer 'even a hint of a solution to the basic problems which exist between Israel and the Palestinians', either in the short run or down the road (Israeli journalist Danny Rubinstein). Its operative meaning became still more clear after the May 1994 Cairo Agreement, which ensured that the territories administered by Arafat would remain 'squarely within Israel's economic fold', as the *Wall Street Journal* observed, and that the military administration would remain intact in all but name. The significance of the agreement was understood at once in Israel. Meron Benvenisti, former Deputy Mayor of Jerusalem and head of the West Bank Data Base Project, and one of the most astute observers in the Israeli mainstream for many years, commented that the Cairo Agreement, 'much as it is difficult to trust one's own eyes when reading it, . . . grants the Military Administration the exclusive authority in "legislation, adjudication, policy execution"', and 'responsibility for the exercise of these powers in conformity with international law', which the US and Israel interpret as they please. 'The entire intricate system of military ordinances . . . will retain its force, apart from "such legislative regulatory and other powers Israel may expressly grant"' the Palestinians. Israeli judges retain 'veto powers over any Palestinian legislation "that might jeopardize major Israeli interests"', which have 'overriding power', and are interpreted as the US and Israel choose. Though subject to Israel's decisions on all matters of any significance, Palestinian authorities are granted one domain as their own: they have 'exclusive responsibility for anything done or not done', meaning that they agree to take upon themselves the debilitating costs of the 28-year occupation, from which Israel profited enormously, and to assume a continuing responsibility for Israel's security. This 'agreement of surrender', Benvenisti observes, puts into effect the extremist 1981 proposals of Ariel Sharon, rejected then by Egypt.

After another Israel–Arafat agreement a year later, Benvenisti commented that 'Arafat once again bowed his head before the infinitely stronger opponent'. He reviewed the terms of the agreement, which left over half the West Bank under 'absolute Israeli control' and the status of another 40 per cent delayed for several years, during which time Israel can continue to use US aid to 'create facts' in the routine manner. The agreement, Benvenisti notes, rescinds the provision of the DOP 'that the West Bank will be considered "one territorial unit, whose integrity will be preserved during the interim stage"'. Little will change from the occupation period, he predicts, except that 'Israeli control will become less direct: instead of running affairs up front, Israeli "liaison officers" will run them via the clerks of the Palestinian Authority'. Like Britain during its day in the sun, Israel will continue to rule behind 'constitutional fictions'. No innovation of course; that is the traditional pattern of the European conquest of most of the world.[24]

The situation is even worse in Gaza, where the Israeli Security Services (Shabak) remain 'an invisible but violent force whose shadowy presence is always felt, wielding a fateful power over Gazans' lives', *Ha'aretz* correspondent Amira Hass reports, adding that Israeli authorities continue to control the economy as well. Since 1991, Graham Usher elaborates, Israel has redirected Gaza's traditional fruit and vegetable production to ornamentals and flowers by various punitive measures, including reduction of arable citrus land by almost a third through confiscations. The goal is only in part to remove valuable territory from eventual Arab control. Israel also intends 'to decouple Gaza's trade with other economies, the better to lock it into Israel's own'. Export from these single-crop sectors is in the hands of Israeli contractors, and very low labour costs in the demoralised Gaza Strip allow Israeli entrepreneurs to maintain their European markets at substantial profit.

By summer 1995, 95 per cent of the population of the Gaza population was 'imprisoned within the region' by Israeli force, the Israeli human rights group Tsevet 'aza reports, with the 'economy strangled' and security forces controlling trade, export, and communications, often seeking to 'produce harsher conditions for the Palestinians'. Under these conditions, few are willing to face the hazards of investment, at least outside the industrial parks set up by Israeli manufacturers to 'exploit the cheap labor of Palestinians'. They report further that Israel continues to refuse to allow Palestinian investors to open small productive facilities, and that fishermen are kept to six kilometres from the coast, where there are no fish during the summer months. The limited water supplies in this very arid region are used for intensive Israeli agriculture, even artificial lakes at elegant resorts, visitors report. Meanwhile water supplies to Palestinians in Gaza have been cut in half since the Oslo Accords, UN human rights investigator Rene Felber wrote in a harshly critical report on prison conditions and water policy. He resigned shortly after, commenting that it is pointless to issue reports that go into the wastebasket.[25]

A year after the DOP, Israel's control of West Bank land reached about 75 per cent, up from 65 per cent when the accords were signed. Establishment and 'thickening' of settlements also continued at a rapid pace, along with the construction of 'bypass roads' that integrate the Jewish settlements into Israel proper, leaving Arab villages cut off from one another and from the urban centres that Israel prefers to relinquish to Palestinian administration. The highway projects are immense, with costs expected to be about US$400 million, according to the Secretary-General of the governing Labor Party. The purpose is to provide settlers with what one calls 'a road where I don't have to see Arabs all around me'. Details are secret, but 'outlines are emerging from settlers' maps', correspondent Barton Gellman reports, including the usual method of quietly putting 'the force of Israeli law' behind projects 'begun illegally by the settlers'. Benvenisti describes the roads as 'political facts that have long-term consequences' within the plan to 'cut the Arab areas into boxes, making *laagers* (encircled camps) out of the West Bank', part of 'a victor's peace, a diktat'.

Government funding for settlements in the territories increased by 70 per cent in the year following the DOP (1994), from a level that was already high by earlier standards. Support for settlers is so lavish that their living standards are among the highest in the country. Newspaper ads 'call on Jews of Tel Aviv and its vicinity to settle in Ma'aleh Ephraim' overlooking the Jordan Valley and linked by bypass roads to Jerusalem, part of the development that virtually splits the West Bank in two. The ads offer 'swimming pools, enormous lawns, and a real countryside atmosphere that will impart a high quality to your life', with government grants of over US$20 000 per family as well as low mortgages, tax exemptions, and other inducements. In June 1995, the mayor of nearby Ma'aleh Adumim announced the building of

6000 new housing units that should more than double the city's population to 50 000 within the next few years, along with shopping malls, a new city hall, and other construction. The Labor Party journal *Davar* reports that the Rabin government has kept the priorities of the ultra-right Shamir government it replaced; while pretending to freeze settlements, Labor 'has helped them financially even more than the Shamir government had ever done', enlarging settlements 'everywhere in the West Bank, even in the most provocative spots', including settlements of the (often American) followers of the (American) Rabbi Kahane, who was barred from Israel's political system because of his advocacy of Hitler's Nuremberg laws and other mimicry of the Nazis.

As a result of such measures, in the year following the DOP the Jewish population in the West Bank increased by 10 per cent, in Gaza by 20 per cent, the Israeli press reports, a process that continues and may be accelerating. General (ret.) Shlomo Gazit, former head of Military Intelligence and West Bank Administrator, observes that programs announced by the Labor Party are intended to double the Jewish population of the West Bank within the five-year 'interim period' following the Oslo Accords. The Foundation for Middle East Peace in Washington, which publishes regular updates, concludes that 'the Rabin government's construction plans for West Bank and Jerusalem settlements rival and in some respects surpass the settlement construction efforts of the Shamir government during 1989–92', with 'a marked increase' planned for the coming years; the Shamir government had previously been the most extremist in opposing Palestinian rights and encouraging Israeli takeover of the territories.

A newly announced plan 'shatters any remnant of the Palestinians' illusion that the Oslo Accord will bring about either an Israeli withdrawal from significant territories in the West Bank, or that East Jerusalem can ever serve as a Palestinian capital', veteran West Bank correspondent Danny Rubinstein commented in

January 1995. Subsequent events only reinforced the conclusion. In June, Ma'ale Yisrael was established as the 145th settlement in the West Bank, against the orders of the government but with its acquiescence. Settlers use heavy equipment and explosives to build access roads near densely settled and heavily patrolled sectors of the West Bank, but the government knows nothing about it, spokespersons tell the press. Arabs are treated rather differently if they commit such crimes as seeking to expand a dwelling on land they own (permits rarely being granted).[26]

All of this is apart from what has been taking place in East Jerusalem and its environs, conquered in the 1967 war. 'Since the annexation of East Jerusalem in 1967', the Israeli human rights group B'Tselem reports, 'the Israeli government has adopted a policy of systematic and deliberate discrimination against the Palestinian municipal population in all matters pertaining to expropriation of land, planning, and building', including 'deliberate settlement of Jews in East Jerusalem [which] is illegal according to international law', but acceptable to the US, the ultimate authority by virtue of its power. 'Extensive building and enormous investment' on the part of the government 'encourages Jews to settle' in formerly Arab East Jerusalem, while the authorities 'choke development and building for the Palestinian population', as elsewhere in the territories and in Israel itself. Most of the expropriated land was privately owned by Arabs, B'Tselem reports: 85 per cent, according to Israel's Absorption Minister Yair Tzaban. 'Some 38 500 housing units were built on this land for the Jewish population, but not one housing unit for Palestinians.' Furthermore, 'building has been barred on most of the area that remains in Palestinian hands'. 'Only 14 per cent of all the land in East Jerusalem is zoned for the development of Palestinian neighborhoods.' 'Green zones' are established as 'a cynical means in the service of the attempt to deprive the Palestinians of the right to build on their land and to preserve these zones as sites for future construction for the benefit of the Jewish population'; implementation of such plans is regularly reported.

The policies were designed by Mayor Teddy Kollek, who has been much admired in the West as an outstanding democrat and humanitarian. Their purpose, Kollek's adviser on Arab affairs Amir Cheshin comments, was 'placing difficulties in the way of planning in the Arab sector'. 'I don't want to give [the Arabs] a feeling of equality', Kollek explained, though it would be worthwhile to do so 'here and there, where it doesn't cost us so much'; otherwise 'we will suffer'. Kollek's planning commission also advised development for Arabs if it would have 'a "picture window" effect', which 'will be seen by a large number of people (residents, tourists, etc.)'. Kollek informed the Israeli media in 1990 that, for the Arabs, he had 'nurtured nothing and built nothing', apart from a sewage system—which, he hastened to assure his listeners, was not intended 'for their good, for their welfare', 'they' being the Arabs of Jerusalem. Rather, 'there were some cases of cholera [in Arab sectors], and the Jews were afraid that they would catch it, so we installed sewage and a water system against cholera'. Under Kollek's successor, Likud Mayor Ehud Olmert, treatment of Arabs has become considerably harsher, according to local reports.[27]

Along with East Jerusalem, Jewish settlements, military facilities, and the highway network of bypass roads, Israel will continue to control West Bank water resources and 'unsettled state lands, which amount to about half of the territory of the West Bank', Aluf Ben reports; total state lands amount to perhaps 70 per cent of the West Bank, according to Israeli press reports. State lands are reserved for the use of Jews; West Bank Arabs are confined to the separated cantons allotted to them. Such restrictions also hold for 92 per cent of the land within Israel, implemented in various ways to bar Israeli Arab citizens not only from almost all land of their country but also from development funds.

Contributions by Americans to realise these objectives are tax-
deductible as charitable donations, spreading the costs among
taxpayers generally; one imagines that government programs to
bar Jews from 92 per cent of New York and from normal services
might be treated a bit differently. As usual, the facts are kept
from those who pay the bills.[28]

Israel has always preferred to deal with Jordan—the 'Palestinian state' of the Shamir–Peres–Baker Plan—rather than the
Palestinians; the two states have always had a shared interest in
suppressing Palestinian nationalism, and cooperated to this end
during the 1948 war. Specifically, US–Israel plans favour arrangements for Jerusalem and the Jordan Valley with Jordan rather
than the Palestinian administration. With these ends in mind, a
small amount of land in the Jordan Valley was returned to Jordan
with great fanfare. We have to turn to the Israeli press to discover
that the Jewish National Fund (JNF) had used heavy equipment
a few weeks before to 'shave' the fertile topsoil and remove it to
Jewish settlements.[29]

Expropriation of Arab property for Jewish settlement
'pose[s] problems as far as the peace process is concerned', Clinton's UN Ambassador Madeleine Albright informed the Security
Council; but 'we do not believe that the Security Council is an
appropriate place to have a discussion about this action'—all
funded by the American taxpayer (including the JNF, officially
a charity), and discussed nowhere else either. 'In Washington-
speak, this translates that the US will veto any Jerusalem resolution that is "hostile" to Israel', correspondent Graham Usher
observes. That is the traditional practice; like the World Court
and other international institutions, the UN does what the US
wants, or it is dismissed; and Israeli expansion at the expense of
the Palestinians is traditional US policy, reaching new levels
under Clinton.[30]

Terror and Punishment

The DOP initially aroused much hope, even euphoria, among Palestinians. That is understandable after years of suffering and struggle culminating in the Intifada, suppressed with great cruelty. But it is never a good idea to be tempted by exalted rhetoric and desperate hope rather than attending to the facts of power, and, in this case, the literal wording of the documents designed by the victors. Inevitably the bleak realities have swept early enthusiasm aside. One consequence has been an upsurge of terror, which has modified the traditional pattern in which the victims were overwhelmingly Arab. Facts are hard to come by, since killing of Palestinians, or other atrocities and abuses directed against them, receive little attention, surely not the prominent coverage and passionate denunciation of 'mindless murder' (*New York Times*) when Israeli Jews are the victims. To select virtually at random, the *Times* editors, and others, expressed no 'revulsion and outrage', or even saw any need to report the facts, when Israel's military death squads established in 1989 were revived, killing seven people in the first week of 1995 alone, four in the village of Beit Liqya; another was saved by the courageous intervention of the Palestinian human rights activist Hanan Ashrawi, formerly on the PLO negotiating team. A rare notice in the US press reports that from the signing of the accords through the following year, 'some 187 Palestinians have died mainly at the hands of an increasingly strained Israeli Defense Force (IDF), which bears the burden of protecting Jewish settlers', along with 93 Israelis; by May 1995, the numbers had risen to 124 Israelis and 204 Palestinians, 'fewer than in previous years'. The Islamic fundamentalist group Hamas, regarded as the primary agency of anti-Jewish terror, has proposed negotiations to 'remove civilians from the circle of war and violence', the Israeli press reports, but Prime Minister Rabin rejected the offer on the grounds that 'Hamas is the enemy of peace, and the only way to deal with it is by a war of extermination'.[31]

Israeli atrocities in Lebanon also regularly pass without mention or comment in the US. More than 100 Lebanese were killed by the Israeli army or its Southern Lebanese Army mercenaries in the first half of 1995, the London *Economist* reports, along with six Israeli soldiers in Lebanon. Israeli forces use terror weapons, including anti-personnel shells that spray steel darts (sometimes delayed action shells to maximise terror), which killed two children in July 1995 and four others in the same town a few months earlier, and seven others in Nabatiye, where 'no foreign journalists turned up' to describe the atrocities, Robert Fisk reported from the scene. The occasional mention is usually in the context of a denunciation of Hizbollah terror against Israelis in retaliation.[32]

No matter who the victim, the reaction of the military authorities is the same: Punish the Palestinians. The most dramatic example was in Hebron after the massacre of 29 Palestinians in the Ibrahimi Mosque in February 1994 by Hebron settler Baruch Goldstein, an American immigrant, like much of the extreme fringe, neo-Nazi in character as Israeli commentators regularly observe. After the massacre, 'the Israeli occupation redoubled the oppression' of Palestinians, Ori Nir reported a year later. New security measures 'to protect the Jewish settlers from revenge' became permanent, with main roads closed and the market that was a regional centre and the basis for Hebron's economy destroyed. The market was closed because it is near the settlement of 50 Jewish families in this city of 120 000 Palestinians, and 'settlers used to turn their stalls upside down in riots, until the Israeli military authorities got tired of being in the middle of the turmoil and simply closed the market', correspondent Gideon Levy reports: 'Now the shops are locked and the entry into the street is permitted for Jews only', including those who 'go to the market with vicious dogs to intimidate the Palestinians', throw stones at them as they march through Palestinian areas with 'weapons ready for action' in the weekly Saturday night riots, and otherwise make clear who the rulers are, with the tolerance of the security forces.

Buses serving Arabs are barred from the city, Nir continues; those used by the tiny minority of Jewish settlers move freely. For Arabs, the 'insane reality' enforced by the military 'subordinates their lives to the settlers' interests'. Life for them has become 'a nightmare' with the destruction of the economy and the constant abuse by settlers who chain dogs to bar passage to Arabs, paint Stars of David on Arab houses and slogans saying 'Arabs out', 'Death to the Arabs', 'Long live Baruch Goldstein', and engage in arbitrary humiliation or worse while the security forces look the other way. They show up, correspondent Ran Kislev adds, but only when Arabs 'try to defend their property' in Hebron or the surrounding villages. The standard consequences are 'that a number of Arabs are wounded and more are imprisoned'.

Perhaps the most severe punishment is the curfews that regularly follow any turbulence, no matter who is responsible. After the Goldstein massacre at the Mosque (the Patriarchs' Cave), confinement of Arabs under virtual (often actual) house arrest for long periods became routine, sometimes in a manner that reveals the grim reality more graphically than the regular atrocities. During the Passover holidays in 1995, for example, a four-day round-the-clock curfew was imposed on the 120000 Palestinians of Hebron so that the few settlers and the 35000 Jewish visitors brought to Hebron in chartered buses could have picnics and travel around the city freely dancing in the streets with public prayers to bring down 'the government of the Left', laying the cornerstone for a new residential building, and indulging in other pleasures under the protective gaze of extra military forces. 'The celebration was brought to a close', Yacov Ben Efrat reports, 'by settlers rampaging through the Old City, destroying property, and smashing car windows . . . in a city magically cleansed . . . of Palestinians', using the opportunity 'to insult the Palestinians imprisoned in their houses and to throw stones at them if they dared to peek out of the windows at the Jews celebrating in their city' (Israel Shahak). 'Children, parents and old people are effectively jailed for days in their homes, which in most cases, are seriously overcrowded', Levy reports, able to turn on their TV sets to 'watch a female settler saying happily, "There is a curfew, thank God"', and to hear the 'merry dances of settlers' and 'festive processions', some to 'the Patriarchs' Cave open only to Jews'. Meanwhile 'commerce, careers, studies, the family, love—all are immediately disrupted', and 'the medical system was paralyzed' so that 'many sick persons in Hebron were unable to reach hospitals during the curfew and women giving birth could not arrive in time at the clinics'.[33]

The extended curfews impose great suffering, sometimes literal starvation, on a population that has been made dependent for survival on menial labour in Israel, under terrible conditions that have been condemned for years in the Israeli press, with graphic descriptions. The only comparative scholarly study concludes that 'the situation of noncitizen Arabs in Israel is worse relative to that of nonnationals in other countries'—migrant workers in the United States, 'guestworkers' in Europe, etc. But those were the good old days. Now Palestinians are being replaced by workers brought in from Thailand, the Philippines, Romania, and other countries where people live in misery. The Labor Ministry reported over 70 000 registered foreign workers by March 1995, while only 18 000 entry permits were granted to Palestinians from the territories, down from 70 000 a year earlier. Investigative reporters report that, along with tens of thousands of illegal migrants, they suffer 'inhuman working hours and withholding of pay on various pretexts', with 'men sold as slaves from one employer to another' and 'women enduring severe sexual harassment and afraid to say a word', knowing that the least protest can lead to expulsion.

These 'silent and hard-working people in many cases live in subhuman conditions', the editor of *Ha'aretz* writes, 'and are often subjected to the oppression of their employers'. They are kept isolated and without rights, family lives, or security. Their condition 'would be the closest thing in our time to slavery' if it were not 'an agreed-upon deal'—thanks to the conditions of 'really existing capitalism' in much of the world. The 'Thai solution' portends further disaster for the Palestinians, he warns, with dangerous consequences for Israel as well.

The curfews and closures 'devastated the Palestinian economy and destroyed 100 000 families in Gaza alone', Nadav Ha'etzni reports. The 'trauma' can only be compared with the mass dispossession and expulsion of Palestinians in 1948. As imported semi-slave labour bars the Palestinian work force from the only employment that had been allowed them, 'the Oslo Accords have created a truly new Middle East', he writes.[34]

Development Programs and Plans

Under Israeli occupation, meaningful development in the territories was banned. An official order of the Israeli Ministry of Defense declared that 'no permits will be given for expanding agriculture and industry which may compete with the State of Israel'. The device is familiar from American practice, and Western imperialism generally, which commonly allowed service regions 'complementary' but not 'competitive development'—one reason why Latin America has been such a disaster area, as well as India, Egypt, and other regions under Western control.

Though Israel's barring of development in the territories was well known, its extent came as something of a surprise even to the most knowledgeable observers when they had an opportunity to visit Jordan after the peace agreements. The comparison is particularly apt, Danny Rubinstein observes, since the Palestinian populations are about as numerous on both sides of the Jor-

dan, and the West Bank was somewhat more developed before
the Israeli takeover in 1967. Having covered the territories with
distinction for years, Rubinstein was well aware that the Israeli
administration 'had purposely worsened the conditions under
which Palestinians in the territories had to live'. Nonetheless, he
was shocked and saddened to discover the startling truth.

'Despite Jordan's unstable economy and its being part of the
Third World', he found, 'its rate of development is much higher
than that of the West Bank, not to mention Gaza', administered
by a very rich society which benefits from unparalleled foreign
aid. While Israel has built roads only for the Jewish settlers, 'in
Jordan people drive on new, multiple-lane highways, well-
equipped with bridges and intersections'. Electricity is available
everywhere, unlike the West Bank, where the great majority of
Arab villages have only local generators that operate irregularly.
The same goes for the water system. In arid Jordan, several large
water projects . . . have turned the eastern bank of the Jordan
valley into a dense and blooming agricultural area', while on the
West Bank water supplies have been directed to the use of settlers and Israel itself—about 5/6 of West Bank water, according
to Israeli specialists. Many villages have no running water at all,
and even such cities as Hebron and Ramallah lack running water
for many hours a day in the summer.

Factories, commerce, hotels, and universities have been developed in impoverished Jordan, at quite high levels. Virtually
nothing similar has been allowed on the West Bank, apart from
'two small hotels in Bethlehem'. 'All universities in the territories
were built solely with private funding and donations from foreign
states, without a penny from Israel', apart from the Islamic University in Hebron, originally supported by Israel as part of its encouragement of Islamic fundamentalism to undermine the
secular PLO, now a Hamas centre. Health services in the West
Bank are 'extremely backward' in comparison with Jordan. 'Two

large buildings in East Jerusalem, intended for hospitals and clinics to serve the residents of the West Bank, which the Jordanians were constructing in 1967, were turned into police buildings by the Israeli government', which also refused permits for factories in Nablus and Hebron under pressure from Israeli manufacturers who wanted a captive market without competition. 'The result is that the backward and poor Jordanian kingdom did much more for the Palestinians who lived in it than Israel', showing 'in an even more glaring form how badly the Israeli occupation had treated them'.[35]

As in the Gaza Strip, 'Nothing symbolises the inequality of water consumption more than the fresh green lawns, irrigated flower beds, blooming gardens and swimming pools of Jewish settlements in the West Bank', two *Financial Times* correspondents observe, while nearby Palestinian villages are denied the right to drill wells and have running water one day every few weeks, polluted by sewage, so that men have to drive to towns to fill up containers with water or to hire contractors to deliver it at fifteen times the cost. Israel claims the right to West Bank water—which provides some 30 per cent of Israeli water usage and half of its water for agriculture—by 'historic use' since the 1967 occupation. It is hard to imagine that it will relinquish this valuable resource to any Palestinian authority, a fact that alone renders discussion of autonomy virtually meaningless.[36]

The huge literature of apologetics tells a different story, lauding the 'benign' occupation that has brought such benefits to the ungrateful Palestinians while 'making the desert bloom'. It also makes much of the great increase in educational opportunities offered to the Palestinian population under Israeli rule—ignoring, however, what Rubinstein reports, as well as some other things. In internal discussion, government officials recommended allowing such educational opportunities as part of the overall plan to 'transfer' Palestinians elsewhere, to the extent pos-

sible. The hope was that 'many of the college graduates may em-
igrate from the region' since there will be no professional
opportunities for them under Israeli rule (Michael Shashar,
spokesman of the military government in the early years of the
occupation). For the Palestinians who remain, there were to be
no options apart from a marginal existence in isolated villages or
menial labour under atrocious conditions in Israel.[37]

The basic contours of the 'peace process' were captured realistically by Tel Aviv University Professor Tanya Reinhart, who
pointed out that it is an error to compare the arrangements currently being imposed with the *end* of Apartheid in South Africa;
rather, they should be compared with the *institution* of that mon-
strous system, with its 'home rule' provisions for new 'independent states', as they were viewed by South African racists and
their loyal friends.[38] The US is pouring in money that is effectively
diverted to land confiscation, construction and development in
the occupied territories, funding security forces, and so on. The
effect will be that the Palestinians will end up as a subject population, lacking rights, or will become desperate enough to try
to leave. Jordan may be eyed as a potential dumping ground,
which it will resist, but perhaps ineffectively as it becomes ab-
sorbed more fully as a dependent region within the far more rich
and powerful Israeli economy.

Israel and Arafat's wing of the PLO can be expected to be
united in firm opposition to democracy in the Palestinian-admin-
istered areas. One can only admire Rabin and Peres for their
forthrightness in announcing that 'if Hamas wins the elections
to the Autonomy council—the agreement is void'. Arafat will naturally applaud, just as he rescinded the November 1994 elections
to the Fatah Council in the Ramallah region, cancelling further
elections, after his supporters were defeated. It is also hardly to
be expected that Israel will end its illegal occupation of southern
Lebanon (in defiance of a March 1978 Security Council demand

that it withdraw immediately and unconditionally) or its terror operations there and elsewhere in Lebanon at will, not only the atrocities that occasionally are noticed, but even the minor cases not reported in the US: for example, the ban on fishing Israel has imposed south of Tyre for almost 20 years; or the kidnapping of a southern Lebanese man announced by the army in July 1994, taken to Israel on suspicion of having participated in operations against the Israeli occupiers and their murderous client army—operations that are legitimate resistance, not terror, according to the major UN resolution on terrorism, passed in December 1986 by a vote of 153–2 with Honduras alone abstaining, but effectively vetoed, since the US voted against it (with Israel); hence unreported, and banned from history.[39]

'Human Dust and the Waste of Society'

The DOP and its aftermath take a long step towards the goals of rational expansionists and rejectionists in the US and Israel. If the Palestinian issue can indeed be swept under the rug, the relations among the major countries can perhaps become public and strengthened, with Israel becoming a technological, industrial, and financial centre while maintaining its military predominance, backed by US power, and continuing to survive on a US dole, incomparable in world affairs. Officially, the US$3 billion current annual grant amounts to over 25 per cent of total US aid. When various other devices are considered, the actual sum is more than twice that, Middle East analyst Donald Neff estimates (loan guarantees, grants, deferred payments, etc.; tax-deductible contributions, also unique, are another public subsidy). Aid to Israel is also without conditions or oversight, unlike all other programs, including the more than US$2 billion regularly given to Egypt to keep it in line with US–Israeli interests.

In contrast, US$100 million goes to Palestinians, all through Arafat's Palestinian National Authority (PNA), mostly for secu-

rity forces. The Clinton Administration cut by US$17 million the
US contribution to UNRWA, the largest single employer in the
Gaza Strip and responsible for 40 per cent of its health and education services. Washington may be planning to terminate
UNRWA, which 'Israel has historically loathed', correspondent
Graham Usher observes, leaving the Palestinians as a 'problem'
to be solved by Israel and the PNA, which is considered a virtual
agency of the Israeli government. Breaking with earlier policies,
the Clinton Administration voted against all General Assembly Resolutions pertaining to Palestinian refugees in 1993 and
1994, on the grounds that they 'prejudge the outcome of the ongoing peace process and should be solved by direct negotiations',
now safely in the hands of the US and its clients. As a step towards dismantling UNRWA, its headquarters are to be moved
to Gaza. That should effectively terminate international support
for the 1.8 million Palestinian refugees in Jordan, Lebanon, and
Syria. The next step will be to defund UNRWA and hand it over
to the PNA, UN sources report.[40]

The funds that go to Israel and Egypt, and the tiny trickle to
the Palestinians, are the component of US aid most strongly opposed by the general public.[41] But policy is sharply divorced from
opinion on a wide range of issues, not just this one.

It might be noted that US payments to Israel are not only
extraordinary in scale, but also illegal. Human Rights Watch
(HRW) recently discussed the matter, pointing out once again
that US law expressly forbids military or economic aid to any
government that engages in systematic torture. And as its extensive report again shows, Israel does 'engage in a systematic pattern of ill-treatment and torture', according to internationally
accepted standards, and on quite a remarkable scale. HRW estimates that 'the number of Palestinians tortured or severely
treated while under interrogation during the intifada [from December 1987] is in the tens of thousands', out of an adult and

adolescent male population of less than 3/4 of a million, only a fraction eventually charged (and sentenced, usually on 'confessions'). Israel is apparently the only industrial democracy in which torture is legally authorised, by recommendation of the official Landau Commission, which concluded that the security services had been using torture for sixteen years but that only certain measures of coercion should henceforth be permitted (spelled out in a classified section); the practices that have been observed and are authorised are considered torture by human rights monitors.[42] Human Rights Watch gives details, as has the Israeli human rights organisation B'Tselem, and other inquiries for 20 years.

It is, however, unfair to single out Israel, since most US aid is illegal for the same reason; for example, half of US military aid to Latin America goes to Colombia, which doesn't only torture but also slaughters on an impressive scale, leading the hemisphere in human rights abuses.

The extreme rejectionist assumptions of the rulers are revealed at every turn. One illustration is the reaction to Arafat's call for a 'Jihad' for Jerusalem. That elicited virtual hysteria in the United States, proving that the devious terrorist cannot be trusted. Meanwhile Israel announced that *its* Jihad was completed: Jerusalem would remain the eternal and undivided capital of Israel, with no Palestinian institutions (let alone rights). That declaration passed without comment in the United States. The (null) reaction to Israel's decision to hand administration of the Holy Places to its Jordanian ally reflected the same rejectionist stance, as does the lack of concern over the expanding borders of the ambiguous area of Jerusalem, and the rapid pace of new construction and settlement there, indirectly financed by the unwitting US taxpayer.

Still another step towards realising US–Israeli rejectionism is the termination of the theoretical right of return or compensation for Palestinian refugees. That was a crucial element of the Universal Declaration of Human Rights (UD): its Article 13 states that 'Everyone has the right to leave any country including his own, *and to return to his country*' (my emphasis). The day after the UD was adopted by the General Assembly it also unanimously adopted Resolution 194, applying Article 13 to the case of the Palestinians. The UD is recognised in US courts and elsewhere as 'customary international law', and as the 'authoritative definition' of human rights standards. Article 13 is surely its most famous provision, invoked annually for many years on Human Rights Day, December 10, with demonstrations and angry appeals to the Soviet Union to allow Russian Jews to leave, their sacred right under Article 13. Always concealed was the fact that those who invoked Article 13 with most passion were its most passionate opponents. The trick was easily accomplished: it was only necessary to suppress the italicised phrase, its meaning spelled out by UN 194. That hypocrisy, at least, is behind us. The first part of Article 13 has lost its relevance, and the Clinton Administration rescinded US support for its second part in December 1993, in its first celebration of Human Rights day, breaking with the 45-year official policy by voting against UN 194, alone as usual (along with Israel).

The victory for US–Israeli rejectionist extremism is an extraordinary accomplishment. It takes another long step towards realising the aspirations of the Zionist leadership from the earliest days, when the Founding Father of modern Zionism, Chaim Weizmann, informed Lord Balfour that 'the issue known as the Arab problem in Palestine will be of merely local character and, in effect, anyone cognizant of the situation does not consider it a highly significant factor'. The current settlement does not depart far from the basic guidelines outlined by former President Haim Herzog in 1972, when he declared that he does 'not deny the Palestinians any place or stand or opinion on every matter',

although 'certainly I am not prepared to consider them as partners in any respect in a land that has been consecrated in the
hands of our nation for thousands of years. For the Jews of this
land there cannot be any partner'. As I mentioned, it falls well
within the range of the various Israeli proposals, from left to far
right, since 1968.

True, the results still fall short of the attitudes Weizmann had
expressed when he remarked, 70 years ago, that the British had
informed him that in Palestine 'there are a few hundred thousand
Negroes, but that is a matter of no significance'. But the outcome
does demonstrate the far-sightedness of Israeli government specialists in 1948, who foresaw that the Palestinian refugees would
either assimilate elsewhere or 'would be crushed': 'some of them
would die and most of them would turn into human dust and the
waste of society, and join the most impoverished classes in the
Arab countries'. And of Moshe Dayan—perhaps the most sympathetic to the Palestinians among the leadership—when, in the
heyday of Labor Party exuberance before the 1973 war, he declared that Israeli control over the territories is 'permanent' and
advised that Israel tell the Palestinians 'that we have no solution,
that you shall continue to live like dogs, and whoever wants to
can leave—and we will see where this process leads . . .'.

Of course, Israel could never have achieved such goals on its
own, and probably would never have dared to pursue them. It
could do so only by becoming a client of the world ruler. The belief
that US power is guided by some kind of 'moral commitment' to
Israel is too ludicrous to merit comment, as Israel will quickly discover if it makes the mistake of crossing the master. As long as the
strategic relationship is maintained, and US domination is maintained without serious challenge internal to the United States itself, questions of justice and human rights can be safely filed away.

Recall the official recognition that the Pentagon budget must
remain high, with intervention forces aimed primarily at the Mid-

dle East, where 'threats to our interests could not be laid at the Kremlin's door'. With that insight into real world, there is good reason to accept the judgment of Shlomo Gazit that, after the Cold War,

> Israel's main task has not changed at all, and it remains of crucial importance. Its location at the center of the Arab Muslim Middle East predestines Israel to be a devoted guardian of stability in all the countries surrounding it. Its [role] is to protect the existing regimes: to prevent or halt the processes of radicalization and to block the expansion of fundamentalist religious zealotry.

To comprehend his words, it is only necessary to carry out the usual translation from Newspeak to ordinary language. The term 'stability' means US control, 'radicalization' means unacceptable forms of independence, and 'fundamentalist religious zealotry' is a special case of the crime of independence. It is immaterial whether the criminals favour secular nationalism, democratic socialism, fascism, liberation theology or 'fundamentalist religious zealotry'. Surely Israel's task is not to undermine the world's most extreme Islamic fundamentalist regime, Saudi Arabia—at least not right now—just as Israel was not called upon to 'block' the extremist Islamic fundamentalist forces of Gulbuddin Hekmatyar, the US favourite of the 1980s who has been tearing the remnants of Afghanistan to shreds after the Soviet withdrawal while expanding his narcotrafficking; or the Islamic fundamentalist groups that Israel was nurturing in the occupied territories a few years ago, to undermine the secular PLO. Nor, for that matter, is Israel expected to 'contain' the United States, one of the more extreme religious fundamentalist cultures in the world.

If Israel reacts intelligently to what *New York Times* Middle East specialist Thomas Friedman called Arafat's 'white flag' of surrender, it will drop the restrictions it has imposed to prevent any development in the territories. The rational stance would be to encourage an inflow of foreign funds, which can be used to establish a service sector for Israeli industry and to benefit Israeli investors and their Palestinian and foreign partners. It would make sense for Israel to move assembly plants a few miles away, where there is no need to be concerned about such matters as labour rights, pollution, and the presence of unwanted Arabs (or even Thai and Romanian workers) within Jewish settled areas. Plants in and near Gaza, and in West Bank cantons, can provide cheap and easily exploitable labour, yielding profits for investors and helping to control the population. Wealthy sectors in Israel should gain considerably from an intelligent exploitation of the territories on the model that Washington maintains in its own neighbourhood.

As for security, it would make sense to leave it mostly in the hands of local client forces—the model followed by the British in India, the US in the Caribbean–Central America region, and rational powers generally. There are many advantages, one of them pointed out by the latest Nobel Peace Prize winner shortly after the DOP was announced. Speaking to the political council of the Labor Party, Prime Minister Rabin explained that Palestinian forces should be able to 'deal with Gaza without problems caused by appeals to the High Court of Justice, without problems made by B'Tselem, and without problems from all sorts of bleeding hearts and mothers and fathers'. That's about right, though outside muscle may be needed, too, as in the traditional imperial pattern.

With good planning, things ought to develop along lines outlined by Asher Davidi in the Labor Party press in February 1993, a few months before the Israel–Arafat agreement in Oslo. He described the 'complete agreement between representatives of the various sectors (banking, industry and large-scale commerce) and the government that the economic dependence of the "Palestinian entity" must be preserved', but with 'a transition from colonialism to neo-colonialism', undertaken jointly with a wealthy fringe of Palestinian investors and subcontractors, as in the standard Third World model.

It is not clear what the settlement might mean for Israeli society internally. One leading Israeli specialist, Sami Smooha, predicts that a peace settlement would 'significantly increase inequality', harming the second-class Jewish citizens of Eastern origin, though improving the status of the third-class Palestinian citizens. Perhaps, though inequality may increase for other reasons. Israel remains highly dependent on American grants and aid, hence more likely than most to follow the US model, abandoning its traditional social contract. As the economy is 'liberalized', the unusually high inequality within Israel can be expected to increase, as it mimics the internal order of the master who keeps it going in return for services rendered.[43]

After the 1967 war, it seemed to me that the most wise and humane course for the victors would have been to revive traditional Zionist ideas about federation of Jewish- and Arab-administered areas, perhaps leading to eventual binationalist integration as links between the communities develop, crossing national lines. That option became even more appropriate, in my opinion, after Kissinger's rejection of the withdrawal provisions of UN 242, still more so after the US quickly and forcefully joined Israel in rejecting the concept of two states when it reached the international agenda in the mid-1970s, and increasingly in the years that followed.[44] With the DOP, it should have been obvious that the two-state option had lost whatever (in my view limited) prospects it had, and that has become still more clear since. Among Israelis, Palestinians, and sympathetic outsiders concerned with peace and justice, a shift towards concern for questions of human rights and democracy rather than increasingly unrealistic political illusions is overdue, and, with it, a return to alternatives that have long been available, and still are.

These might have prevented the 1973 war, which was a close call for Israel, the terrible invasion of Lebanon and its aftermath, and much other destruction and suffering, which is by no means at an end.

Throughout the whole affair, we observe clearly the leading principles of world order: world affairs are governed by the Rule of Force, while intellectuals are counted upon to disguise realities to serve the needs of power. It takes some discipline to miss the point. The arrangements now unfolding are degrading and shameful, but no more so than the rather similar pattern being instituted throughout much of the world as the operative ideals—not those of the fairy tales—have overcome many popular barriers to their realisation. Some have progressed more than others in 'turning into human dust and the waste of society', but that is the direction in which much of the world is going, and will go, if the masters are permitted to design a world order in which 'What We Say Goes'.

7

The Great Powers
and Human Rights:
the Case of East Timor

Forbidden Territory

I've been asked to speak about the great powers and human rights. That's actually a very brief talk.

There are two versions of the story. The official one is familiar: upholding human rights is our highest goal, even 'the Soul of our foreign policy', as President Carter put it. And if we are at all at fault, it is in maintaining this noble standard too rigorously to the detriment of the famous 'national interest'.

A second version is given by the events of history and the internal record of planning. It was outlined with admirable frankness in an important state paper of 1948 (PPS 23) written by one of the architects of the New World Order of the day, the head of the State Department Policy Planning Staff, the respected statesman and scholar George Kennan. In the course of assigning each region of the world its proper role within the overarching framework of American power, he observed that the basic policy goal is to maintain the 'position of disparity' that separates our enormous wealth from the poverty of others; and to achieve that goal

'We should cease to talk about vague and . . . unreal objectives such as human rights, the raising of the living standards, and democratization', recognising that we must 'deal in straight power concepts', not 'hampered by idealistic slogans' about 'altruism and world-benefaction'.

Clearer minds have never veered far from such precepts, in internal discussion or, more importantly, in action.

The thinking of statesmen is not uniform, of course, and we should not overlook the variations within the spectrum. Thus Kennan was removed from his position shortly after because he was considered too soft and moralistic for this tough world, replaced by the more realistic Paul Nitze, who outlined the framework of world order a few months before the outbreak of the Korean War in another important state paper (NSC 68, April 1950).

There are two forces in the world, NSC 68 explained: the 'slave state' and the defender of 'civilization itself'. They are polar opposites, by their very nature.

The 'fundamental design' of the 'inescapably militant . . . slave state' is 'the complete subversion or forcible destruction of the machinery of government and structure of society' everywhere, so that it will gain 'absolute authority over the rest of the world' and 'total power over all men'. Since this 'implacable purpose' and 'compulsion' is an essential property of the slave state, evidence is irrelevant (so none is adduced in this lengthy and critically important document), and the paths of diplomacy are excluded by definition, except as a mask to placate public opinion. No accommodation is conceivable, so the adversary must be destroyed—by virtue of its essential nature, not ours.

The absolute evil of the slave state is highlighted still more starkly when contrasted with the absolute perfection of the defender of civilisation, which is 'founded upon the dignity and worth of the individual' and marked by 'marvelous diversity', 'deep tolerance', 'lawfulness', a commitment 'to create and maintain an environment in which every individual has the opportunity to realize his creative powers'. Its 'fundamental purpose' is 'to assure the integrity and vitality of our free society' and to safeguard its values throughout the world. The perfect society 'does not fear, it welcomes, diversity' and 'derives its strength from its hospitality even to antipathetic ideas'. The 'system of values which animates our society' includes 'the principles of freedom, tolerance, the importance of the individual and the supremacy of reason over will'. The essential tolerance of our world outlook, our generous and constructive impulses, and the absence of covetousness in our international relations are assets of potentially enormous influence', particularly among those who have been lucky enough to experience these qualities at first hand, as in Latin America, which has benefited from 'our long continuing endeavors to create and now develop the Inter- American system'; nothing is said about the results.[1]

Nitze's hard-headed conception served as the foundation for the 'rollback' policy that replaced the more compassionate approach of his predecessor, who failed to grasp properly the nature of the forces of light and of evil. The unending conflict between these opposite extremes—soft-hearted moralism and tough-minded realism—cannot be ignored when we consider the great powers and human rights.

The lessons of history and the documentary record tell us a good deal about that topic. But unfortunately what they tell us is politically incorrect, to adopt a term of contemporary ideological warfare, so they must be relegated to the memory hole. And so they are, with marvellous facility along with the thousands of pages of documentation that show how effectively and consistently the guiding values are implemented, even articulated, unless the wrong ears are listening. I might mention at although the unusual importance of the two state papers just cited is fully recognised in the scholarly literature, their actual contents and wording tend to be evaded, and they are little known beyond, as the curious can readily discover. As for what they imply, that is beyond the pale.

I want to talk here about a particular case, one that is rather typical but happens to shed an unusually brilliant light on the general topic, and the gap—or more accurately the chasm—that separates doctrine from reality: the case of East Timor. It teaches us quite a lot about the free and very privileged societies in which we live, which, as we know, have not gained that privilege through their rigorous adherence to the 'Western values' hailed by respected thinkers. These important matters aside, this issue is of critical importance because it is one of the great crimes of the century, and one of the easiest to bring to an end. This isn't Iraq–Kuwait, or Bosnia, or Angola, or Rwanda. There is no ambiguity, no complication about the proper resolution, and no need to threaten to use force to achieve it, even sanctions. UN peace-keepers or mediators are unnecessary. It would be enough for the accessories to the crime to desist, the United States and Australia prominent among them, though they are not alone. The rogues' gallery includes Britain (particularly under Thatcher and Major), France, Japan, and many others who share Kennan's understanding of world order and its guiding values—which means leading circles just about everywhere. It is likely that the withdrawal of the partners in crime would suffice to induce Indonesia to remove the piece of gravel from its shoe, in the words of Foreign Minister Ali Alatas—much to the relief of many Indonesians who have been able to penetrate the heavy censorship that the government imposed to keep the truth from its own population, in time-honoured fashion.

Just as it is wrong to deny the divergence of thinking among world leaders, illustrated by the Kennan–Nitze spectrum for example, so it would be unfair to leave the impression that world leaders recognise no limits to criminal atrocities. True, some do not reach threshold; in the case we are considering, a death toll that international human rights monitors estimate at more than a quarter of the population with half the remnants driven by 1979 into closed camps where they suffered famine comparable to Biafra and Pol Pot's Cambodia, the second highest infant mortality rate in the world, destruction of 90–95 per cent of livestock and collapse of agricultural production; and on, and on, to the present moment. But really significant crimes do not pass unnoticed, and in one case were severe enough to lead to the threat of sanctions against Indonesia. In November 1993, on behalf of the non-aligned movement and the World Health Organisation (WHO), Indonesia submitted to the UN a resolution requesting an opinion from the World Court on the legality of the use of nuclear weapons. In the face of this atrocity the guardians of international morality leaped into action. The US, UK, and France threatened Indonesia with trade sanctions and termination of aid unless it withdrew the resolution, as it did. Traditional clients understand when a message from the powerful is to be heeded.

Citizens of the free world were fortunate to have the information readily available to them; in this case, in the Catholic Church press in Canada.[2]

Freedom of information has limits, however. In June 1994 the World Court was scheduled to take up the WHO request for an opinion, despite a furious campaign by the US, UK, and their allies to prevent this outrage. The matter is of some importance. Even consideration of the issue by the Court would be a contribution to the cause of non- proliferation; even more so a decision that use of nuclear weapons is a crime under international law— hence by implication, possession as well. I found no word on the matter at the time (or since, in the mainstream), though the non-proliferation treaty was a topic of lead headlines, particularly the threat to its impending renewal posed by the nuclear weapons programs of 'rogue states'.

Asian Values

With regard to East Timor, the situation in the West has been improving, though we are a long way from emulating the courage of people like George Aditjondro, the Indonesian scholar who exposed the crimes of his government and forthrightly condemned them, and finally had to seek refuge in Australia. Or the Indonesian student associations that called upon their government, 'for the sake of humanity and our common well-being, [to] reconsider the fake process of integration in East Timor', demanding that Indonesia withdraw its forces and grant 'a full and free "right of self-determination" to the people of East Timor'. Or the director of the Jakarta Institute for the Defence of Human Rights, H.J.C. Princen, who called on his 'Dear friends in Australia' in September 1994 to join him in 'defending the right of self-determination of the island of East Timor' and not to 'be deceived by the sweet words of our politicians who are only concerned about power and money'. Or Luhut Pangaribuan, the Director of Indonesia's Legal Aid Institute, who, on a visit sponsored by the Australian government, combined a 'scathing assessment of his country's abuse of human rights' with a plea to Australia to fulfil its 'moral duty to Timor' and its 'international obligation to forcefully criticise Indonesia for violations of human rights' instead of putting trade issues first.[3]

Needless to say, for Indonesians to take a public stand on these matters is a shade more difficult than for us to respond to their pleas.

When people here, or elsewhere in the West, speak of the need for good relations with Indonesia, the question we should ask is: 'Which Indonesia do they have in mind?'. General Suharto's family and cronies and the affiliates of foreign investors? That's one Indonesia, but there is another Indonesia, too, a land of people struggling for freedom and justice. In that Indonesia we find human rights activists, independent intellectuals, and student associations; the judge who overruled the government's order banning the major newsweekly *Tempo*; the independent journalists' association that defies government orders to disband; the advocates of a more free and open society who meet twice weekly under the rubric of Petition 50 in defiance of rules against unlicensed assembly at the home of former Marine Corps commander Ali Sadikin, who has been punished for his criticism of Suharto's 'totalitarian system' and tells an American reporter in Jakarta that 'the Americans talk about democracy but it is only talk while Mr. Suharto makes profits for the Americans and the capitalist world'; the labour leaders tossed into jail to clean the place up for the 1994 APEC summit; and the thousands of workers who, in the face of harsh repression, continue to meet, strike and demonstrate in protest against abysmal working conditions in a country with wages at half the level of China and no independent unions—but exempted from human rights conditions by the Clinton Administration. The other Indonesia includes the vast majority of people, who would join the protest if they were able to learn the truth and react without fear—as we can, with no difficulty at all.[4]

The common argument that criticism should be withheld because we must 'respect Asian values' and 'maintain good relations with Indonesia' is meaningless at best, mere delusion, unless we are told which Asia and which Indonesia the speaker has in mind. The choice is usually tacit, reflecting not a 'pragmatic course' as cynically maintained, but rather the values of those who advance the argument and the outcomes they prefer. These are simple truths, which should be brought to the surface.

Western Values

For a long time, the 'voluntary censorship' of free societies (to borrow Orwell's phrase) was unusually rigorous in the United States, while Washington furnished the decisive military and diplomatic support for the worst slaughter relative to population since the Holocaust. The reason is not, as later claimed by apologists, that sources were lacking or that this corner of the world was too remote to elicit attention. Sources were always ample in comparison to other cases kept prominently in view because blame could be assigned to official enemies, a contrast so dramatic in those years that it has taken some discipline to 'miss it'. And prior to the Indonesian invasion, coverage of East Timor was quite high in the press, because something was at stake that mattered to Western values: the fate of the Portuguese empire, then causing much concern. The invasion and subsequent atrocities were accompanied by a sharp decline in attention. Media coverage reached flat zero in 1978 (as it did in Canada), when the Indonesian assault reached its peak of near-genocidal ferocity while President Carter—of human rights fame—sent new deliveries of arms to expedite the slaughter. Before the total cutoff in 1978, the limited reporting and commentary rarely strayed from State Department lies denying atrocities, and pronouncements of Indonesian generals, presented as fact. The US role was blacked out, and still is.[5]

That situation, however, has changed significantly. By now there is some coverage of the facts and editorial condemnations are consistently strong and fairly regular, though the decisive US role remains virtually unmentionable and other major issues are off the agenda, including the crucial significance of oil in the Timor Gap. And the ugly media record of earlier years is suppressed in favour of more useful stories about the courage and integrity of the sharp-eyed tribunes of the people who never relax their vigilance in exposing the iniquity of the powerful. The iniquity that was at last recognised is that the US 'averted its eyes from East Timor' and 'could have done far more than it did to distance itself from the carnage' (James Fallows). We didn't do enough to stop what the New York Times finally condemned as the 'shaming of Indonesia'—not the shaming of the United States and its ideological institutions.

In this mood of regret, we therefore recognise that the US 'could have done far more than it did to distance itself' from its enthusiastic and decisive contribution to the ongoing slaughter, carried out with US arms, with instant supplies of new counterinsurgency equipment to the invaders. That takes care of the silence of the press and intellectuals while these events were unfolding before their eyes, and while Carter stepped up the arms flow when Indonesia was running short because of the ferocity of its assault, even arranging shipment of US jets via Israel to avoid the (slight) danger of public exposure. And while, from the outset, the US acted to render the United Nations 'utterly ineffective in whatever measures it undertook' because 'The United States wished things to turn out as they did' and 'worked to bring this about', as explained with great pride in his 1978 memoirs by the agent of the crime, UN Ambassador Daniel Patrick Moynihan, lauded ever since for his high-minded defence of international law and unwavering condemnation of (properly chosen) foreign devils.

At the critical extreme, we now hear that 'There's something troubling about the way we select our cases for intervention'— Harvard historian Stanley Hoffmann, unusual for his refusal to abide by the rules, who notes further that there has been no 'international cry to intervene in ethnic bloodshed in East Timor'. Putting aside the fact that 'ethnic bloodshed' is not quite the term applied to the Soviet invasion of Afghanistan or Iraq's invasion of Kuwait, some questions surely come to mind: just who might call for such intervention, and how should it proceed? By bombing Washington and London, the main supporters of Indonesia's aggression and mass slaughter? Suppose that a commentator in pre-Gorbachev Russia had found something troubling about Soviet intervention policy, wondering why Russia did not intervene to prevent the imposition of martial law in

Poland or repression in Czechoslovakia and Hungary. Would we even laugh? How could Moscow intervene to bar the policies it actively supported? In a properly disciplined intellectual culture, these questions cannot arise. No one laughs. Respectable British opinion is scarcely different. Writing in the (London) *Times Higher Education Supplement*, Leslie Macfarlane, emeritus politics fellow at St John's College in Oxford, recognises that the US and UK, 'to their shame, failed to put pressure on President Suharto to refrain from invasion' of East Timor. But the 200 000 or more deaths 'cannot be attributed to "the West"', he adds, reproaching Edward Herman for including them in his account of Western-backed state violence: no 'Western promotion or support for the invasion and pacification of East Timor in the early 1980s [*sic*] is laid at the West's door', Macfarlane instructs us.[6]

Even the sporadic and narrowly bounded coverage is too much for some prominent figures: Australian Foreign Minister Gareth Evans, for example, who 'took the opportunity' of a meeting with *New York Times* editors 'to complain about that paper's criticisms of human rights violations in Indonesia' and its 'continued harping on the Indonesian invasion of East Timor'. Senator Evans is right; things have changed from the good old days of silence or denial. Even the editors of the *Wall Street Journal*, for whom no crime in which the US has a hand could be criminal, advised Suharto to remove the pebble from its shoe and 'get rid of the East Timor albatross'—not out of concern for the victims, to be sure. Congressional concerns are substantial, extending across the political spectrum. There is an effective solidarity movement that distributes information (most of it from Australia, as has been the case from the outset). And there is a fair amount of public awareness.[7]

For years, the burden in the United States was carried by a handful of mostly young activists, who achieved quite a lot, although the pace was painfully slow. One direct consequence is the growing attention in the media that so distresses the Foreign Minister. The way that happened is instructive, a story that should be told some day, though perhaps not right now. It does not quite fit the self-congratulatory version that emanates from the inner sanctum, and seems to be believed by the foreign press. The record does, however, include cases of real journalistic integrity from the early 1980s, and shows what can be done if even a few people dedicate themselves to the task—an important lesson.[8]

Public protest has begun to hamper Washington's participation in the ongoing atrocities. Congress banned small arms sales and cut off funds for military training, compelling the Clinton Administration to take some complex manoeuvres to evade the law. Delicately selecting the anniversary of the Indonesian invasion, the State Department announced that 'Congress's action did not ban Indonesia's purchase of training with its own funds', so it can proceed despite the ban, with Washington perhaps paying from some other pocket. The announcement received scant notice and no comment in the press, Senator Evans must have been pleased to learn. But it did lead Congress to express its 'outrage', reiterating that 'it was and is the intent of Congress to prohibit U.S. military training for Indonesia' (House Appropriations Committee): 'we don't want employees of the US Government training Indonesians', a staff member reiterated forcefully but without effect.[9]

The justification for the military aid and training is the familiar one, offered reflexively to explain the wisdom of extending a helping hand to torturers and killers. 'There is widespread agreement that . . . [military training] serves a very positive function in terms of exposing foreign militaries to U.S. values', a State Department official informed the press in response to inquiries about the US$100 million in arms sales to Indonesia authorised by the Administration in 1994, and the plans to renew training without constraint or evasion. Democratic Senator Bennett Johnston, who spearheaded the Clinton Administration's efforts to undermine congressional restrictions, took the same stand. His evidence was a statement by the Commander of the US forces in the Pacific, Admiral Larson, who said that 'by studying in our schools' Indonesian army officers 'gain an appreciation for our value system, specifically respect for human rights, adherence to democratic principles, and the rule of law'. Arms sales too facilitate a constructive 'dialogue' and allow us to maintain our 'leverage and influence'. We have seen the results for many years in Latin America, Haiti, the Philippines, and other places where military aid and training have instilled 'an appreciation for our value system'.[10]

The Washington director of Human Rights Watch/Asia noted that Indonesian officers have been trained in the US since the 1950s, without 'discernible improvement'. But the comment reflects the perverse standards of the human rights monitors, who do not properly appreciate the successes in instilling the right values, exhibited most dramatically, perhaps, by the US-trained officers who helped organise the 'staggering mass slaughter' as the current government of Indonesia took power in 1965, a 'boiling bloodbath' that gave 'hope where there once was none', providing 'the West's best news for years in Asia'.[11]

US military assistance played a significant role in that triumph, Secretary of Defense Robert McNamara reported to President Johnson. It 'encouraged' the army to act 'when the opportunity was presented'. Training and instruction were particularly valuable, McNamara continued, singling out the programs that brought Indonesian military personnel to the United States for training at universities, 'very significant factors in determining the favourable orientation of the new Indonesian political elite' (the army). Congress agreed, noting the 'enormous dividends' of US military training of the killers and continued communication with them while they were cleansing the society.

Apart from inculcating our value system, the contacts established by US training and aid provided 'leverage and influence' in other ways, also facilitating the flow of arms and other military equipment to implement the announced policy 'to exterminate the PKI' (the Indonesian Communist Party). Washington and the media could hardly contain their delight over these successes. US Deputy Chief of Mission Francis Galbraith, later Ambassador, 'made clear' to high-ranking officers that 'The embassy and the USC were generally sympathetic with and admiring of what the army was doing'. The leading administration dove, George Ball, noted that US military aid and training 'should have established clearly in the minds of the army leaders that the US stands behind them if they should need help', but instructed the Jakarta embassy to exercise 'extreme caution lest our well-meaning efforts to offer assistance or steel their resolve may in fact play into the hands of Sukarno and [his political associate] Subandrio', targeted for removal as part of the army takeover and massacre. Secretary of State Dean Rusk added that 'If the army's willingness to follow through against the PKI is in any way contingent on or subject to influence by the United States, we do not want to miss the opportunity to consider U.S. action'.

The press completely agreed. Under the headline 'A Gleam of Light in Asia', the leading liberal commentator of the *New York Times*, James Reston, assured his readers on the basis of his close contacts with high government officials that the US had played much more of a role than it was admitting, and that 'it is doubtful if the coup' by General Suharto and the welcome events that followed 'would ever have been attempted without the American show of strength in Vietnam or been sustained without the clandestine aid it has received indirectly from here'. The editors recognised that 'the situation . . . raises critical questions for the United States', but praised Washington for answering them correctly, having 'wisely stayed in the background during

the recent upheavals', recognising that the 'Indonesian moderates' who had just littered the country with some half a million
corpses might be harmed by too warm and public an 'embrace'—
the only 'critical question' that comes to mind. Washington had
also shown its wisdom by rewarding the moderates 'with generous pledges of rice, cotton and machinery' and resumption of the
economic aid that was held back before the 'staggering mass
slaughter' set matters right.[12]

The same training expedited the war crimes in Timor, and
much else. Surely it is only reasonable for it to continue.

Indonesia is not a departure from the norm. It is easy to miss
the significance of policy decisions by focusing too narrowly on a
specific time and place; a great power has a broader vision, and
a serious inquiry will trace actions back to their source, in which
case a good deal falls into place. Turning to another part of the
world in the same years, after the overthrow of the parliamentary
regime of Brazil by US-backed neo-Nazi generals, the Kennedy
liberals who were still largely running the show took a closer look
at the results of their historic decision to shift the mission of the
Latin American military to 'internal security'. In June 1965, Mc-
Namara's Defense Department issued a (secret) memorandum
entitled 'Study of U.S. Policy Toward Latin American Military
Forces', expressing satisfaction over the success in 'attaining the
goals set for' the programs of military training and aid, which had
improved 'internal security capabilities', established 'predominant
U.S. military influence', and given the military 'the understanding
of, and orientation toward, U.S. objectives', in particular, the need
'to protect and promote American investment and trade', the
'economic root' of policy that had become 'stronger' than others.
That understanding and orientation is of particular importance
in 'the Latin American cultural environment', where the military
must be prepared 'to remove government leaders from office
whenever, in the judgment of the military, the conduct of these

leaders is injurious to the welfare of the nation'. Since the military are 'probably the least anti-American of any political group [*sic*] in Latin America', they must take a leading role in the 'revolutionary struggle for power among major groups' that the reigning Marxists in Washington saw in process, as they had just done with such success in Brazil, and were soon to do throughout much of Latin America. The same reasoning holds, and was soon applied, in Indonesia, the Philippines, Thailand, Greece, and elsewhere.

Recall that this is the evaluation at the liberal dovish extreme, drawing from the earlier insights of George Kennan that 'we should not hesitate before police repression by the local government' and that 'It is better to have a strong regime in power than a liberal government if it is indulgent and relaxed and penetrated by Communists'. Recall also that the latter term is construed quite broadly, including virtually anyone who gets in the way, and that the problem posed by the 'Communists' is sometimes squarely faced. As President Eisenhower and Secretary of State Dulles concluded ruefully in internal discussion, the 'Communists' can 'appeal directly to the masses' and 'get control of mass movements', 'something we have no capacity to duplicate', because 'The poor people are the ones they appeal to and they have always wanted to plunder the rich'. It is therefore necessary to turn to the military, who, with proper training at American universities and military installations, will gain 'the understanding of, and orientation toward, U.S. objectives' as to who should plunder whom. The subsequent history of Indonesia is a case in point, to which we turn directly.[13]

Returning to Clinton's evasion of congressional restrictions, with the support of Senate Democrats the Administration was also able to block human rights conditions on aid to Indonesia. Trade Representative Mickey Kantor announced that Washington would suspend its annual review of Indonesian labour practices. Agreeing with Senator Johnston, who was impressed by 'the steps Indonesia has taken . . . to improve conditions for workers in Indonesia', Kantor commended Indonesia for 'bringing its labor law and practice into closer conformity with international standards'—a witticism that is in particularly poor taste, though it must be conceded that Indonesia did take some steps forward, fearing that Congress might override its friends in the White House. 'Reforms hastily pushed through by the Indonesian government in recent months include withdrawing the authority of the military to intervene in strikes, allowing workers to form a company union to negotiate labour contracts, and raising the minimum wage in Jakarta by 27 per cent' to about US$2 a day, the *Guardian* reported. To be sure, the reforms still left something to be desired. The new company unions that are magnanimously authorised must join the All-Indonesia Labour Union, the state-run 'union'; and to prevent any misunderstanding, authorities also arrested 21 labour activists. A year later, in June 1995, Amnesty International issued an update on workers' rights in Indonesia, reporting that 'advocates of workers' rights have continued to operate under threat of intimidation, arrest, imprisonment, torture and ill-treatment', while recent demonstrations 'have been broken up violently by police', among other abuses.

'We have done much to change and improve', Indonesia's Foreign Minister said, 'so according to us there is no reason to revoke' trade privileges. Clinton liberals agreed. Suharto is 'our kind of guy', as a senior Clinton Administration Asian specialist observed, commenting on his warm reception in Washington.[14]

One effect of the activism of the 1960s was the pressure on Congress to impose human rights conditions on aid, trade, and military sales. Every administration from Carter until today has had to seek ways to evade such constraints. In the 1980s, it became a sick joke, as the Reaganites regularly assured Congress (always happy to be deceived) that its favourite assassins and torturers were making commendable progress. Clinton is forging no new paths with his Indonesia chicanery.

In early 1995, Washington stepped up its efforts to return to full participation in Indonesian atrocities. On March 15, Ambassador to Indonesia Robert Barry in a speech in Washington, announced plans to seek authority from Congress to renew the military training program, confirmed the next day by Admiral William Owens, vice-chairman of the Joint Chiefs of Staff, who reported the Pentagon's view that the Indonesian military is addressing American concerns over the situation in East Timor.

Admiral Owens didn't specify what he had in mind. Perhaps the execution of six villagers in Liquica a few weeks earlier. Or perhaps he was thinking of the experiences of the Australian health worker Simon de Faux in a church-run health program: an 8-year-old child with half his face bashed in by a soldier wielding a rifle butt and his eye 'virtually hanging out of his face'; other children with similar stories screaming 'please help'; hideous torture and repeated rape; the appalling health conditions among people unwilling to go to Indonesian doctors or take medicines for fear that it was 'part of a "genocide"'; the terror and murders in Dili by 'Ninjas' who were 'actually Red Beret commandos'; the reports by clergy of six massacres 'of equal magnitude' after the November 1991 Dili massacre that killed hundreds; the 19-year-old Timorese boy who took the great risk of helping de Faux escape from a town after threats from the military, saying 'I grew up in tears, I live in tears, I will die in tears, I was dead from the minute I was born' as he reported the fate of his family—his mother raped, his father killed, a missing brother, the kind of story de Faux heard everywhere.

De Faux's account merited no report in the United States, not even his testimony to the UN Decolonisation Committee in New York. But it was presumably available to US intelligence, hence the Joint Chiefs, since de Faux had met in Timor with Canadian diplomats including the Ambassador, and had also described his experiences to a visiting Australian diplomatic party including the Ambassador and his first secretary, who 'did not want to know what I had seen', de Faux felt, and urged him to 'back off' and 'not to speak to the media'.[15]

Without difficulty, one can add other illustrations of the improvements that impressed the Joint Chiefs.

On the day that Admiral Owens announced the Clinton Administration's plans, John Shattuck, the Assistant Secretary of State for Human Rights, informed Congress that the human rights situation in East Timor, 'which began worsening in late 1994, worsened further in January this year'. Human Rights Watch/Asia had just put out a report on 'Deteriorating Human Rights in East Timor', describing 'extrajudicial executions, torture, disappearances, unlawful arrests and detentions' and other abuses. Citing these (generally unreported) facts, the editors of the pro-Clinton *Boston Globe* commented that 'the most generous way to describe the Clinton administration's approach to human rights is to call it ambivalent'—meaning that the words spoken quietly at home are often decent enough, though the actions taken contradict them with grim consistency.[16]

That is a fair summary of the topic I was asked to address in this talk.

A few months later the Secretary of State offered to sell more F-16 jets to Indonesia. The Postal Service quietly issued new rules announcing a 'country change': 'East Timor is deleted. It is part of Indonesia'. At the Jakarta APEC conference in November 1994, the US Information Service had distributed a paper stating that the US 'does not contest the integration of East Timor into Indonesia'. And Clinton refused comment on Timorese demands for self-determination while announcing his trust in the government's promise that there would be 'no retribution' against Timorese demonstrators 'for exercising their political expression and bringing their concerns to us' in their courageous action at the US embassy in Jakarta.

Despite all this, some feel that the Administration is adopting too harsh and uncompromising a stance. Foreign Minister Evans criticized Clinton's 'tough approach', saying that his 'blunt representations to Indonesia's President Suharto in November on the issue of autonomy in East Timor had failed'. It is not easy to comment.[17]

Washington's efforts to extend its partnership in crime persist, but so do the efforts of people who continue to be appalled by what is being done in their name. These efforts have had notable success: in the halls of Congress, the media, and, more importantly, among the general public, which can bring important pressures to bear. Indonesia has been compelled to turn elsewhere for arms, primarily Britain, where the government and corporations are delighted with the new opportunities for profit, unimpeded so far by large-scale popular protest, though John Pilger and some others have been putting many pieces of gravel in the shoes of Foreign Secretary Douglas Hurd and the like; and Pilger particularly is receiving plenty of flak in high places in London and his native Australia, greatly to his credit.

Britain had joined in as atrocities peaked in 1978. France declared its strong support for Indonesia at the same time, announcing that it would sell arms to Indonesia and protect it from any public 'embarrassment' over its Timorese escapade; French intellectuals kept silent, preferring to parade before the cameras with much anguish about the other fellow's comparable crimes in Cambodia—the usual posture. By the 1980s, under Thatcher's guiding hand, Britain had taken first place in the highly profitable enterprise of war crimes. The reasoning was explained by Defence Procurement Minister Alan Clark: 'I don't really fill my mind much with what one set of foreigners is doing to another' when there is money to be made. That aside, it is understood that Britain must continue to 'reserv[e] the right to bomb niggers', as the noted statesman Lloyd George described the mission of civilisation 60 years ago.

In November 1994, Pilger reported new evidence that British- supplied Hawk aircraft were being used to attack civilian targets, and that, contrary to official tales, the Foreign Office knew that 'they are for offensive purposes' (former FO official Mark Higson, who testified to the Scott Commission on similar 'fictions' with regard to arms sales to Saddam Hussein, part of the 'culture of lying', he said). A few days earlier, the London *Observer* had reported that 'Britain is assembling a huge arms deal with Indonesia, in defiance of international calls for a weapons embargo because of the country's appalling human rights record', a 'secret deal worth an estimated £2 billion'. Included are new Hawk jets. 'Britain is also working hard to reach agreement on a huge range of other military equipment', while also 'pushing to train Indonesian troops denied access to US training programmes because of the human rights issue'. These reports surfaced a week after the High Court judgment against Douglas Hurd for using overseas aid as a 'sweetener' for arms deals. Canada too 'reserves the right to bomb niggers'. In the face of popular protest, its Conservative government had stopped selling arms after the Dili massacre, but the Liberal government that replaced it has reversed that policy, issuing new permits that are close to the level authorised through the entire 1980s.[18]

As I landed at the Sydney airport, the first headline to greet me announced that Australia intended to sell Indonesia $100 million worth of rifles, 'considered to be the most advanced and deadly rifle in the Asia-Pacific', 'the largest and most lucrative defence deal Australia has struck with Indonesia'. Doubtless the rifles will contribute greatly to the defence of Indonesia and Australia from the foreign aggressors falling upon them from every side; particularly Australia, in the light of the fact that 'Indonesia is the country most favourably placed to attack Australia', as the

Department of Defence noted 20 years ago, reporting that it already had the capacity for 'low-level harassment that would create difficult problems'.[19]

It's easy enough to understand why Australia wants to sell advanced assault rifles that Indonesia is likely to put to the obvious use. Like Britain and Canada, Australia hopes to profit from the new 'niche market' that has opened as a result of barriers to such sales from the United States. That 'makes sense', the editors of the *Australian* conclude: 'the interests of our long-term relationship with Indonesia and the continuing viability of our domestic defence industry make it desirable that this opportunity . . . be pursued as vigorously as possible'. 'The commercial reality for Australia is that the international arms industry is too valuable to ignore', whatever 'one set of foreigners is doing to another', as Thatcher's Minister put it. Anyway, there are plenty of others who 'would move quickly into any market vacuum'.

That is true enough. Under Bush and Clinton, the US had taken over 3/4 of the arms market for Third World countries— 85 per cent of the sales going to 'nondemocratic governments' as defined by the State Department, a policy that is opposed by 96 per cent of the population. But others are trying hard. The Congressional Research Service reports that France just took the lead in direct arms transfer agreements, perhaps impressed by the results of French arms and protection for government killers in Rwanda, though Washington arms control specialists consider this 'a brief hiatus' and the US retains a hefty lead in total government-authorised arms sales, with 52 per cent of all arms deliveries and 35 per cent of all agreements.[20]

In any event, the standard argument, repeated by the editors of the *Australian*, is absolutely correct. Rational people should therefore only applaud when it comes to be applied, with equal validity, to other meritorious enterprises. It surely is absurd, for example, to leave the international narcotics racket in the hands of rank amateurs (often indirectly abetted by the great powers), when it could easily be taken over by new government agencies dedicated openly to the sale of lethal drugs, another market that is 'too valuable to ignore' in these days of government austerity.

In the United States, popular protest has had other effects, one very recently in Boston, where a Federal Court awarded US$14 million in damages to Helen Todd, whose son—a citizen of New Zealand and a university student in Sydney—was murdered by Indonesian forces in the series of killings called the 'Dili massacre'. The defendant was General Sintong Panjaitan, one of the architects of the massacre, which was considered in poor taste in the West. Massacres are supposed to be conducted in secret, out of the range of TV cameras; and it is considered bad form to beat and almost kill American reporters, even if they are freelance dissidents as in this case (Alan Nairn and Amy Goodman). That technical error calls forth a routine response. First dismay over the 'aberrant behaviour by a section of the military which had been responded to in a reasonable and credible way by the Indonesian government' (Senator Evans). Then a judicial cover-up, and praise for the 'moderates' who are responsible for this and much worse atrocities and are now showing their honour and courage by facing up 'in a reasonable and credible way' to the aberration that happened to be accidentally exposed. Following the routine, light sentences were given to a few low-ranking soldiers, while survivors were sentenced to many years in prison, up to life sentences, for such crimes as expressing hostility to their benefactors. Meanwhile, it is well to avoid the reaction of the architects of the error, for example, General Try Sutrisno, Commander of the Armed Forces (later Vice-President), who said that the demonstrators had 'spread chaos' by unfurling posters discrediting the government and shouting 'many unacceptable things', and when 'they persisted with their misdeeds . . . they had to be shot. These ill- bred people have to be shot . . . and we will shoot them'.[21]

The operation was conducted smoothly, a tribute, perhaps, to the skill of the public relations firm that handles Indonesia's affairs. Human rights monitors were appalled, but the important people were properly impressed. Nevertheless, it was thought expedient to send General Panjaitan out of the country. According to the Center for Constitutional Rights, which conducted the successful civil suit, he was dispatched to Harvard University, perhaps to refine his skills in the manner described by Defence Secretary McNamara and Congress after the 'staggering mass slaughter' of 1965. When local activists in Boston learned about it, they checked with the university, who denied that he was there. Further inquiries located the unknown general, leading to an article in the Boston press on the first anniversary of the Dili massacre with the headline 'Indonesian general, facing suit, flees Boston'. He was tried in absentia, and sentenced, telling Reuters: 'Just assume it is a joke'. Apparently the Australian government agreed, welcoming him a few months later as part of an Indonesian delegation studying civil and defence research technology. That was quite proper, Foreign Minister Evans explained, because although General Panjaitan 'was held responsible for the killings in Dili, he was not the one who gave the order to fire on the demonstrators' in this 'aberration', which the UN rapporteur had determined to be 'a planned military operation against unarmed civilians'.[22]

The Panjaitan affair is an almost exact replay of events a year earlier in Boston, in this case involving Guatemalan General Hector Gramajo, who was responsible for tens of thousands of killings in the Guatemalan highlands in the early 1980s (with the fervent support of the Reagan Administration). He was being groomed by the State Department for the next step up, perhaps even the presidency, and was sent to Harvard for further training. Local activists learned about it from the Central American press and checked with Harvard, who had never heard of him. Further inquiry revealed that he was indeed there. A civil suit for torture and other atrocities was brought against General Gramajo by the Center for Constitutional Rights. The subpoena was served by Alan Nairn, who originally exposed the US initiatives behind the organisation of death squads in Central America, and has a marvellous record for courageous independent journalism, and also a flair for the dramatic. He raced up and handed the subpoena to the general as he was receiving his diploma at the graduation ceremonies, so there would be no ambiguity about where he was, and no problem of public knowledge, at least locally. Gramajo too fled the country, and was sentenced in absentia for crimes (including torture of an American nun), with a US$47 million fine.[23]

These matters are of no slight importance. It is useful to make it clear that not everyone appreciates the exploits of the State Department's favourite killers. Furthermore, training of military officers in American universities has an acknowledged and admired role, as already discussed.

'The Welfare of the World Capitalist System' and 'The Problem of Indonesia'

To understand what has been happening it is necessary to look more closely at the background.

We should begin from the end of World War II, when 'the United States assumed, out of self-interest, responsibility for the welfare of the world capitalist system'. I'm quoting diplomatic historian Gerald Haines, also senior historian of the CIA, in a highly regarded study of the US takeover of Brazil as part of this welfare program. 'American leaders tried to reshape the world to fit U.S. needs and standards', Haines continues. They looked forward to an 'open world'—open to exploitation by the rich, but not completely open even to them. The US desired a 'closed hemispheric system in an open world', Haines explains. Furthermore, it had no intention of allowing others to interfere with its control over the crucial Middle East region, as discussed in the preceding chapter. And internally, the US, which had fully half the world's wealth at the time, not only retained but in fact dramatically expanded the historic role of the state in protecting and subsidising US- based 'free enterprise, now under the guise of "defense"'.[24]

The responsibility for the welfare of the rich and privileged was taken very seriously. US business and political leaders had been carrying out sophisticated global planning during the war, looking ahead to the domination of the world that they anticipated, and the plans were implemented to the extent possible in its aftermath. The main task was to reconstruct the rich societies, crucially the 'the great workshops', Germany and Japan. That was understood to be necessary for the welfare of the rich at home, who had to find markets for the US manufacturing surplus and opportunities for lucrative foreign investment in the global economy they envisioned. A major concern of Dean Acheson and others was the 'dollar gap', which impeded exports. Several devices were tried to overcome it, including the Marshall Plan (in large measure, a subsidy from the US taxpayer to US corporations from which Europeans gained indirect benefits). But what finally worked was a vast rearmament program, what historian William Borden calls 'international military Keynesianism' in his important work on postwar reconstruction (*The Pacific Alliance*). The point was well understood by the business world. Reflecting the general understanding, the *Magazine of Wall Street* saw military spending as a way to 'inject new strength into the entire economy', and found it 'obvious that foreign economies as well as our own are now mainly dependent on the scope of continued arms spending in this country', which finally succeeded in reconstructing state capitalist industrial societies abroad, overcoming the dollar gap and also laying the basis for the huge expansion of multinationals, mainly US-based.

It was also understood early on that to implement the project it would be necessary to restore something like the old colonial system. Part of the US responsibility for the welfare of the rich was to guarantee 'the colonial economic interests' of the Western European allies (CIA memorandum, 1948), and in the Asia–Pacific region, to restore Japan's 'Empire toward the South', as George Kennan advised; now Japan's New Order would be under US control, hence no longer a problem. In fact, it was no real problem before either, except that the US was not being granted privileged entry to it, one of the many interesting aspects of World War II that never managed to see the light of day during the patriotic frenzy whipped up for the 50th anniversary.

One effect of the reconstruction of the colonial order in a different guise was to be the establishment of triangular trade patterns, whereby the second-level industrial powers would earn dollars from US import of raw materials from former colonies, enabling them to absorb US exports. More generally, planners assigned each part of the world its specific role. Independent nationalism would interfere with the project, hence could not be tolerated. For most of the world, 'complementary development' was the most that could be allowed; there are interesting exceptions in the region of Japanese influence, where the two major former Japanese colonies, largely under the stimulus of Vietnam War 'military Keynesianism', were able to renew the rapid economic development that had taken place under the harsh colonial rule of Japan, which, unlike the West, developed its colonies. From the outset, the US was on a collision course with Third World nationalism, one of the major themes of postwar history, generally concealed in a Cold War framework.

The Western hemisphere and the world's major energy resources of the Middle East were assigned to the global ruler itself. Africa was to be handed over to its traditional colonial masters to be 'exploited', as George Kennan put it, for their reconstruction, an opportunity that might also give Europeans a needed psychological lift, he felt. Southeast Asia was to 'fulfill its major function as a source of raw materials for Japan and Western Europe' (Kennan's State Department Policy Planning Staff) within the triangular trading system, and for the US as well. The principle of self-determination was not forgotten, but in due time. Sumner Welles, a high official who was particularly close to President Roosevelt, felt that true self-government might come to the Belgian Congo in a hundred years. Even self-determination for Portuguese (East) Timor was contemplated, though 'it would certainly take a thousand years', Welles felt.[25]

The technical term for this commitment to self-determination is 'Wilsonian idealism'; it is regarded by more hard-headed 'realist' thinkers as a moralistic flaw that undermines the 'national interest'.

In this context, Southeast Asia took on major importance, in particular Indonesia, the richest prize. In 1948, Kennan described 'the problem of Indonesia' as 'the most crucial issue of the moment in our struggle with the Kremlin'.

We may note in passing that the phrase 'struggle with the Kremlin' is another technical term. It refers in practice to the conflict with independent nationalist tendencies that interfere with the designated service role—sometimes turning to the Russians for defence and thus becoming agents of the Kremlin conspiracy to gain 'absolute authority over the rest of the world'. When enough time has passed after the defeat of the upstarts, the story undergoes a conventional revision: it now turns out that nationalism was 'misunderstood' as a Kremlin conspiracy, a natural error traced to the 'defensive stance' that is a deeply rooted element of our culture and to our hopeless naivety about the ugly world beyond.

Russia itself had become an enemy for similar reasons. In 1917, it departed from the 'main function' it had fulfilled from pre-Columbian times as a service area for developing Western Europe, later extending its imperial sway to other such regions and even parts of the industrial West itself. The effort to restore the former status quo is a component of 'the Cold War' that has yet to be properly recognised.

In Indonesia, there was no 'struggle with the Kremlin' in 1948, except in the technical sense. After the war, British forces (as elsewhere in the region) overthrew the 'already functioning, if rudimentary, Indonesian government' of the nationalist leaders Sukarno and Hatta, Audrey and George Kahin observe in an important scholarly study, rearming 'whole regiments of Japanese troops' in their effort to restore Dutch imperial rule; the Dutch were also assisted by 'Australian military power'. The US gave 'discreet and largely indirect' support for the Dutch reconquest, in accord with the general plans for the region. 'Some of the most influential American policymakers regarded the Netherlands East Indies as the cork on which much of the Dutch economy had floated— providing some 20 per cent of national income', and feared 'the growth of radical political forces' in Holland if it were not able to exploit Indonesia's rich resources for its reconstruction. Marshall Plan aid to France and Holland, they note, approximately equalled what they were spending to reconquer their former colonies in Southeast Asia, with US weapons. Destruction and loss of life would have been far less in Vietnam and Indonesia had it not been for US–British support for the colonial powers, George Kahin points out, suggesting further that 'the agenda for socioeconomic change in the [Indonesian] Republic would have been considerably more progressive than it in fact became' with Indonesian leaders 'conscious of the immense shadow cast by Anglo- American might standing behind the Dutch'.

US policy shifted when Sukarno and Hatta put down a 1948 revolt 'by a disorganized group of Soviet-oriented Indonesian

Communists' (the Madiun rebellion), with the aid of the 'nationalist Communists' whose socioeconomic program was even more hostile to Western economic interests in Indonesia than that of their now-subdued pro-Soviet rivals'. Much to the distress of the Dutch, Washington began to support the Indonesian army and the Sukarno–Hatta government, in part out of fear that the 'anti-Stalinist, strongly nationalist Communists' and other 'socioeconomic radicals' would extend their popular support if the bloody Dutch war of aggression continued. The CIA even broke the Dutch blockade to fly Indonesian officers from Yogyakarta, the capital of the Indonesian republic, to US military facilities for special training—the origins of the training programs that became so important in subsequent years, if we can believe the Pentagon.[26]

Despite his ritual invocation of 'the struggle with the Kremlin', Kennan was clear-sighted enough to understand the real reasons why he took 'the problem of Indonesia' to be the 'most crucial' issue of international affairs in 1948. 'Indonesia is the anchor in that chain of islands stretching from Hokkaido to Sumatra which we should develop as a politico-economic counter-force to communism', he continued, and a 'base area' for possible military action beyond. A Communist Indonesia would be an 'infection' that 'would sweep westward' through all of South Asia. The fear—growing in subsequent years—was that elements committed to programs of independent development not geared to 'the welfare of the world capitalist system' might win a political victory—a few years later, the Indonesian Communist Party (PKI), which aligned with China in the early 1960s. Indonesia specialists consider those prospects not unrealistic. Harold Crouch writes that 'the PKI had won widespread support not as a revolutionary party but as an organisation defending the interests of the poor within the existing system', developing a 'mass base among the peasantry' through its 'vigor in defending the interests of the . . . poor'.[27]

One can see why the prospects of democracy in Indonesia aroused such concern. The fears are the standard ones, even the terminology in which they are expressed ('struggle with the Kremlin', 'infection', etc.). In one typical case, Kissinger described democratic Chile as a 'contagious example' that could 'infect' not only Latin America but even southern Europe, sending to Italian voters the message that democratic social reform was a possible option. It was therefore necessary to overthrow the government and impose a brutal military dictatorship, another familiar feature of the postwar world. Democracy is a fine thing, and we love it as much as human rights—but only when conditions guarantee that a 'free choice' will satisfy our demands.

Concerns persisted through the 1950s. In 1958, Secretary of State John Foster Dulles informed the National Security Council that Indonesia was one of three major world crises, along with Algeria and the Middle East, emphasising with the 'vociferous' agreement of President Eisenhower that there was no Soviet role in any of these cases. The fundamental problem was the threat of democracy. Though the documentary record is being concealed to an unusual extent, parts have recently been released, including cables from the US embassy in Jakarta in 1958 reporting that the Sukarno government was 'beginning to reach conclusion Communists could not be beaten by ordinary democratic means in elections. Program of gradual elimination of Communists by police and military to be followed by outlawing of Communist Party [is] not unlikely in comparatively near future'. The Joint Chiefs of Staff, the same day, urged that 'action must be taken, including overt measures as required, to insure either the success of the dissidents or the suppression of the pro-Communist elements of the Sukarno government'.

The 'dissidents' were the 'Revolutionary Government' that had been established in a rebellion in the outer islands, where the oil and US investments were mostly to be found. The rebellion had substantial US support that is still being concealed. Australia too was involved, apparently for the same basic reasons: fear of democracy. The officially released documents scarcely hint at the extraordinary level of the US government efforts revealed by the Kahins in their study, though what has been released indicates the ambivalence in Washington because the likely outcomes were unclear. In particular, there was fear that the US involvement was alienating pro-American Indonesian generals on whom the US was relying, and inducing them to turn to the Russians. US intervention was of course known to the Indonesians, though denied at home, where the press angrily denounced Indonesia for its accurate account—'manifestly false', the *New York Times* thundered, as proven by the 'emphatic . . . declaration' of the Secretary of State that the US was not involved. The US intervention, the most extreme of the Eisenhower years, remains 'one of the most zealously guarded secrets in the history of U.S. covert overseas operations', the Kahins comment.

After the collapse of the rebellion and the exposure (in Indonesia) of US involvement, intelligence concluded that 'Events in Indonesia during the last year have greatly strengthened the position of the Indonesian Communists (the PKI). If the national elections scheduled for 1959 are held, the PKI will probably emerge as the largest party in Indonesia and be in a strong position to demand cabinet representation'—something completely unacceptable in the case of a political organisation that defends the interests of the overwhelming majority, according to prevailing democratic theory.[28]

Though the rebellion collapsed, the US intervention did succeed in the primary goal of undermining the threat of democracy. 'The most immediate and at the same time most long term of the effects of the civil war were the destruction of parliamentary government', the Kahins conclude, noting that Indonesia 'has never again enjoyed a representative government'. The civil war also 'struck a devastating blow against any future prospects for a devolution of power from the central government in Jakarta to authorities in the regions or any measure of decentralization and local autonomy'. Indonesia became an 'authoritarian centralized polity', and has so remained, under presidential–military rule. The rebellion left the country with a 'tense and brittle tripolarization of just three major political forces, each now stronger than before', they continue: the army, the Communist party, and Sukarno. The next task was to ensure the victory of the army, which had the right priorities. Unlike the PKI, Crouch points out, its 'conception of economic development', implemented once it took power, was 'primarily oriented toward the interests of the elite and the white-collar middle class' and the 'comprador' class associated with foreign corporations, 'the military elite and the civilian bureaucrats and business groups—both domestic and foreign—closely linked to it'. If the right plunderers could be put in charge, all would be well.[29]

The early 1960s were a tense and difficult period as the three forces jockeyed for power. There were also international complications, in part related to Britain's attempt to construct a Malaysian federation, supported by Australia 'as the best way of keeping the territories under Western influence', Gregory Pemberton reports, reviewing just-released Cabinet records. In March 1963, the Defence Minister noted Australia's concern 'at Indonesia's growth as a military power, her declared opposition to the Malaysian federation, and her use of military power in support of diplomatic aims'. There was no principled objection to such use of military power; a few months earlier, in December 1962, a British–Australian military operation had 'forcibly suppressed a popular movement in Brunei which challenged the undemocratic rule of the Sultan and his support for Malaysia', actions that Indonesia used as a 'pretext' for its opposition to Britain's Malaysia confederation, the Cabinet held, bringing 'Australia into potentially direct conflict with Indonesia in 1963' (Pemberton).[30]

For Indonesia itself, the Western priority was to ensure that the army would emerge triumphant in the tripolar power struggle. To achieve this end, the US adopted the standard operating procedure for overthrowing civilian governments that get out of hand: cut down assistance, but continue military aid and training, keeping contacts with the only force that can do the job. By the time the goal was finally achieved with the 1965–66 coup and massacre, the US had 'trained 4000 Indonesian army officers—half the total officer corps, including one-third of the general staff' (Toohey and Pinwill).[31]

As I've already mentioned, Washington liberals were following the same course in Latin America at the time, with successes that they and the business community found heartening as parliamentary governments were overthrown in favour of brutal military dictatorships. The same methods were tried in Iran after the fall of the Shah, but failed. The technique is an understandable one; it is not easy to think of an alternative, given the acknowledged inability to 'appeal directly to the masses' and 'get control of mass movements' as the 'Communists' can do, using the unfair advantages they gain from 'defending the interests of the poor'—'Communist' here used in the technical sense that covers also militant anti-Communists with the wrong priorities.

The Problem Solved

By the early 1960s, US experts were urging their contacts in the Indonesian military to 'strike, sweep their house clean' (Guy Pauker of the Pentagon-sponsored RAND Corporation in a study published by Princeton University Press); 'if the officer corps appreciated its historic role, it could be the nation's salvation', he wrote in a University of California study. University of Pennsylvania specialist William Kintner, formerly of the CIA and then at a CIA-subsidised research institute, advised that with

Western help, 'free Asian political leaders—together with the military—must not only hold on and manage, but reform and advance while liquidating the enemy's political and guerrilla armies'.
The threat was urgent, he warned, because 'If the PKI is able to
maintain its legal existence and Soviet influence continues to
grow, it is possible that Indonesia may be the first Southeast Asia
country to be taken over by a popularly based, legally elected
communist government'. The 'armies' were 'political', as he knew,
but he felt that it should be possible to liquidate them with US
help, so that we could have 'democracy'. Pauker was not so sure
it could be done, fearing that the US favourites 'would probably
lack the ruthlessness that made it possible for the Nazis to suppress the Communist Party of Germany . . . [These right-wing
and military elements] are weaker than the Nazis, not only in
numbers and in mass support, but also in unity, discipline, and
leadership' (RAND memorandum, 1964).

Again, it is well to recall that the policies emanate from a
central source, Washington, and are therefore likely to be similar
over quite a range (as in Latin America, at the same time). Just
a year earlier, the Kennedy Administration had expressed the
same concerns over Vietnam, where plans were in process to
overthrow the Diem government for fear that it was going to act
on its threat to call for the US invaders to withdraw and to reach
a political settlement with North Vietnam. Ambassador Henry
Cabot Lodge explained to President Kennedy that 'Viet-Nam is
not a thoroughly strong police state . . . because, unlike Hitler's
Germany, it is not efficient' and is thus unable to suppress the
'large and well-organized underground opponent strongly and
ever- freshly motivated by vigorous hatred'. The Vietnamese 'appear to be more than ever anxious to be left alone', and though
they 'are said to be capable of great violence on occasion', 'there
is no sight of it at the present time', an impediment to US efforts
to defend South Vietnamese democracy.[32]

In Vietnam, the Kennedy-backed coup took place, but the Generals never met the standards of the liberals of Camelot. Their Indonesian allies and students showed a better understanding of the values of their tutors, and 'swept their house clean' in the 'staggering mass slaughter' of 1965–66 that elicited such utter euphoria across the spectrum in the United States, understandably. The party that was serving the interests of the poor majority was 'liquidated' along with what Crouch calls a 'holy war of extermination' in areas where the PKI had virtually no presence, destroying plantation workers, landless peasants, and numerous others with army support and encouragement. Pauker recognised that his earlier pessimism had been unfounded; and the military had shown the 'ruthlessness that I had not anticipated a year earlier'.

The scale of the slaughter is debated, but it was certainly huge. The CIA ranked it 'as one of the worst mass murders of the 20th century, along with the Soviet purges of the 1930s, the Nazi mass murders during the Second World War, and the Maoist bloodbath of the early 1950s. In this regard, the Indonesian coup is certainly one of the most significant events of the 20th century'. The goal of eliminating the PKI as a political force was achieved. The country was quickly turned into a 'paradise for investors', and the threat of a political victory by a party representing the wrong people was put off for a long time.[33]

As I've mentioned, the US supported the massacres, hesitating only out of concern that overt involvement might play into the hands of President Sukarno, who was ousted shortly after. The record of unrestrained joy over the 'boiling bloodbath' has to be read to be believed. I have surveyed it in some detail for the US. I don't know whether that has been done elsewhere, though I suspect that the reaction was much the same. It would be worth a careful look.

Recall Defense Secretary McNamara's testimony about the value of the military aid and training of Indonesian officers, which had given them the right 'orientation', as in Latin America. His pride seems justified. In the major scholarly study of the massacre, Robert Cribb points out that 'In most cases, the killings did not begin until elite military units had arrived in a locality and had sanctioned violence by instruction or example', and in the countryside, where 'by far the worst massacres' took place, 'the main killers were army units'. One can see the importance of sending General Panjaitan to Harvard.

Apart from the open jubilation, the most interesting reactions had to do with the US wars in Indochina, then well on their way to their eventual toll of some four million killed. Freedom House published a statement by leading scholars hailing the 'dramatic events' in Indonesia, offering them as justification for what we would call 'the US attack against South Vietnam' if a shred of honesty were imaginable. US forces in Vietnam provided a 'shield' that encouraged the Indonesian Generals to do their necessary work, Freedom House and its 'distinguished Americans' argued, agreeing with James Reston and others.

Years later, top planners spelled out their delayed reaction to the 'dramatic events'. McGeorge Bundy, National Security Adviser under Kennedy and Johnson and former Harvard dean, finally came to realise, he said, that 'our effort' in Vietnam should perhaps have been brought to an end after October 1965, when 'a new anti-communist government took power in Indonesia and destroyed the communist party'. With Indonesia now protected from infection, it may have been 'excessive', he felt, to continue to demolish Indochina at inordinate cost to ourselves. The rest of the region was being immunised in a similar if not quite so spectacular way, while the virus of independent nationalism in Indochina was destroyed so completely that by the early 1970s, the business press recognised that the US had basically won the war. It had, if we consider the fundamental goals, though maximal goals were not achieved, so the partial victory can only be construed as a humiliating defeat, and the essential questions remain largely foreign to the intellectual culture apart from an occasional nod of the Bundy type.

Robert McNamara, the chief architect of the war in Vietnam, added his commentary in his 1995 memoirs, in which he apologised with much emotion—to Americans, for what he did to them and their society. Omitted is any reference to his pride in the Pentagon role in the 'staggering mass slaughter', though he does note that Indonesia 'reversed course' after the killing of '300,000 or more PKI members . . . and now lay in the hands of independent nationalists led by Suharto'. He reviews his frustration over the stubborn and irrational refusal of the Vietnamese enemy to accept his forthcoming offer of a negotiated settlement in which they would lay down their arms and become part of an 'independent, non-Communist South Vietnam'. Suharto's Indonesia is the model of 'independent nationalism' that McNamara was offering—without shame or probably even comprehension—to what he must have known to be the only 'truly mass-based political party in South Vietnam' (government Indochina expert Douglas Pike). At least, that has the merit of consistency, considering the general reaction that he shared to the fate of the major political organisation in Indonesia.[34]

No concerns were expressed in Congress about the slaughter, no major relief agency offered aid. The World Bank restored Indonesia to favour, soon making it the third largest borrower. Western governments and corporations followed along.

Within a few years, the roles had been reversed. In 1977, one old Asia hand, George McArthur, wrote that the PKI had 'subjected the country to a bloodbath', placing their necks under the knife in a major Communist atrocity. As for the 'quietly determined' leader Suharto with his 'almost innocent face' and 'scrupulously constitutional' reliance on 'law not on mere power' (*Time*), the 'Indonesian moderate' admired by the *New York Times* who was presiding over the massacres and 'encouraging as wide as possible participation . . . as a way of committing fence-sitters to the victory of the anti-communist cause' (Cribb), he retained his moderate status as he proceeded to compile one of the world's worst human rights records in Indonesia, not to speak of some exploits beyond.

'Many in the West were keen to cultivate Jakarta's new moderate leader, Suharto', after the dramatic events of 1965–6, the *Christian Science Monitor* reported years later, though some recognised that his human rights record is 'checkered' (*Times* Southeast Asia correspondent Philip Shenon). The London *Economist* described the great mass murderer and torturer as 'at heart benign'—towards foreign investors, at least—while denouncing the 'propagandists for the guerrillas' in East Timor and Irian Jaya with their 'talk of the army's savagery and use of torture'—including the Bishop and other church sources, thousands of refugees in Australia and Portugal, Western diplomats and journalists who have chosen to see, the most respected international human rights monitors, all 'propagandists' rather than intrepid champions of human rights because they have quite the wrong story to tell. The events of 1965 are not evaded, however, in an upbeat story about Suharto's achievements in the *Wall Street Journal*: one sentence reads: Suharto 'took command of the effort to crush the coup attempt, and succeeded'. The editor of its Asia counterpart, Barry Wain, described how Suharto 'moved boldly in defeating the coup makers and consolidating his power', using 'strength and finesse' to take total control. 'By most standards, he has done well', Wain continues, though, like Shenon, he recognises that his human rights record is 'checkered', citing government involvement in the killing of several thousand alleged criminals from 1982 to 1985. Putting aside some questions about earlier years, an equally laudatory column in *Asiaweek* a few weeks before had reported yet another massacre in Sumatra, where armed troops burnt a village of 300 people to the ground, killing dozens of civilians, part of an operation to quell unrest in the province. But nothing could sully the reputation of the 'moderate' who is 'at heart benign'.

By now, reconstruction of history has become almost surreal. On the 50th anniversary of Indonesia's independence, the government released Sukarno's close associate Subandrio, now 81, and two others who had been jailed in 1965. They were pardoned by 'President Suharto, who came to power in the midst of the bloodshed in the 1960's' and 'is credited with putting down the . . . coup attempt that led to the deaths of hundreds of thousands of people', the Southeast Asia correspondent of the *New York Times*, Philip Shenon, reported. The charge against them was that they 'were instrumental in plotting the coup attempt in 1965 that brought down President Sukarno, Mr Suharto's predecessor'—'following the massacre of ethnic Chinese', the editors add, referring also to the 'touchy' question of East Timor, where 'famine claimed tens of thousands, and unrest has persisted ever since'.[35]

The Problem of East Timor

The reaction to the 1965–66 events casts an interesting light on Western civilisation. Small wonder that it has disappeared from the record.[36] It also provides part of the context for the Western reaction to the Indonesian invasion of East Timor ten years later. The Indonesian generals had liquidated the party of the poor, destroyed the threat of democracy, and opened the country to foreign plunder. With affairs of state safely in the hands of mass murderers with the right priorities, Indonesia at last was no longer a 'crucial issue in our struggle with the Kremlin', and could proceed to 'fulfill its main functions'. These are services to Western values that are not easily overlooked. Another 'staggering mass slaughter' could hardly be expected to disrupt the friendly relations that had been established by the successful emulation of the Nazis, relieving earlier doubts.

There were, of course, more particular reasons for the West to lend its hand to new atrocities. The fate of the Portuguese empire was a matter of much concern. As I mentioned, coverage of East Timor was quite high in the US, in that context. And it is well to remember that not only East Timor was subjected to a devastating Western-backed assault. The same was true of Portugal's former colonies in Africa. The distinguished historian of Africa Basil Davidson writes that 'all those responsible for the "contra" subversions in Angola and Mozambique will be cursed by history for enormous and terrible crimes, which will long weigh heavily on the whole of Southern Africa'. The scale of these crimes is indicated by a UN study that estimates over US$60 billion in damages and 1.5 million dead during the Reagan years alone, by way of South Africa, with US–British support under the guise of 'constructive engagement'. In Angola, the terror has continued, at a level worse than Bosnia in the same years. From the outset, the concerns were the usual ones: the virus of nationalism that might be 'independent' in something other than the Suharto style, and the risk that it might spread, assigned the Cold War justifications in the usual ways as well. There is reason to believe that the same was true of Indonesia's invasion of East Timor, and Western support for it; the invasion was 'motivated by the fear that an independent Timor would become a source of subversion in Indonesia itself', Harold Crouch writes.[37]

How would East Timor carry out such 'subversion'? Only by the dread 'demonstration effect' that has always inspired such terror, often called 'concealed aggression', 'internal aggression', or even 'outright aggression'. Thus, in a 1955 study, the Joint Chiefs of Staff outline two 'basic forms of aggression' in addition to aggression in the literal sense: 'Overt armed attack from within the area of each of the sovereign states', and 'Aggression other than armed, i.e., political warfare, or subversion'. An internal uprising against a US-imposed police state, or elections that come out the wrong way, are forms of 'aggression', which the US and its allies have the right to combat by arbitrary violence; unwanted political activities constitute 'subversion', something that no society can tolerate however democratic it may be, not even the defender of 'civilization itself' with its 'deep tolerance' and famed 'hospitality even to antipathetic ideas'. The premises are a constant feature of the record, both public and internal, and concern that East Timor might 'foment subversion' in such ways is not at all far-fetched, by prevailing standards.

Apart from these matters, there was also concern over 'East Timor's enormous strategic significance in Southeast Asia (especially for Australia)' (Gerry Simpson), and the related matter of deep-water passage for nuclear submarines off of its coasts. But I suspect that if the record is released, we will find that a major factor was the one emphasised by Australian Ambassador to Jakarta Richard Woolcott in August 1975 when he advised (in secret) that Australia go along with the invasion he anticipated because it could make a better deal on the oil reserves in the Timor Gap with Indonesia 'than with Portugal or independent Portuguese Timor', 'a pragmatic rather than a principled stand', he added, noting accurately that 'that is what the national interest and foreign policy is all about'. The interests of energy corporations are 'the national interest' virtually by definition, though it is a bit misleading to say that the recommended approach is not 'principled'; the principle is quite clear, and, in the real world, pursued with rare consistency.[38]

Australia's *de jure* recognition in 1979 of Indonesia's 1976 annexation of the occupied territory was in that context, it seems. The treaty to rob East Timor's oil was signed in 1989 and ratified by Parliament shortly after. It was put into effect immediately after the Dili massacre, when the Indonesia–Australia joint authority began signing exploration contracts with major oil companies to exploit the oil of what the Treaty calls 'the Indonesian Province of East Timor'—which does not merit the inalienable right of self-determination, we are told, because it is not viable economically. The Indonesia–Australia Timor Gap Treaty, which offers not a crumb to the people whose oil is being taken, 'is the only legal agreement anywhere in the world that effectively recognises Indonesia's right to rule East Timor', the Australian press observes.[39] Of course, Australia affirms the sacred right of the people of East Timor to self-determination, as it insisted before the World Court. There is no need to go into the casuistry that accompanies the solemn affirmation of this right in principle while Indonesia's right to abrogate it is endorsed in practice.

In his treatise on Australian Foreign Policy, Foreign Minister Evans offers the Timor Gap Treaty as 'an example of a non-military solution to a problem that historically has often led to conflict', a model for the world to follow. Pretty impressive. More recently, he has suggested it 'as a model to resolve a dispute in the South China Sea over the Spratly Islands'. This pursuit of non-violence perhaps falls under what Evans calls 'good international citizenship', which 'demands no less than acting to help secure universal adherence to universal rights' and pursuit of 'purposes beyond ourselves'. Pragmatic guidelines do not suffice.[40]

It should be noted that neither legal nor moral considerations are affected by the 1995 decision of the World Court not to consider the merits of the issue on the procedural grounds that Indonesia rejects its jurisdiction, while reaffirming that 'the territory of East Timor remains a non-self-governing territory and its people has the right to self-determination for these reasons'. The issue 'is not the law but justice', the Thai press had commented accurately as the Court proceedings opened, and

by the standards of justice 'there can be no defence of the cynical oil exploration agreement Australia signed with Jakarta',
though 'at the same time, the contract has no bearing on the
daily suffering of the East Timorese . . . There are few places in
the world where human rights are so systematically trampled as
in East Timor'.[41]

At least the 'Western values' so loftily proclaimed are understood somewhere.

The record of the Indonesian invasion in December 1975 and
its aftermath is familiar to Australians at least, and I will not re-
count it. The US, Britain, and Australia were well aware from August that Indonesia was planning to invade and was indeed
carrying out military operations within East Timor—including special forces, regular troops, heavy weapons, and air and naval bom-
bardment—in preparation for the full- scale invasion that took
place on December 7, delayed a few hours so as not to embarrass
President Ford and Henry Kissinger, then visiting Jakarta.[42] All
three countries effectively authorised the invasion, which was carried out with US arms and with diplomatic support, as UN Ambassador Moynihan testified. New arms were sent at once to
enhance the slaughter. So matters continued through the 1970s,
while the decisive Western complicity in vast crimes was dismissed
with shameful apologetics, or simply suppressed.

The story did begin to get some attention by 1980, when it
was becoming a little hard to miss the similarity to the Pol Pot
atrocities of the same years. Leading journalists still considered
the story unworthy of attention. At the left extreme, in the *Nation*,
former *Times* correspondent A.J. Langguth dismissed concern over
Timor on the grounds that 'If the world press were to converge
suddenly on Timor, it would not improve the lot of a single Cambodian', the latter 'worthy victims' whose tragic fate can be blamed
solely on official enemies (with a suitable narrowing of vision). In
the *Washington Journalism Review*, a leading journal of media cri-

tique, Asia specialist and foreign correspondent Stanley Karnow ridiculed a January 1980 news report on East Timor that he couldn't even bring himself to read because 'it didn't have anything to do with me', while respected TV commentator Richard Valeriani dismissed it as a waste of space because 'I don't care about Timor', obviously the wrong story, with the wrong lessons. They added approvingly that '99.99 per cent of the American people don't care about Timor', while disparaging 'that long story about Timor in the *New York Times*' that might let some of them in on the secret, in which case they would surely care, unlike their betters, particularly if they were to learn about the still-hidden US role.

Times UN correspondent Bernard Nossiter refused an invitation to a press conference at the UN on East Timor in October 1979 because he found the issue 'rather esoteric', and also chose not to report on the UN debate, including testimony from Timorese refugees and others on the continuing atrocities at the wrong hands.[43] The *Wall Street Journal* devoted an editorial to the 'interesting campaign' that was shaping up on East Timor, noting that several hundred thousand people may have died and that 'it sounds suspiciously like Cambodia, some people are saying', though 'this one is ours', conducted with US arms. This charge, the *Journal* explained, 'tells us less about Timor than it does about certain varieties of American political thinking', which fail to comprehend that the US could do nothing because 'the violence that has cursed the place is the wholly unsurprising mark of a disintegrating world order', and 'talk about the evils of US power is likely to hasten that disintegration, not arrest it'. By seeking to bring awareness of US government actions to the general population, critics of US policy are therefore contributing to the atrocities carried out with US arms and support; it is those who suppress the facts who are engaged in the humanitarian effort to help the victims.

It's doubtful that Pravda could have risen to more exalted heights.

The comparison to Cambodia was put to rest shortly after, when the State Department explained that the two cases were quite distinct. The US was supporting the Khmer Rouge-based government in exile because its 'continuity' with the Pol Pot regime 'unquestionably' makes it 'more representative of the Cambodian people than the Fretilin is of the Timorese people'. Though unreported, the official position settles the issue.[44]

The issue reached awareness again when Iraq invaded Kuwait. Again, it took discipline to miss the parallels. But the crucial differences were eloquently explained by leading scholars and other commentators. I'll spare you the details, which merely go to show how little has changed, apart from a decline in the quality of the rhetoric, from the days when Pascal recorded with suitable mockery 'how the casuists reconcile the contrarieties between their opinions and the decisions of the popes, the councils, and the Scripture', so that we may adhere faithfully to the preachings of the Gospel that 'the rich are bound to give alms of their superfluity, [though] it will seldom or never happen to be obligatory in practice', thanks to 'the utility of interpretations'.

World attention focused again on East Timor after the Dili massacre, the technical error I already mentioned, but briefly, and without effect on more important matters such as the takeover of the oil resources of East Timor.

Let me just conclude with what is most important. This horror story can be brought to an end, if Westerners can exhibit even a fraction of the integrity and courage shown by Indonesians who are protesting what their government is doing, under conditions vastly more onerous than any of us dream of—I do not even speak of the incredible courage of the Timorese, which shames all of us, Australians in a special way because of the debt of blood remaining from World War II, as I am sure you know.

We are, I think, at an important turning point. With enough energy and commitment to change Western policies, there is reason to suspect that the government of Indonesia can be encouraged to remove the piece of gravel from its shoe, that one of the world's major atrocity stories can be brought to an end, and that the people of East Timor may come to enjoy their inalienable right of self-determination—perhaps in less than a thousand years.

East Timor
and World Order

I very much appreciate the opportunity to discuss some current issues with you. There are quite a few that seem urgent and pressing. I'd like to focus on one that is surely a shared concern, and on which we even have a kind of special relationship. It also happens to be very timely, of great human significance, and a kind of microcosm of the basic principles of world order on which any hope for a decent future rests: the issue of East Timor. At stake is the fate of a people who have suffered miserably, and still do, and to whom Australia owes a unique debt, as you know. Also at stake are foundations of world order and international law, including the crucial principles of the UN Charter on the use of force and the inalienable right of self-determination, a binding obligation on all states. The issue takes on further importance because it may be at a turning point, perhaps a decisive one, and because it is so easily resolved, in comparison to other much thornier ones. It gains further significance because it casts a cruel and brilliant light on the nature of our own free and democratic societies, and the intellectual culture that prevails within them—perhaps the hardest question to face honestly, and one of the most important.

That last aspect relates to the special relationship I mentioned. Much of what I know about the topic comes from Australian sources, including the press. The reason is simple. When I became seriously concerned after the Indonesian invasion, American sources largely dried up, and the quality of what remained was disgraceful. Meanwhile, my tax dollars were being used to provide 90 per cent of Indonesia's arms—restricted to self-defence, according to the law—with new arms shipments designed for counter-insurgency immediately after the invasion and a renewed increase in 1977–78 as atrocities peaked and press coverage reached zero. There was ample information available from highly credible sources including congressional testimony, but it was scrupulously withheld from those who were footing the bills, not only in the press but even the journals of opinion.[1] My own talks, testimony at the United Nations, and publications relied substantially on Australian sources. That's the reason for the special relationship—and it already teaches us quite a bit about how free societies function, if we choose to learn.

The situation has changed in the last few years. Arms sales to Indonesia have declined as a result of popular and congressional pressures, the result of work by a few very dedicated activists with the support of the Church and others. Britain has taken over the lead role in enriching itself though bloodshed, with a degree of cynicism in high places that is startling, even by its traditional standards. While US media coverage has improved, it remains unimpressive. To take one crucial example, apart from the extreme margins the issue of oil in the Timor Gap has been under wraps, and it is not the only one.

The Rule of Law

The basic facts of the matter are about as clear as anything is in world affairs. The Indonesian invasion of December 1975 following several months of military actions that were well known to Australia, the US, and Britain was an unprovoked act of aggression, a war crime, which makes all participants war criminals, from Henry Kissinger on down. The aggression was immediately condemned by the UN General Assembly. Responding to the recommendation that it take 'urgent action', the Security Council unanimously called upon Indonesia to withdraw all its forces 'without delay', called upon 'all States to respect the territorial integrity of East Timor as well as the inalienable right of its people to self-determination', and requested the Secretary-General to act to implement the resolution.[2]

That position has a firm basis in international law. I would like to say a few words about that, but with a preliminary qualification. I am not really concerned here with the technicalities, but rather the principles that underlie them. It is unfortunate but true that we live under the rule of force, not the rule of law, in the sense that the great powers do what they choose, as do others if they can get away with it, irrespective of law and high-sounding principles. A dramatic recent example is the effort by Nicaragua to use the peaceful means required by international law in response to US terrorist attack. Nicaragua went to the World Court; the US reacted by withdrawing its acceptance of ICJ jurisdiction. When the Court nonetheless issued a judgment, the US simply dismissed it. Nicaragua then turned to the UN Security Council, which passed a resolution calling on all states to obey international law (11–1, three abstentions; blocked by US veto). Nicaragua tried the General Assembly, where the US again vetoed resolutions in two successive years, once joined by Israel and El Salvador, the second time by Israel alone; a negative US vote amounts to a veto. The media paid no attention, correctly regarding world opinion as irrelevant when the most powerful state so decides.

It would be misleading to say that the ruling of the World Court was ignored. The Court called upon the US to terminate its 'unlawful use of force' against Nicaragua—another war crime—and its illegal economic warfare, and to pay substantial reparations,

also explicitly determining that all assistance to the US-run terrorist forces attacking the country is 'military aid', not 'humanitarian
aid'. There was an immediate response. Congress sharply increased
the military aid to the terrorist forces. The press and intellectual
opinion—including well-known advocates of world order and international law—condemned the Court for discrediting itself by issuing its judgment, the essential contents of which were never
reported. Military aid continued until the US imposed its will
(termed 'humanitarian aid' in Congress and the press). After the
shattered country finally accepted US demands, it was compelled
to withdraw its request for reparations as it collapsed into a major
humanitarian disaster, declining rapidly into chaos, misery, and
hopelessness after traditional US control was finally established;
the facts are not reported apart from an occasional sarcastic reference to Sandinista incompetence and crimes. More grotesque yet,
the outcome is widely hailed across the spectrum of articulate opinion as yet another illustration of how the United States has 'served
as an inspiration for the triumph of democracy in our time'—a triumph illustrated well enough throughout the regional horror cham-
ber, a topic that is also not within the realm of discussion in
respectable circles.[3]

This is only a tiny sample. It would be hard to design a
clearer illustration of the ugly reality.

For such reasons, I will discuss the backgrounds in international law only insofar as they reveal, as I think they do, the principles to which decent people should be committed, and which
they should compel their governments to observe—impossible
in many countries, easy enough in ours, if we choose.

The UN resolutions on East Timor and the obligations they
impose on all states gain further significance from the fact that
the resolutions merely affirm, for this particular case, the language of two critically important resolutions adopted unanimously by the UN General Assembly in 1970 and 1974: the

Declaration of Principles of International Law Concerning Friendly Relations and Co-operation among States, and the Resolution on the Definition of Aggression.[4] These resolutions declare unequivocally that 'No territorial acquisition resulting from the threat or use of force shall be recognized as legal', and that no 'special advantage resulting from aggression shall be recognized as lawful': in both cases, not *should*, but *shall*, an obligation. The application of these principles to the Indonesian invasion of East Timor shortly after is immediate, and was so recognised by the Security Council in its call on all states to uphold the principles of international law that they had just so ringingly affirmed.

The Friendly Relations Declaration has a uniquely important status in international law, as has repeatedly been affirmed. It was adopted in celebration of the 25th anniversary of the United Nations, after years of careful drafting. To its credit, the government of Australia took an active role throughout and co-sponsored the final draft. Australia's official position was that the declaration does not amend the UN Charter but merely 'elaborates some of its most important principles', in particular, those concerning the use of force and the right of self-determination. Australia described the Declaration as a contribution to 'the progressive development and codification of international law', quoting from Article 13 of the UN Charter which confers that role on the General Assembly.

Australia's very principled position has been affirmed repeatedly since, beginning at once, in 1971, when the World Court issued its *Namibia Advisory Opinion*, which obligated all states to refrain from recognising South Africa's illegal occupation of Namibia, and further declared that 'member States are under obligation to abstain from entering into treaty relations with South Africa in all cases in which the Government of South Africa purports to act on behalf of or concerning Namibia'. The Court added that 'all States should bear in mind that the injured entity is a people which must look to the international community for assistance in its progress towards the goals for which the sacred trust was instituted', referring to the 'sacred trust of civilisation' that affirmed the principle of non-annexation and the responsibility of the international community for the well-being and development of people who had not yet attained independence.

Four years before the event, the Court judgment reads as a virtual prescription of the obligations of all law-abiding states in the case of Indonesia and East Timor, specifically with regard to recognition of the illegal occupation and annexation, and with regard to any treaty that Indonesia might attempt to implement concerning the conquered territory.

'There could not be a more compelling call to action on behalf of the people of East Timor', Bill Bowring comments. An understatement, perhaps, since, however objectionable, the South African occupation of Namibia, as Roger Clark points out, was not 'of the same ilk as East Timor where the right to self-determination was denied by a simple invasion across international boundaries'.[5]

The most striking reaffirmation of the Friendly Relations Declaration, perhaps, was in the World Court decision on the US and Nicaragua, which singled it out as demonstrating that the treaty obligation of the UN Charter to abstain from force is a binding obligation under customary international law, accepted as valid by all states that endorsed the Declaration, notably Australia, given its leading role.

The Declaration gains further force, directly applicable to the present case, from the 1974 Vienna Convention on the Law of Treaties, also endorsed by Australia without reservations, which declares a treaty 'void' if it conflicts with international law: the International Law Commission that drafted the Convention singled out the Friendly Relations Declaration as the basis for determining when a treaty is void, and subsequent commentary has done so as well.

It seems simple enough to figure out what the Namibia Opinion, the Vienna Convention, the Resolutions, and the basic principles that underlie them, and 'the sacred trust of civilisation' entail about a treaty based on the acquisition of territory by force and denial of the inalienable right of self-determination, and offering 'special advantage' to its signatories, a treaty in which a conqueror purports to act on behalf of helpless people still denied the right of self-determination who must rely on the international community for defence of their rights. I know of only one such treaty, namely the Timor Gap Treaty that was implemented five years ago where we are meeting, by the Australian Parliament, dealing with the rich oil resources of the area that the Treaty describes as lying between 'the Indonesian Province of East Timor and Northern Australia'.

In brief, the issue of war crimes seems about as clear as such things ever are, and the obligations of all states to refrain from endorsing them or gaining special advantage from them as well. One could hardly find a clearer case to determine whether international law and world order mean anything at all, beyond their utility as weapons to beat official enemies.

The results of the experiment are dramatically clear. The model of international behaviour was established at once by the world's most powerful state, which also holds a commanding lead in its high-minded invocation of exalted principles and impressive flights of self- congratulatory rhetoric for upholding them. The United States responded to the Security Council Resolution by rapid escalation of its decisive participation in the crime, in direct violation of the injunction to all states it has just endorsed. The endorsement of the high principles was public; the instant renunciation of them was secret, also concealed by the media, which had the evidence but chose to suppress it. The reason for the secrecy was, as usual, hatred of democracy: fear that the primary enemy, the domestic public, might not appreciate what is being done in their name and with their money. Secretary of State Henry Kissinger at once stepped up the flow of arms and instructed his UN Ambassador to block any diplomatic reaction to Indonesia's criminal aggression, adopting the stance that Australian diplomat Richard Woolcott—again in secret—admiringly called 'Kissingerian realism', a technical term for cowardly thuggishness and criminality. Woolcott urged Australia to follow the same course, and his advice was taken.

In the United States, no one is more revered for his defence of international law and its universality than Senator Daniel Patrick Moynihan, who was UN Ambassador at the time of the outright invasion in December 1975, and was kind enough to tell us in his memoirs just how he defended these high principles. In his own words:

> The United States wished things to turn out as they did and worked to bring this about. The Department of State desired that the United Nations prove utterly ineffective in whatever measures it undertook. This task was given to me, and I carried it forward with no inconsiderable success.

He goes on to explain how 'things turned out', noting that within a few months some 60 000 people had been killed, '10 percent of the population, almost the proportion of casualties experienced by the Soviet Union during the Second World War'. Having compared himself proudly to the Nazis, Moynihan goes on to other matters, secure in the knowledge that his reputation as a great humanitarian and the nation's leading advocate of international law will be unsullied. A former professor himself, Moynihan's assessment of the intellectual community proved quite accurate, another comment on free societies.

There is no need to review the parade that followed suit as diplomats caught the scent of money and power, always solemnly proclaiming their profound devotion to the principles of international law and righteously denouncing those who violated its sacred principles (in properly selected cases), and basking in the acclaim of the respectable intellectual community, with rare exception.

International Responsibilities

Dispensing with that sordid tale, let us turn rather to Australia's official stand on these matters. I'm no expert on Australian foreign policy, so you'll pardon me, I hope, if I rely on secondary sources. A natural place to look is the 1991 treatise *Australia's Foreign Relations* by Foreign Minister and legal scholar Gareth Evans, presumably an authoritative guide.[6] He writes that 'Australia has always taken its international responsibilities very seriously . . . Once we subscribe to a treaty we abide by its requirements in every detail', unlike other more negligent states. That this is indeed Australia's public stand is underscored by its principled role in spelling out the obligations of all states to uphold the inalienable right of self-determination, and to refuse either to recognise the acquisition of territory by force or to gain any 'special advantage' from such crimes.

Australia's official commitment to the high principles formulated by the Foreign Minister was reiterated forcefully by Prime Minister Hawke, who warned that 'big countries cannot invade small neighbours and get away with it'. Thanks to the virtuous Anglo-Americans and their associates, the weak will 'feel more secure because they know that they will not stand alone if they are threatened', and 'would-be aggressors will think twice before invading smaller neighbours'. 'All nations should know that the rule of law must prevail over the rule of force in international relations', the Prime Minister declared. One could hardly be more clear and explicit. All of this is in reference to Iraq's invasion of Kuwait, which Senator Evans properly denounced as 'naked indefencible aggression by a strong ruthless and ambitious sovereign country over a weaker neighbour'.[7]

Australia's principled stand was illustrated further by the decision of the Fraser government to revoke the *de jure* recognition of the incorporation of the Baltic countries into the USSR, solemnly reaffirmed by Prime Minister Hawke in 1983 as 'demonstrat[ing] our continuing commitment to the purposes and principles of the United Nations Charter [drawn up five years after the Baltic states were taken over again by Russia] and to the cause of democracy and freedom in the world'. With respect to East Timor, Australian attitudes were clarified further with the release of Cabinet records from the early 1960s. The Menzies Cabinet then resolved that neither Australia nor the Western powers would accept an armed takeover of East Timor, though Australia would have no alternative but to acquiesce in Indonesian annexation if it were achieved by peaceful means—not exactly what occurred.[8]

With this background, one can only be perplexed to read on in the Foreign Minister's study of Australia's foreign relations. There is nothing about the norms of international law that Australia played such a prominent role in establishing as the obligations of all states. Nor is there a word about the application of these high principles to the Indonesian invasion of East Timor, as articulated unanimously by the UN Security Council—with utter cynicism, as the US Ambassador casually observed. In fact, there are only a few sentences on the whole topic. One mentions the *de jure* recognition of Indonesia's annexation of East Timor by the same government that revoked the recognition of the Soviet annexation of the Baltic states. There is a single phrase about 'The Indonesian takeover of East Timor in 1975, when the military moved with less than decent haste to take the place of the hastily departed Portuguese colonialists, with five Australian journalists being killed in the process'—in some unspecified way; Roger East apparently lost his life in some different way. That is the full record: the problem was the *less than decent haste*, which was embarrassing, not the crime of aggression or crimes against humanity, or the behaviour of the accessories, who are always ready with uplifting rhetoric, when it serves the needs of money and power. We can only conclude that the matter of Australia's international obligations is considered irrelevant to foreign policy. If so, Australia is in good company: that of the United Nations from A to Z.

The irrelevance to foreign policy of law and principle—even mere fact—is clarified more fully by Senator Evans in his review of 'The Case for Australian Participation' in the Gulf War.[9] The high principles are forcefully reiterated, and Iraq's violation of them, resolutely condemned. Iraq's invasion of Kuwait 'demonstrated that the habits of millennia— greed, violence, the unbridled quest for dominance and power—were still with us and guiding the behaviour of at least some nations', namely Iraq, which invaded and annexed another country, pillaged it, and committed many crimes, 'all in defiance of the strongest possible expressions of international abhorrence and a body of international law'. Such behaviour is deeply offensive to Australia, which had to respond because of 'the gravity of Iraq's affronts to international law and the norms of civilised behaviour'. Particularly contemptible was Iraq's 'use of military power and influence in pursuit of their objectives', the 'blatant and indisputable breach of international law and norms', and 'the stark and indisputable nature of Iraq's actions: the invasion, military occupation and annexation of one sovereign country by another'. Given its commitment to international righteousness, 'Australia had a very strong interest in demonstrating both that acts of aggression of this kind were not tolerable, and that the international community had the will and the means to respond to them'. With the Cold War over, Australia's honour and interests lie in denying the right of 'regionally based-powers to pursue hegemonic ambitions and have recourse to unprovoked aggression against their neighbours'.

Does this sound familiar, right on Australia's doorstep? Evans is not unaware of the similarity, of course, but dismisses it on the grounds that the cases are not comparable. That is indeed true. The Western-backed atrocities in East Timor were (and remain) incomparably more serious than anything charged to Saddam Hussein in Kuwait. And no country entered into a treaty with Iraq to rob Kuwait's oil. But these differences Evans does not mention; rather, far more marginal ones. East Timor was 'not sovereign in its own right, but was a colonial dependency whose future was in dispute'; disputed, that is, by the conqueror, not the world community, at least in its rhetorical reaction at the United Nations. And 'there was a significant civil conflict' in East Timor, namely, the uprising sponsored by Indonesia (as the Foreign Minister knows well even from the diplomatic cables that have been leaked) and that had ended several months before the outright invasion. And if there was no 'civil conflict' in Kuwait, it is because the large majority of its population, including the semi-slaves who did most of the work, were not part of the small super- privileged minority of actual citizens and feared to open their mouths in protest, let alone civil conflict.

Evans also omits the most obvious difference between the two cases, the one that in fact determined the differential reaction: in the case of East Timor, support for war crimes and crimes against humanity was highly profitable to Australia and served the interests represented by policymakers; the conquest of Kuwait harmed those interests. The same is true of its equally high-minded allies.

The same trivially obvious facts were somehow 'missed' by an impressive array of distinguished diplomats and commentators, or simply denied, with arguments no less powerful than those of the Foreign Minister. The lesson is instructive for those who care to understand something about 'the sacred trust of civilisation', taking its place in a rather full library of similar cases, past and present.

A further consideration in Australia's principled stand after Iraq's invasion in August 1990, the Foreign Minister continues, was 'the early evidence of Iraq's determination to stay in Kuwait', and Saddam's later behaviour as he 'flatly refuse[d] to consider withdrawal'. The Iraqi tyrant—a great friend and ally of the West before his crime of disobedience, the first one that mattered—'had abundant opportunities to explore negotiated ways out but had ignored or rebuffed them all', Evans asserted as unqualified fact.

I do not know whether the Australian press has reported the ample information that was available from late August 1990 until the US bombing began in January 1991 concerning Iraqi offers to withdraw, and the instant and unqualified rejection of them by the US government, which, without qualification or exception, refused its 'abundant opportunities to explore negotiated ways out'. It is hard to imagine that no one, even in Australian intelligence, read the front-page story by New York Times chief diplomatic correspondent Thomas Friedman on August 22 under the heading 'Bush's hard line', explaining Washington's refusal to consider 'a diplomatic track' for fear that negotiations might 'defuse the crisis' and restore the previous status quo at the cost of 'a few token gains in Kuwait' for the Iraqi dictator. The token gains were 'a Kuwaiti island or minor border adjustments', both matters long under dispute: the 'island' was an uninhabited mudflat assigned to Britain's Kuwaiti colony in the imperial settlement to ensure that Iraq would remain landlocked; the adjustments of an ambiguous border involved the Rumailah oil field, 95 per cent within Iraqi territory and exploited by slant digging from Kuwait according to Iraq. It does not seem beyond the realm of possibility that diplomacy might have resolved such issues, as Washington feared, and the literate world knew. And as could have been understood more clearly, at least by people in New York, where every newsstand a week later featured blaring headlines in *Newsday* on the Iraqi offer that apparently prompted Friedman's article, and the acknowledgment in the *Times* the following day, in very small print, that it had had the story but had not published it.

It is however possible that other published information escaped the notice of Australian commentators and the intelligence services, for example, the report by Washington correspondent Knut Royce on the January 2, 1991, disclosure by US officials of Saddam's offer 'to withdraw from Kuwait if the United States pledges not to attack as soldiers are pulled out, if foreign troops leave the region, and if there is agreement on the Palestinian problem and on the banning of all weapons of mass destruction in the region', an offer described by high officials in Washington as 'interesting' because it dropped the border issues and 'signals Iraqi interest in a negotiated settlement'. It was 'a serious prenegotiation position', a State Department Mideast expert observed, though Washington 'immediately dismissed the proposal'.[10] It is true that the media laboured mightily to suppress the unwanted facts, and still do, and that they are joined by scholarship in this endeavour. But the facts were certainly available.

It is also hard to imagine that Australian intelligence could not inform the Foreign Minister that the greatest fear of President Bush and his advisers from the day of Iraq's invasion was that the Arab states would accept the Iraqi withdrawal that they anticipated, leaving behind a puppet regime (mimicking what the US had just done in Panama). These facts at least are recognised even by scholars who bend over backwards to try to present US–UK actions in the most favourable light, suppressing all of the crucial documentary evidence to this end, but conceding that 'Saddam apparently intended neither officially to annex the tiny emirate nor to maintain a permanent military presence there. Instead, he sought to establish hegemony over Kuwait, ensuring its complete financial, political and strategic subservience to his wishes'— again, like the US in Panama a few months earlier.[11]

Evans's account of these matters illustrates that fact is as irrelevant as principle when 'the national interest' is at stake, as it is construed by the powerful and privileged. Not by the population, as we know for the United States at least. Days before the bombing, by two to one, Americans advocated a diplomatic settlement along the lines of Iraq's latest proposal, though virtually no one was aware of the (well- suppressed) facts; had the media and intellectuals not carried out their tasks with such success, the ratio would surely have been much higher, and it might not have been so easy to 'ignore or rebuff all' of the many opportunities for a diplomatic settlement, questions that are worth pursuing, and perhaps may even enter the permissible agenda in some distant future.

The jacket cover of Evans's treatise is graced with warm words by Indonesian Foreign Minister Ali Alatas for 'My good friend and colleague, Gareth Evans', sentiments that were reciprocated as Senator Evans presented the Honorary Award in the Order of Australia to 'my Indonesian counterpart and friend, Foreign Minister Ali Alatas', expressing his 'delight' in doing so. Shortly before Alatas had praised the book, he had restated Indonesia's position on East Timor at the National Press Club in Washington: 'Although the Indonesian people welcomed the expressed desire of the East Timorese people for integration, the Government declared that it would not accede to it until after a proper exercise of the right of self-determination had been conducted. Hence, a provisional People's Assembly of East Timor was formed . . . In the capital city of Dili on May 31, 1976, this Assembly, in a public session . . . formally cast its vote to choose independence through integration with the Republic of Indonesia'.[12]

Comment is hardly necessary.

In December 1989, perhaps as Senator Evans was completing his study of Australia's foreign relations, he took time off to

drink champagne with his 'good friend and colleague' on an aeroplane over the Timor Gap as they signed the treaty dividing up
the spoils of Indonesia's armed conquest, endorsed by Parliament as the book was going to press. The Treaty offers nothing
to the people of East Timor, but fortunately, Senator Evans explained, 'Our conclusion of the Timor Gap Treaty with Indonesia
in no way infringes the rights of the East Timorese people', whose
resources are being stolen by the criminal and its accessory.[13]

The Foreign Minister's comments on the good fortune of the
Timorese were made after the decision of the World Court not
to consider 'the merits' of the case brought by Portugal against
Australia on the matter of the Treaty, because Indonesia refused
to accept the Court's jurisdiction. It surely remains clear enough
that, independently of Indonesia's attitude towards international
law, Australia is committed to the principle that treaties are void
if they conflict with the obligations of all states enunciated in the
UN Charter, spelled out under Australia's lead in international
instruments, binding on all states, which declare illegal any acquisition of territory by force and any special advantage that
might be gained by the improper acquiescence in such crimes,
principles applied directly to the Indonesian invasion by the UN
Security Council. Whatever the World Court might decide, the
Timor Gap Treaty definitively and explicitly renounces everything
that Australia stands for, according to the Foreign Minister and
official stands over many years.

The Evans study of Australia's foreign relations does mention
the Timor Gap Treaty: it is 'an example of a non-military solution
to a problem that historically has often led to conflict'. Apart
from the facts about how the solution was achieved, you will, I
am sure, recall the secret cable sent by Ambassador to Jakarta
Richard Woolcott in August 1975, advising that Australia approve the likely invasion because favourable arrangements to
gain a share of East Timor's oil 'could be much more readily ne-

gotiated with Indonesia . . . than with Portugal or an independent East Timor'. And the report by Michael Richardson a year later that Indonesia was prepared to offer Australia generous terms in exchange for recognition of the Indonesian invasion. All of this paved the way to an exemplary contribution to world order, a fine model of a 'non-military solution'.[14]

All in all, a pretty stunning performance.

In parliamentary debate, the Foreign Minister has explained his position more fully, stating that 'There is no binding legal obligation not to recognise the acquisition of territory that was acquired by force'. So much for the Friendly Relations Declaration, which states that 'No territorial acquisition resulting from the threat or use of force shall be recognised as legal', wording affirmed by the World Court as a binding legal obligation under international law, and understood by Australia to be no more than an elaboration of the meaning of the UN Charter, the basic treaty obligation of all states.

Senator Evans also stated that the legal status of the Friendly Relations Declaration has 'long been hotly contested'. That was nine years ago, and we still await the evidence, which, so far, legal scholars have been unable to unearth, as Roger Clark observed in an as-yet-unanswered challenge, in the most prominent discussion of the Treaty (see note 5). Evans elaborated further that 'the world is a pretty unfair place, littered with examples of acquisition by force', which may therefore be recognised freely by those who hope to gain 'special advantage' by so doing; it should not have troubled us unduly had Libya signed a treaty with Iraq to divide up Kuwait's oil. In the same breath, the Foreign Minister banned official contacts with the PLO because of its 'consistently defending and associating itself with Iraq's invasion of Kuwait'—though he did not, I believe, accuse the PLO of granting official recognition to a gross violation of the Friendly Relations Declaration or signing a treaty to gain 'special advantage' from Iraq's aggression by dividing up Kuwait's oil reserves with the conqueror.[15]

I am sure that any competent law student can show that all of this is a perfect model of consistency. But, as I mentioned, I'm interested now in a different topic: what really guides the acts of the powerful, how these are served up to the general public, and what stand honest people should take, as citizens of democratic societies.

Pragmatism and National Interest

After all of this, it's a relief to turn to a straightforward honest account of what is going on. The best I know is in Ambassador Richard Woolcott's August 1975 cable, in which he recommended 'a pragmatic rather than a principled stand' with regard to the forthcoming Indonesian invasion, because 'that is what national interest and foreign policy is all about'. The Woolcott doctrine neatly cuts through the Gordian knots. There are no problems, no inconsistencies, no need for further casuistry once all principles have been abandoned and it is frankly acknowledged that the powerful do what they like, acting with 'Kissingerian realism'. This position is far preferable, in my opinion, to the inflated and self- congratulatory rhetoric intended for the public—for 'domestic population control', to borrow some of the terminology of pacification theory.

I do have one suggestion, however. The phrase 'national interest' is a residual Orwellism that should be removed, in the cause of semantic hygiene. The term is conventionally used to designate the special interests of those whose domestic power allows them to craft state policy for their own ends, an insight that we can trace back at least as far as that unregenerate Marxist extremist Adam Smith, who observed that the 'merchants and manufacturers' of England are 'the principal architects' of policy, and use their power to ensure that their own interests are 'most peculiarly attended to', however 'grievous' the impact on others.

Plainly, there are other conceptions of 'the national interest'. There may well be Australians who feel that 'Timor's petroleum smells better than Timorese blood and tears', in the bitter words of the Timorese priest who chronicled the horrible Kraras massacre of 1983. But as you know much better than I, there are plenty of Australians who would reject this concept of the national interest with contempt and disgust. Many of them have been quite outspoken about it, not only in the press and journals. Michelle Turner's moving oral history gives many examples. Take, say, Paddy Kenneally, who landed in Timor in 1942 with Australian forces, shortly after Australia invaded the Portuguese colony, setting off a war with Japan in which perhaps 60 000 Timorese died, including many who helped protect the Australian commandoes at a terrible cost to the people of Timor. They died, and continued to die after Australian troops departed, while preventing a likely Japanese invasion of Australia. As for the Timor Gap Treaty, Kenneally says 'with us it's only greed . . . In 1942, if the Timorese had said, "Well, your wounded or your feeding are none of our business", not many of us would have come back', and many Timorese would have survived. He goes on to express his bitterness about Australia's 'betrayal'. He is far from alone in conceiving of the 'national interest' in terms of elementary morality and integrity.[16]

The debt in blood aside, most Australians surely would not accept the 'pragmatic' concept of 'national interest', which is precisely why it is articulated in secret, and why such efforts were made to suppress it after it surfaced. The fact that government secrecy is largely motivated by fear of democracy becomes very evident when one ploughs through declassified records, and is known to diplomatic historians. The US State Department's Historical Advisory Committee—not exactly a gang of radicals—just wrote a formal letter to the Secretary of State objecting to the violations of the traditional rules on declassification, an interference with freedom of information initiated by Reaganite statist reactionaries who strongly believed that the increasingly powerful state they nurtured should be protected from public scrutiny. The committee of historians wrote that 'the refusal to declassify material derives from fear of embarrassment rather than national security'. They could have added that secrecy largely serves that function in the first place.

Apart from the interest of people everywhere in living up to the ideals that are impressively intoned when advantage is to be gained thereby, and even apart from the special debt that Australians owe to the Timorese people, we might ask just what are the great costs to 'the national interest' in the technical sense if Australia decides to adhere to its obligations under international law and elementary justice. Perhaps, as Ambassador Woolcott felt, Australia could make a more lucrative deal with Indonesia to exploit Timor's oil resources. But what is an independent East Timor going to do with its oil? Drink it, perhaps? As everyone knows, they'll call in the same oil companies, possibly on slightly different terms. Even on grounds of Kissingerian realism, are these sufficient grounds for Australia to take the lead in endorsing and profiting from terrible crimes?

What about relations with Indonesia generally? Are they likely to suffer if Australia takes a quiet, dignified, and principled stand? The two countries have complementary socioeconomic systems and major common interests, both economic and strategic, and that is a firm basis for interactions, without the need to barter the lives of suffering people whose only crime is that they are small and weak.

That brings us to the question of Indonesia's 'national interest'. Again, the same questions arise. Which Indonesians are we talking about? Which ones do we choose to support? The interests of General Suharto's family and cronies are not those of Indonesians who are struggling for freedom and justice. There are many of them, including people who are calling on their 'dear friends in Australia' to join them in 'defending the right of self-determination of the island of East Timor' and not to allow themselves to be 'deceived by the sweet words of our politicians who are only concerned about power and money' (Indonesian human rights activist H.J.C. Princen). The reason why the Indonesian government has imposed harsh censorship on its Timor exploits is the usual one: to protect itself from its own population. No one else is fooled, unless they choose to be. The government feared, and rightly, that the people of Indonesia are likely to have the wrong concept of 'national interest'. They might turn out to be less than happy that the budget needed by the armed forces for East Timor 'has drastically reduced the state budget allocated to education and health', as the courageous Indonesian activist and scholar George Aditjondro reports, citing scholarly studies. Or about the tens of thousands of reported casualties and the costs of war, terror, and occupation. And they are no less able to perceive the moral issues than Australians, which is why there have been many protests in Indonesia once the facts began to seep through along with strong calls for withdrawal and the grant of the 'full and free "right of self-determination" to the people of East Timor'.[17]

Such domestic reactions are a good part of the famous piece of gravel in the shoe that troubled Foreign Minister Alatas, and that his government might well decide to remove, to the relief of Indonesians who have their own concept of the national interest.

It has repeatedly been argued here that Indonesia cannot rid itself of the piece of gravel for fear of strengthening separatist movements or perhaps national honour, the same arguments put forth to justify Russia's hold on the Baltic countries, or its current vicious assault on Chechnya, to mention merely two examples of an infamous list. In many such cases, the issues are not trivial, and include complex questions of value and judgment about federalism and independence or centralisation of state power. Each case has to be looked at on its merits; the arguments in the present case are hardly impressive. The proper role of outsiders is to try, as much as possible, to help the affected people gain the right and power to make their own decisions—the *affected people*, not their autocratic rulers, or foreign investors, or the 'principal architects of policy' in our own countries. The rule of outsiders is surely not to pre- empt that choice by firmly placing the boot on the necks of suffering people.

It is also not the role of outsiders to affect a high moral stand, as when a Douglas Hurd—of all people—solemnly explains that the West cannot 'export Western values [on human rights] to developing nations', values that the Third World has learned all about well enough, thank you. As for denunciations of others for their crimes, there are not too many people, and no institutions of power, that are in a very strong position to take such a stance.

My own view, for what it is worth, is that we should look primarily at ourselves. In 1980, the US press finally did begin to give some recognition to what had happened in East Timor, after four terrible years. The *New York Times* had a powerful editorial entitled 'The Shaming of Indonesia'. I wrote a letter, which they would not publish though some NGOs did, suggesting that the title and thrust of the editorial should have been 'the shaming of the United States' (or the shaming of the *New York Times*, though I didn't suggest that, in the vain hope of passing through those august portals). We have our own crimes to consider in the case of East Timor, serious and critical ones, and we are hardly in a position to issue a blanket condemnation of Indonesia, whose people had no way to find out what was going on, and did not, with a few exceptions like George Aditjondro, who needs no lectures from us.

The point generalises, but I won't elaborate. The implications seem obvious.

I'll wind up by reiterating something that should also be obvious. I have been speaking of one of the great crimes of the modern era, one in which we have had and still have a primary role. It is also one of the easier cases to resolve, in world affairs. The piece of gravel can be removed, and we could help ease the way, if we so choose.

Endnotes

Chapter 4

1 Rocker, *Anarchosyndicalism* (Secker & Warburg, 1938); 'Anarchism and Anarchosyndicalism', appended essay in P. Eltzbacher (Freedom Press, 1960).

2 Brady, *Business as a System of Power* (Columbia, 1943). On corporate propaganda, see particularly the pioneering work of Alex Carey, some now collected in his *Taking the Risk out of Democracy* (UNSW, 1995); and on postwar America, Elizabeth Fones-Wolf, *Selling Free Enterprise: the Business Assault on Labor and Liberalism, 1945–1960* (U. of Illinois Press, 1995), the first American academic study of the general topic. See also William Puette, *Through Jaundiced Eyes: How the Media View Organized Labor* (Cornell U. Press, 1992); William Solomon and Robert McChesney, eds., *New Perspectives in U.S. Communication History* (Minnesota, 1993); McChesney, *Telecommunications, Mass Media & Democracy* (Oxford, 1993).

3 Particularly illuminating on these matters is the work of Harvard legal historian Morton Horwitz, including *The Transformation of American Law, 1870–1960*, vol. II (Oxford, 1992).

4 Gary Zabel, ed., *Art and Society: Lectures and Essays by William Morris* (George's Hill, Boston, 1993). Hugh Grant Adams, cited by Ronald Edsforth, *Class Conflict and Cultural Consensus* (Rutgers U. Press, 1987, 29). See also Patricia Cayo Sexton, *The War on Labor and the Left* (Westview, 1991).

5 See my Russell memorial lectures, *Problems of Knowledge and Freedom* (Harper & Row, 1971), for discussion. On Dewey, see particularly Robert Westbrook, *John Dewey and American Democracy* (Cornell U. Press, 1991).

6 Buchanan, *The Limits of Liberty: Between Anarchy and Leviathan* (Chicago, 1975), 92.

7 Stephen Kinzer, *New York Times*, Oct. 14, 1994.

8   *New York Times*, Oct. 7, 1994.

9   Justin Burke, et al., *Christian Science Monitor*, July 26, 1995.

10 Poll, Maria Lopez Vigil, *Envio* (Jesuit University of Central America, Managua), June 1995. Colum Lynch, *Boston Globe*, Sept. 15, 1994; apparently the only report in the mainstream press. See also Alexander Cockburn, *Nation*, Nov. 7, 1994.

11 Clive Ponting, *Churchill* (Sinclair-Stevenson, 1994), 132.

12 For some efforts at comparison, and review of the meagre literature on the topic, see my *Year 501* (South End, 1993); also *World Orders, Old and New* (Columbia, 1994). I'll skip the reaction, though it is of some interest.

13 Montgomery, *The Fall of the House of Labor* (Yale, 1987), 7; Jon Bekken, in Solomon and McChesney, *op. cit.*; Fones-Wolf, *op. cit.* On similar developments in England a few years later, see Edward Herman and N. Chomsky, *Manufacturing Consent* (Pantheon, 1988), ch. 1.2.

14 George Melloan, *Wall Street Journal*, May 16, 1994.

15 Ware, *The Industrial Worker 1840–1860* (Chicago: Ivan Dee, 1990, reprint of 1924 edition); Montgomery, *Citizen Worker* (Cambridge, 1993).

16 Von Humboldt, see my *Cartesian Linguistics* (Harper & Row, 1966), 'Language and Freedom', 1969, reprinted in *For Reasons of State* (Pantheon, 1973) and James Peck, ed., *The Chomsky Reader* (Pantheon, 1987). Also *Problems of Knowledge and Freedom*. Smith, see Patricia Werhane, *Adam Smith and His Legacy for Modern Capitalism* (Oxford, 1991), and *Year 501*. De Tocqueville, Jefferson, see John Manley, 'American Liberalism and the Democratic Dream', *Policy Studies Review* 10.1, 1990; 'The American Dream', *Nature, Society, and Thought* 1.4, 1988.

17 Rajani Kanth, *Political Economy and Laissez-Faire* (Rowman and Littlefield, 1986); see *World Orders*, for further discussion. *New York Times* April 28, 1995.

19 *Fortune*, May 1, May 15; *Business Week*, March 6, 1995.

20 *Business Week*, Jan. 30; May 15, 1995.

Chapter 5

1   Lake, *New York Times*, Sept. 26, 1993; Sept. 23, 1994.

2   Friedman, *New York Times* Week in Review, June 2, 1992. Huntington, *International Security* 17:4, 1993.

3   Schoultz, *Human Rights and United States Policy towards Latin America* (Princeton, 1981); Maechling, *Los Angeles Times*, March 18, 1982.

4   Johnson, Nov. 1, 2; *Public Papers of the Presidents*, 1966, Bk II, 563, 568. Crossette, 'U.N. Finds That Its Reputation Has Slumped for Many in the U.S.', *New York Times*, June 25, 1995. Bernstein, *New York Times Magazine*, Jan. 22, 1984. For more on these illuminating topics, see my *Deterring Democracy* (Verso, 1991; Hill & Wang, Vintage, 1992); *Letters from Lexington* (Common Courage, 1993). The suppression of the

record is as remarkable as the expression of attitudes.

5   Hans Morgenthau, *The Purpose of American Politics* (Vintage, 1964).

6   Bairoch, *Economics and World History* (Chicago, 1993).

7   Prasannan Parthasarathi, Who Was Rich and Who Was Poor in the Eighteenth Century ms. Harvard, May 1995; to appear in *Past and Present*, and, much more fully, in a forthcoming Harvard PhD dissertation.

8   See my *World Orders, Old and New* (Columbia, 1994), for review of these and other cases, including the renewal of the story as the US took over after World War II. Britain's restrictions on development in the American colonies were already discussed by Adam Smith, who also bitterly condemned its crimes in India.

9   Davidson, *Black Man's Burden* (Times Books, 1992). On Ireland, see Lars Mjmset, *The Irish Economy in a Comparative Institutional Perspective* (National Economic and Social Council, Government Publications, Dublin 1992).

10 Sciolino, *New York Times*; Manuela Saragosa, *Financial Times*; Nov. 17, 1994. On the Seattle conference, see *World Orders*.

11 Korb, *Washington Post Weekly*, July 17; John Aloysius Farrell, *Boston Globe*, June 11; Robert Simison and Neal Templin, *Wall Street Journal*, May 18, 1995.

12 See Richard Du Boff, *Accumulation and Power* (M. E. Sharpe, 1989); my *Year 501* (South End, 1993).

13 See *World Order* for further discussion and sources. Also Sidney Plotkin and William Scheurman, *Private Interests, Public Spending* (South End, 1994).

14 E. Childers, 'The Demand for Equity and Equality: The North–South Divide in the United Nations'. Conference of the Jamahir Society, 2 July, 1994, Geneva.

15 *Excelsior* (Mexico), Nov. 21, 1992. AP, *BG*; Katherine Seelye, *New York Times*; Kenneth Cooper and Dan Morgan, *Washington Post*; all June 9, 1995. UNIDO, Ian Hamilton Fazey, *Financial Times*, July 3, 1995. Aid levels, attitude studies, Robin Wright, *Los Angeles Times*, June 13, 1995.

16 Steven Kull, *Bulletin of Atomic Scientists*, March/April 1995. Bosnia, Reuters, *BG*, July 23, 1995. Aid, Robin Toner, *New York Times*, Nov. 16, 1994; the figures presented are misleading, not distinguishing discretionary spending.

17 *The State of Working America, 1994–95* (Sharpe, 1994). *Fortune*, June 12, 1995.

18 Carothers, *In the Name of Democracy* (California, 1991); in Abraham Lowenthal, ed., *Exporting Democracy* (Johns Hopkins, 1991).

19 See *Deterring Democracy*, ch. 10, for a review.

20 Oxfam UK/Ireland, *Structural Adjustment and Inequality in Latin America*, Sept. 1994. Nicaragua News Service, April 30–May 6, 1995. See *World Orders*, for further detail.

21 See my article in *Z magazine*, Nov. 1994, for details.

22 For recent discussion of how it looks to me, see *World Orders*, and 1995 articles in *Z magazine* and elsewhere.

23 *Business Week*, June 5; Richardson, *The Bulletin*, Jan. 17; Prowse, *Financial Times*, June 19, 1995. Prowse's commentaries frequently depart from the standards of the journal, which, like the business press generally, tends to keep free of ideological passions in its reporting.

24 Maureen Dowd, *New York Times*, Dec. 15, 1994. *New York Times*, June 5; David Wessel and Rick Wartzman, *Wall Street Journal*, June 8, 1995. National Public Radio news review 'All Things Considered', May 12, 1995.

25 Richard Morin, *Washington Post Weekly*, Jan. 9, 1994. Lawrence Korb, *New York Times Magazine*, Feb. 26, 1994; *op. cit. Jane's Defence Weekly*, Jan. 28, 1995. *Los Angeles Times*, April 18; Christopher Georges, *Wall Street Journal*, May 17, 1995.

26 *Christian Science Monitor*, July 11, 1995.

27 Jonathan Elliot, ed., *The Debates in the Several State Conventions on the Adoption of the Federal Constitution*, 1787, Yates's Minutes, vol. 1, second edn (Lippincott, 1836), 450. Jules Kagian, *Middle East International*, Oct. 21, 1994.

28 Nedelsky, *Private Property and the Limits of American Constitutionalism* (Chicago University Press, 1990).

29 Shipler, *New York Times*, Weekly Book Review, concluding that the marginal National Public Radio system 'challenges some venerable American doctrine' by not following government orders. On the gift of radio to corporations under the guise of democracy, see Robert McChesney, *Telecommunications, Mass Media & Democracy* (Oxford, 1993).

30 Peter Applebome, *New York Times*, Aug. 1, 1994.

31 M. R. Kelley and T. A. Watkins, *Technology Review*, April 1995; *Science*, April 28, 1995. Chandler, 'The Role of Business in the United States: a Historical Survey', *Daedalus*, Winter 1969.

32. Eric Schmitt, *New York Times*, Feb. 23; Reuters, *BG*, March 3, Eyal Press, *Christian Science Monitor*, Feb. 23; William Hartung, *Nation*, Jan. 30, 1995. *Jane's, op. cit.* Bush program, see *Deterring Democracy*, ch. 1.2.

33 Chambliss, *Social Problems* 41.2, May 1994; *New Left Review*, Spring 1994. Drugs, see *Deterring Democracy*, chs 4–5.

34 Paulette Thomas, *Wall Street Journal*, May 12, 1994.

35 S. Hewlett, *Child Neglect in Rich Societies* (UNICEF, 1993).

36 Michael McCarthy, *Wall Street Journal*, Nov. 8, 1994.

37 Stein, *New York Times*, July 30, 1995.

38 Lawrence Mishel and Jared Bernstein, *The State of Working America: 1994–95*, (M. E. Sharpe, 1994); Edward Wolff, *Top Heavy* (Twenty Century Fund, 1995).

39 *Fortune*, May 15, May 1; *Business Week*, July 17, 1995.

40 For details, see *World Orders*. Japan–US figures, 1993 UN World Investment Report, cited by Vincent Cable, *Daedalus*, Spring 1995.

41 Felix, 'The Tobin Tax Proposal', Working Paper #191, June 1994, UN

Development Program; *Challenge*, May/June 1995. *Wall Street Journal*, May 9, 1994.

Chapter 6

1   What follows is based on notes for a talk at Macquarie University in January 1995, updated with some more recent material, some adapted from my articles in *Ha'aretz* (Feb. 4, 1994) and *Struggle* (Ben-Gurion University, October, 1994). Unless indicated, sources can be found in my *World Orders, Old and New*, along with more extensive discussion.

2   Military correspondents Michael Gordon and General (Marine, ret.) Bernard Trainor, *New York Times*, Oct. 23, 1994, excerpt from their forthcoming book *The Generals' War* (Little, Brown, 1995). The revelations, confirming earlier reports, elicited no comment.

3   See my article in *Z magazine*, Feb. 1990; *Deterring Democracy*, ch. 5. correspondent Charles Glass, who noted further that 'the U.S. has become Iraq's largest trading partner'. His lonely campaign in the mainstream media to expose Iraqi atrocities and the critically important US backing for the regime elicited regular evasion or denials from Washington, reported as fact.

4   *Mideast Mirror* (London), March 15; *Wall Street Journal*, April 8; Cowell, *New York Times*, April 11, 1991; Ron Ben-Yishai, interview with retiring Israeli Chief of Staff Gen. Dan Shomron, *Ha'aretz*, March 29; Shalom Yerushalmi, 'We are all with Saddam', *Kol Ha'ir*, April 4; Moshe Zak, *Jerusalem Post*, April 4, 1991 (the last of these, at least, read by US journalists and commentators). For further detail, see my articles in *Z magazine* in 1990 and 1991; also *Deterring Democracy*, ch. 6, Afterword (in 1992 edition); and in Cynthia Peters, ed., *Collateral Damage* (South End, 1992).

5   Powell cited in Gordon and Trainor, *op. cit.* On Panama, see *Deterring Democracy*, ch. 5; *World Orders*, ch. 1. Ropp, 'Things Fall Apart: Panama after Noriega', *Current History*, March 1993.

6   On the relevant US and UK documents, and a review of what was known at once about diplomatic efforts though scarcely reported in the US (even less in the UK, apparently), see *Deterring Democracy*, ch. 6; also Afterword, and in Peters, *op. cit.* On the most highly praised work of scholarship, by Lawrence Freedman and Efraim Karsh, see my 'World Order and its Rules', *Journal of Law and Society* (Cardiff), Summer 1993.

7   Cited by Gabriel Kolko, *Main Currents in American History* (Pantheon, 1984); Gordon Connell-Smith, *The Inter-American System* (Oxford, 1966). The 'naughty children' specifically in mind were Mexican, at that moment. See my *Turning the Tide* (South End, 1985), for elaboration.

8   For discussion of the matter then, see my 1977 article in *Le Monde diplomatique*, reprinted in *Towards a New Cold War* (Pantheon, 1982), ch. 11.

9   See Morris, 'Falsifying the Record: A Fresh Look at Zionist Documen-
    tation of 1948', excerpted from Hebrew and French publications
    in *Journal of Palestine Studies*, Spring 1995.

10 See my *Fateful Triangle* (South End, 1983), ch. 7, and *The Culture of Ter-
    rorism* (South End, 1988), ch. 8. Also Jonathan Marshall, Peter Dale
    Scott, and Jane Hunter, *The Iran-Contra Connection* (South End, 1987),
    ch. 8.

11 The congressional origins of the human rights campaigns have been in-
    vestigated; see Lars Schoultz, *Human Rights and US Policy*. A closer
    look, yet to be undertaken systematically, leads back to 1960s activism.

12 See Frank Costigliola, in Thomas Paterson, ed., *Kennedy's Quest for Vic-
    tory* (Oxford, 1989). On the contempt for Britain and other European
    allies, see Costigliola, 'Kennedy and the Failure to Consult', *Political
    Science Quarterly*, Spring 1995. Kissinger, *Towards a New Cold War*, 457;
    World Orders, ch. 3.

13 There was a small Jewish community, about 10 per cent of the population,
    at the time when Britain declared its commitment to a 'national home
    for the Jewish people' in 1917; but they were mostly anti-Zionist, and
    their descendants largely remain so, quite militantly for the most part.

14 Abraham Foxman, National Director, Anti-Defamation League, letter,
    Wall Street Journal, Aug. 8, 1995, denouncing Edmund Hanauer, who
    made the 'outrageous' comparison in a letter. The ADL, many years
    ago a genuine civil rights organisation, has become something radically
    different since 1967.

15 Cited in Irwin Wall, 'U.S., Algeria, and the Fourth French Republic',
    Diplomatic History, Fall 1994.

16 See *Deterring Democracy*, ch. 1.2.

17 *La Epoca*, May 4, 1991; Foreword, Thomas Fox, *Iraq* (Sheed & Ward,
    1991). On Third World reactions, see my articles in *Z magazine*, May,
    October, 1991, and Peters, *op. cit.*

18 See *Towards a New Cold War*, ch. 6; pp. 406–7; *World Orders*, ch. 3.

19 The documentary record thoroughly refutes later claims about the al-
    leged positions of US negotiator Arthur Goldberg. The leading propo-
    nent of these inventions is Eugene Rostow. See the exchange in the
    New Republic between Rostow and State Department official David
    Korn, who refutes Rostow's version, as he tacitly acknowledges in his
    evasive response; Oct. 21, Nov. 18, Nov. 25, 1991.

20 Tessler, *A History of the Israeli–Palestinian Conflict* (Indiana University
    Press, 1994) pp. 817–18.

21 *Middle East Justice Network*, Dec. 1994.

22 On the journalistic record of the 1980s, particularly the remarkable per-
    formance of the *Times* Jerusalem correspondent and Pulitzer Prize- win-
    ner Thomas Friedman, see my *Necessary Illusions* (South End, 1989).
    Israeli commentary on the Lebanon war is extensively discussed there
    and in earlier sources, among them my *Pirates and Emperors* (1986:

Claremont, Amana, Pluto, Black Rose); see *World Orders* for review.

23 Julan Ozanne, *Financial Times*, Aug. 8, 1995.

24 Rubinstein, *Ha'aretz*, Aug. 30, 1993; *Wall Street Journal*, May 2, 1994; Benvenisti, *Ha'aretz*, May 12, 1994 (Israel Shahak, 'Translations from the Hebrew Press', June 1994); *Ha'aretz*, July 6, 1995 (*The Other Front*, Jerusalem, July 11).

25 Hass, talk at Tel Aviv University *News from Within* (Jerusalem), July 1995; Usher, *Race & Class*, July–Sept., 1994; Haim and Rivca Gordon, Tsevet 'aza, 'The Situation in the Gaza Strip—July 1995' (Hebrew); Felber, AP, *Boston Globe*, Feb. 4, 1995. On the background, see Sarah Roy, *The Gaza Strip* (Institute for Palestine Studies, 1995).

26 Sarah Helm, *Independent*, Oct. 3; Patrice Claude, *Le Monde*, Oct. 5 (*Guardian Weekly*, Oct. 16), 1994; Gellman, *Washington Post* (*Guardian Weekly*, Jan. 22, 1995); Yerah Tal and Ziv Maor, *Ha'aretz*, Jan. 12; Gidon Schmerling, *Kol Ha'ir*, Jan. 20; Hannah Kim, *Ha'aretz*, Jan. 20 (see Israel Shahak, Report No. 149, Jan. 29); *Ha'aretz*, June 8 (*News from Within*), 1995; Editorial, *Davar*, Dec. 29; Motti Basuk, *Davar*, Dec. 30, 1994 (Shahak, Report No. 148, Dec. 30); Gazit, *Yediot Ahronot*, Jan. 22, and Rubinstein, *Ha'aretz*, Jan. 10, 1995; cited in *Report on Israeli Settlement in the Occupied Territories*, Foundation for Middle East Peace (Washington), March 1995. Barton Gellman, *Washington Post Weekly*, July 3–9, 1995.

27 *B'Tselem Report*, May 1995, citing former Jerusalem City Planner and City Council member Sarah Kaminker; summary and excerpts in *Ha'aretz*, May 15; *News from Within*, June 1995. Also Aaron Back and Eiten Felner, senior staff members of B'Tselem, *Tikkun* 10.4, 1995. Tsaban, Olmert, *Middle East International*, May 12, 1995. See also Clyde Haberman, *New York Times*, May 14, 15, 1995.

28 Ben, *Ha'aretz*, Feb. 7, 1995. For further information and background, see Israel Shahak, *Ideology as a Central Factor in Israeli Policies* (Hebrew), May–June 1995. On land and development fund restrictions, see *Towards a New Cold War*, ch. 9; Walter Lehn with Uri Davis, *The Jewish National Fund* (Kegan Paul, 1988). For further background see also Ian Lustick, *Arabs in the Jewish State* (University of Texas, 1980).

29 Amir Rozenblit, *Jerusalem Post*, Sept. 9, 1994.

30 *Middle East International*, May 12, 1995.

31 Shyam Bhatia, *Observer* (London), Jan. 8; 'Mindless Murder in Israel', editorial, *New York Times*, July 27, 1995. John Battersby, *Christian Science Monitor*, Dec. 5, 1994; May 17, 1995. Rony Shaked and Yovel Peleg, *Yediot Ahronot* (American edition), Nov. 4, 1995.

32 *Economist*, July 15; Reuter, *Guardian*, July 10, 1995. Fisk, *Independent*, Oct. 22, 1994.

33 Nir, *Ha'aretz*, Feb. 15 (Shahak 'Translations', April); Levy, *Ha'aretz*, May 14, April 23 (Shahak 'Translations', August); Kislev, *Ha'aretz*, Jan. 17, 1995. Ben Efrat, *Challenge* No. 32, 1995. Shahak, *Ideology*.

34 Moshe Semyonov and Noah Lewin-Epstein, *Hewers of Wood and Drawers of Water* (Cornell, 1987). Shlomo Abramovitch, 'The Land of Opportunities', *Sheva Yamim*, March 3; editor Hanoch Marmari, *Ha'aretz*, March 9 (Shahak 'Translations', April); Ha'etzni, *Ma'ariv* May 5, 1995.
35 Rubinstein, 'Two Banks of the Jordan', *Ha'aretz*, Feb. 13, 1995 (Shahak, 'Translations', April). Haim Gvirtzman, *Ha'aretz*, May 16; interview, *Al Hamishmar*, March 12, 1993; Gvirtzman alleges that the Labor Party settlement program in the West Bank (which he supports) was designed in such a way as to ensure permanent Israeli control over West Bank water; for extensive quotes, see *World Orders*, ch. 3.5.
36 Julan Ozanne and David Gardner, *Financial Times*, Aug. 8, 1995.
37 Yosef Cohen, *Kol Ha'ir*, Dec. 9, 1988, citing Shashar's diaries.
38 Reinhart, *Ha'aretz*, May 27, 1994.
39 Shmuel Toledano, *Ha'aretz*, Aug. 7; Fatah elections, *Yediot Ahronot*, Nov. 18, 1994. Fishing ban, Robert Fisk, Tyre, *Independent*, Feb. 19, 1995. Kidnapping, Eitan Rabin, *Ha'aretz*, July 24, 1994; one of many cases.
40 Neff, *Middle East International*, March 31, July 21, 1995. Usher, *Middle East International*, Jan. 6, 1995.
41 Chicago Council on Foreign Relations, *American Public Opinion and US Foreign Policy*, 1995.
42 Human Rights Watch, *Torture and Ill-Treatment: Israel's Interrogation of Palestinians from the Occupied Territories* (New York, 1994); B'Tselem reports on interrogation of Palestinians, March 1991, March 1992.
43 Smooha, 'Peace: Who Gains, Who Loses', *Iton Aher*, Dec. 1993.
44 See my essays from the late 1960s collected in *Peace in the Middle East?* (Pantheon, 1974), and later ones in *Towards a New Cold War* (ch. 9, 1975; afterword, 1981). Also *Fateful Triangle*.

Chapter 7

1 For much further discussion and sources, see, inter alia, my *On Power and Ideology* (South End, 1987) and *Deterring Democracy*. See *Year 501*, ch. 4, for references not cited below on Indonesia and US relations to it.
2 *Catholic New Times*, Jan. 9, 1994. See also John Pilger, *New Statesman and Nation*, June 3, 1994, the only professional journalist to have investigated, to my knowledge. On the costs of the invasion, see, among others, George Aditjondro, *In the Shadow of Mount Ramelau* (INDOC, Leiden, 1994), an appalling account based mainly on Indonesian sources; and Ian Robinson, in Michael Cranna, ed., *The True Cost of Conflict* (New Press, 1994), citing Amnesty International, Human Rights Watch, USAID, and a wide range of other sources.
3 Aditjondro, *op. cit.*, Yogyakarta Students Association and eleven Javanese student councils, Nov. 1991, *ibid.* See also Aditjondro's interview in the weekly *Sinar*, 19 Nov., 1994, calling on Indonesia to put into practice 'the spirit of the Constitution', which upholds the right of in-

dependence 'for all peoples' and demands that 'colonialism should be eradicated from the Earth'; and Herbert Feith, 'George Aditjondro and East Timor', including a transcript of an ABC TV interview with Aditjondro (East Timor Talks Campaign, Fitzroy, Australia). Political asylum, *Australian*, June 6; *West Australian*, June 9; *Far Eastern Economic Review*, June 29, 1995. Princen, Sept. 30, 1994; *Inside Indonesia*, Dec. 1994. Pangaribuan, Stuart Rintoul, *Australian*, Feb. 23, 1995.

4   For many examples of the bravery of Indonesian students, workers, and others, see John Pilger, 'The rising of Indonesia', *New Statesman*, June 16, 1995. *Tempo*, Patrick Walters, *Australian*, May 8, 1995. Charles Radin, *Boston Globe*, Nov. 20, 1994. Wages, *Economist*, April 2, 1994. On labour action and the shocking work conditions, see Jeremy Seabrook, 'Indonesian workers risk freedom for rights', *Guardian Weekly*, Oct. 23; Merrill Goozner, 'Asian labor: Wages of shame, Western firms help to exploit brutal conditions', *Chicago Tribune*, Nov. 6, 1994.

5   For a review, see my 'East Timor: the Press Cover-up', *Inquiry*, Feb. 19, 1979; and for more detail, Chomsky and Edward S. Herman, *The Political Economy of Human Rights (PEHR)*, vol. 1 (South End, 1979); and subsequent updates in *Towards a New Cold War* and elsewhere. One illustration of how the doctrinal system was operating is that the article cited is the first in any American journal devoted to Timor, with the exception of one on Indonesia with emphasis on Timor by Arnold Kohen ('The Cruel Case of Indonesia', *Nation*, Nov. 26, 1977), whose contributions in these years have saved many thousands of lives and would certainly have won him a Nobel Peace Prize, if it were awarded on merit.

6   Fallows, *Atlantic Monthly*, June 1982. Anthony Flint, *BG*, March 4, 1994, reporting a conference on intervention at Tufts University opened by Hoffmann's address. Macfarlane, review of Alexander George, ed., *Western State Terrorism*, *Times Higher Education Supplement*, June 26, 1992.

7   Brian Toohey, *Australian Financial Review*, Nov. 24, 1994. Editorial, 'Indonesia's Pebble', *WSJ*, Nov. 17, 1994.

8   See references of note 6. For the image, see Peter Wilson, *Australian*, Aug. 1, 1995.

9   Reuters, *New York Times*, Dec. 8, 1993, a few lines on an inside page; Irene Wu, *Far Eastern Economic Review*, June 30, 1994.

10 Jeffrey Smith, *Washington Post*, March 18, 1995. Johnston, letter, *Nation*, April 1994.

11 *New York Times*, *Time*, *US News and World Report*, *Time*, respectively.

12 See *Year 501*, ch. 4, for review of US participation and reaction. Policy 'to exterminate the PKI', cited by Audrey and George Kahin, *Subversion as Foreign Policy* (New Press, 1995).

13 McNamara to National Security Adviser McGeorge Bundy, June 11, 1965; see my *On Power and Ideology*, ch. 1. Kennan, *ibid.* Dulles–Eisenhower, see *World Orders*, ch. 1. On Brazil and the background thinking

as expressed by the Framers of the Constitution, see ch. 5, above.

14 *Counterpunch* (Institute for Policy Studies, Washington), Feb. 15, March 15; Nicholas Cumming-Bruce, *Guardian*, Feb. 16, 1994; AI, 'Indonesia: Workers' rights still challenged', June 1995; David Sanger, *New York Times*, Oct. 31, 1995.

15 'US Military Training', *FEER*, March 30, 1995. De Faux, Gary Hughes, *Age*, May 16; UN testimony, July 11, 1995, distributed by TAPOL (London). Eyal Press, *National Catholic Reporter*, Aug. 11, 1995; the only US report, to my knowledge.

16 Editorial, *Boston Globe*, April 3, 1995.

17 *International Herald Tribune*, Aug. 3, 1995; *Postal Bulletin*, International Rates and Fees, effective July 9, 1995. Charles Radin, *BG*, Nov. 15, 1994. Cameron Stewart and Colleen Egan, *Australian*, June 14, 1995.

18 Pilger, *Distant Voices* (1994); *New Statesman*, Nov. 25, 1994. France, *PEHR*, Michael Durham and Hugh O'Shaughnessy, *Observer*, Nov. 13, 1994. *Briarpatch* (Saskatchewan), July 1995. Lloyd George, cited by V. G. Kiernan, *European Empires from Conquest to Collapse* (Fontana, 1982).

19 J. R. Walsh and G. J. Munster, *Documents on Australian Defence and Foreign Policy 1968–1975* (Hong Kong, 1980), p. 219. The book was suppressed by court action but the most important documents in it are frequently quoted. Among others, see *PEHR*; Brian Toohey and Marian Wilkinson, *The Book of Leaks* (Angus & Robertson, 1987); Geoffrey Gunn, *A Critical View of Western Journalism and Scholarship on East Timor* (Journal of Contemporary Asia Publishers, Manila, 1994). Gunn points out that the book is scarcely available in Australia, even at public libraries. Arms sales, Cameron Stewart, *Australian*, Jan. 17, 1995.

20 *Ibid.*; editorial, *Australian*, Jan. 17, 1995. Eric Schmitt, *New York Times*, Aug. 8; letter, David Isenberg, Centre for Defence Information, *New York Times*, Aug. 13, 1995.

21 Evans, cited by Gunn, *op. cit.*, 250. Gen. Sutrisno, cited in *Power and Impunity* (Amnesty International, 1994), p. 54. In March 1995, Evans reiterated that the Dili massacre was 'never assessed . . . as distinct from just grossly aberrant local behaviour', explaining why it receives no mention in the new edition of his book *Australia's Foreign Relations* (see note 41, below); *Melbourne Herald-Sun*, March 12, 1995.

22 Randolph Ryan, *BG*, Oct. 25, 28; Reuters, Oct. 25, 27; Michael Ellis, *Sydney Morning Herald*, Oct. 29, 1994. Brian McGrory, *BG*, Nov. 12, 1992. Cameron Stewart, *Australian*, March 16, 17; Geoffrey Barker, 'Dili massacre general's visit sure to outrage Timorese, *Australian Financial Review*, March 15, 1995. UN rapporteur, David Watts (London), *Australian*, Dec. 21, 1994, citing *London Times* and AFP; unreported in the US (data base check).

23 Judy Rakowsky, *BG*, April 13, 1995.

24 For references and further discussion, see *Year 501*, chs 2, 4, 7, 11; and

World Orders. Also chs 4, 5, above.

25 See Wm. Roger Louis, *Imperialism at Bay* (Oxford, 1978), p. 237. Towards a *New Cold War,* p. 373, for further discussion.

26 Kahin and Kahin, *op. cit.* George Kahin, 'Democracy in Indonesia', in David Bourchier and John Legge, eds, *Democracy in Indonesia,* Monash Papers on Southeast Asia No. 31, 1994.

27 Crouch, *Army and Politics in Indonesia* (Cornell, 1978), pp. 351, 155; China alignment, 64n.

28 *Foreign Relations of the United States, 1958–1960,* Vol. XVII, *Indonesia* (Washington, 1994); April 8, Aug. 12, 1958. Kahin & Kahin, *op. cit.* Australian involvement, see particularly Brian Toohey and William Pinwill, *Oyster* (Heinemann, 1989), p. 69ff.

29 *Ibid.* Crouch, *op. cit.,* pp. 273, 299, 303.

30 *Weekend Australian,* Jan. 1–2, 1994, on Cabinet records released Jan. 1.

31 *Op. cit.,* p. 93. The USSR had by then given Indonesia US$1 billion in aid, they report.

32 See my *Rethinking Camelot* (South End, 1993), for details and background, from the recently declassified record. Pauker, Kintner, cited by Peter Dale Scott in Malcolm Caldwell, ed., *Ten Years' Military Terror in Indonesia* (Spokesman, 1975); see *Year 501* for review. Pauker (UC) in Toohey and Pinwill, *op. cit.*

33 CIA report cited by Robert Cribb, ed., *The Indonesian Killings of 1965–1966* (Monash Papers on Southeast Asia, no. 21, 1991).

34 Bundy cited by David Fromkin and James Chace, *Foreign Affairs* (Spring 1985). McNamara, *In Retrospect* (Times Books, 1995). Pike, *Viet Cong* (MIT, 1965).

35 McArthur, *International Herald Tribune,* Dec. 5, 1977. *Time,* July 15, 1966. Editorial, *NYT,* Dec. 22, 1965. Cribb, *op. cit.* John Murray Brown, *CSM,* Feb. 6, 1987. Shenon, *NYT,* Sept. 3, 1992. *Economist,* Aug. 15, 1987. Richard Borsuk, *WSJ,* June 8, 1992. Wain, *WSJ,* April 25, 1989. *Asiaweek,* Feb. 24, 1989, cited in *TAPOL Bulletin,* April 1989. Shenon, Editorial, NYT, Aug. 17, 1995.

36 Cribb cites Arnold Brackman's *Communist Collapse in Indonesia* and an unpublished PhD dissertation 'for a summary of international responses to the killings'; the former, at least, avoids the matter almost entirely. The only published review at the time Cribb wrote was Peter Dale Scott's in Caldwell's *Ten Years' Military Terror,* a book that Cribb mentions dismissively for its failure 'to dig deeply into the details of the killings'.

37 Davidson, comment on William Minter, *Apartheid's Contras* (Zed, 1994). 'Inter-Agency Task Force, Africa Recovery Program/Economic Commission, *South African Destabilization: the Economic Cost of Frontline Resistance to Apartheid,* NY, UN, 1989, p. 13. Crouch, *op. cit.,* p. 341.

38 Walsh and Munster, *op. cit.,* p. 200. Simpson, 'Judging the East Timor Dispute', *Hastings International and Comparative Law Review,* University

of California, Winter, 1994.

39 Ian Verrender, *Sydney Morning Herald*, Nov. 19, 1994. See Roger Clark, 'Timor Gap Treaty', *Pace Yearbook of International Law*, 1992; and Christine Chinkin, 'Australia and East Timor in International Law', in *International Law and the Question of East Timor* (Catholic Institute of International Relations, 1995).

40 Evans and Bruce Grant, *Australia's Foreign Relations* (Melbourne University Press, 1991), p. 109. Gordon Feeny, *Melbourne Herald-Sun*, Aug. 1, 1995. Evans (quoting Hedley Bull on 'purposes' . . .) cited by Scott Burchill, *Australia's International Relations* (Australian Institute of International Affairs and Deakin University, 1994), pp. 8, 67.

41 ICJ, Year 1995, General List No. 84, Portugal v. Australia. June 30, 1995. *Bangkok Post*, Feb. 21; cited in *Daily Telegraph Mirror*, Feb. 21, 1995.

42 For details, see the cable traffic in Toohey and Wilkinson, *op. cit.*

43 For a look at what he did consider worth reporting at that time, see *Towards a New Cold War*, pp. 346, 475.

44. For a detailed review of these years, see *Towards a New Cold War* and essays on East Timor and Cambodia reprinted in James Peck, ed., *Chomsky Reader* (Pantheon 1988).

Chapter 8

1 The sole exception was Arnold Kohen, 'The Cruel Case of Indonesia', *Nation*, Nov. 26, 1977. My article 'East Timor: the Press Cover-up', *Inquiry*, Feb. 19, 1979, based on earlier UN testimony, was the first in the country specifically devoted to East Timor after over three years of horrendous US-backed atrocities.

2 For the documents, see *Background Information* (Commission of the Churches on International Affairs, World Council of Churches, 1995/1). For extensive discussion, see *International Law and the Question of East Timor* (Catholic Institute of International Relations, 1995).

3 *New Republic*, March 19, 1990. For a review, see my *Necessary Illusions* (South End, 1989). On the aftermath, see *Deterring Democracy* and *World Orders, Old and New*.

4 The primary source on the legal aspects of the question is Roger Clark, 'Timor Gap Treaty', *Pace Yearbook of International Law*, 4, 1992, from which I am drawing here, unless otherwise indicated. See also his paper and others in *International Law*.

5 Bowring, *ibid.*; Clark, *ibid.*; Gerry Simpson, 'Judging the East Timor Dispute', *Hastings International and Comparative Law Review*, Winter 1994.

6 Evans and Bruce Grant, *Australia's Foreign Relations* (Melbourne University Press, 1991).

7 Cited by Gunn, *Critical View*, citing an Evans 'Backgrounder' on the

Gulf War. For other sources, here and below, see my *Year 501*, ch. 4.

8   Evans and Grant, *op. cit.*; Hawke, Clark, in *International Law*. Cameron Stewart, Gregory Pemberton, and AAP, *Weekend Australian*, Jan. 1–2, 1994.

9   Murray Goot and Rodney Tiffen, *Australia's Gulf War* (Melbourne University Press, 1992).

10 Knut Royce, *Newsday* (New York), Aug. 29, 1990; Jan. 3, 1991.

11 Lawrence Freedman and Efraim Karsh, *The Gulf Conflict 1990–1991: Diplomacy and War in the New World Order* (Princeton, 1992). See ch. 6, above. For discussion at the time and since, see my articles in *Z magazine*, *Boston Globe*, and London *Guardian* from September 1990 to January 1991, and further elaboration in *Deterring Democracy* and *World Orders*. I also reported the facts (which were, after all, public for those who chose to know) on national radio in many countries in the same months, including Australia, if my memory is correct.

12 Evans, Press Release, March 29, 1995; Alatas, March 1992, cited by Simpson, *op. cit.*

13 Press release, June 30, 1995. Signing, Gunn, *op. cit.*, p. 160.

14 Richardson, *Australian Financial Review*, Oct. 19, 1976, cited by Simpson, *op. cit.*

15 See *Year 501*, ch. 4, for references.

16 Turner, M., *Telling: East Timor, Personal Testimonies* (University of New South Wales Press, 1992). See preceding chapter.

17 Aditjondro, *Shadow*; Robinson, in Cranna, *True Costs*.

Index

303

Also Available from Haymarket Books by Noam Chomsky

After the Cataclysm
  The Political Economy
  of Human Rights—
  Volume II
  with Edward S. Herman
  $27, ISBN: 9781608463978

Conversations on Palestine
  with Ilan Pappé
  $11.95, ISBN: 9781608464708

Culture of Terrorism
  $23, ISBN: 9781608463985

Gaza in Crisis
  Reflections on the US-Israeli
  War Against the
  Palestinians
  with Ilan Pappé
  $16.95, ISBN: 9781608463312

Hopes and Prospects
  $17, ISBN: 9781931859967,
  trade paperback
  $39.95, ISBN:
  9781931859974,
  unabridged audiobook

Intervenciones
  Foreword by Eduardo
  Galeano
  $16, ISBN: 9781931859592

Masters of Mankind
  Essays and Lectures, 1963–
  2013
  Introduction by Marcus
  Raskin, $12.95, ISBN:
  9781608463633

On Power and Ideology
  The Managua Lectures
  $16, ISBN: 9781608464005

Pirates and Emperors,
Old and New
  International Terrorism in the
  Real World
  $18, ISBN: 9781608464012

Propaganda and the Public Mind
  with David Barsamian
  $18, ISBN: 9781608464029

Powers and Prospects
  Reflections on Nature and the
  Social Order
  $18, ISBN: 9781608464241

Rethinking Camelot
  JFK, the Vietnam War, and
  U.S. Political Culture
  $16, ISBN: 9781608464036

Rogue States
  The Rule of Force in World
  Affairs
  $18, ISBN: 9781608464043

Turning the Tide
  U.S. Intervention in Central
  America and the Strug-
  gle for Peace
  $19, ISBN: 9781608464050

The Washington Connection
and Third World Fascism
  The Political Economy of
  Human Rights—
  Volume I
  with Edward S. Herman
  $19, ISBN: 9781608464067

Year 501
  The Conquest Continues
  $16, ISBN: 9781608464074

About the Author

 Noam Chomsky is widely regarded as one of the foremost critics of U.S. foreign policy in the world. He has published numerous groundbreaking books, articles, and essays on global politics, history, and linguistics. Among his recent books are *Masters of Mankind* and *Hopes and Prospects*. This book and its companion volume, *After the Cataclysm*, are part of a collection of twelve new editions from Haymarket Books of Chomsky's classic works.

CPSIA information can be obtained
at www.ICGtesting.com
Printed in the USA
JSHW030305230720
6829JS00004B/24